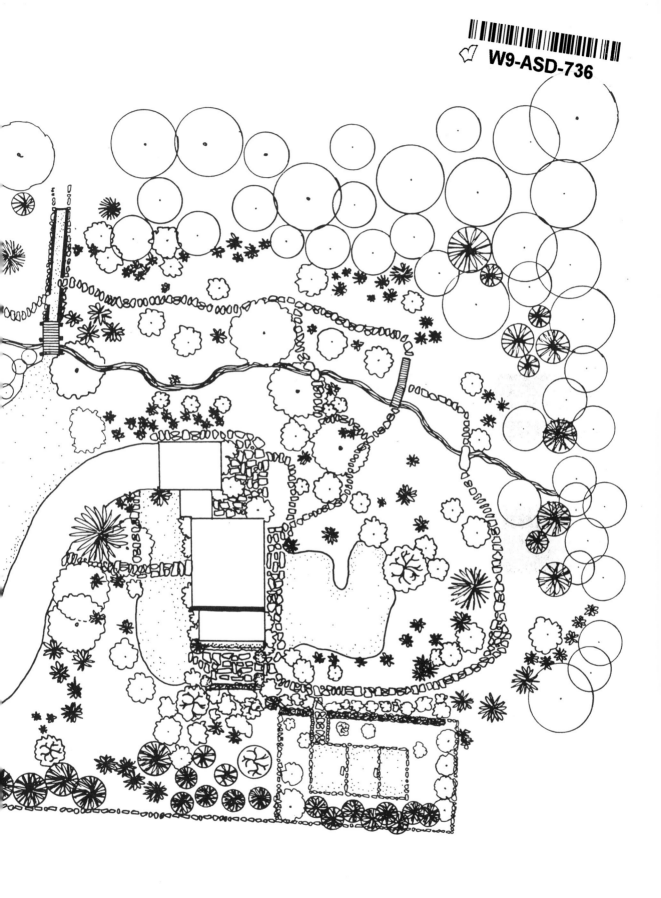

A YEAR AT NORTH HILL

ALSO BY WAYNE WINTERROWD

Annuals for Connoisseurs

A Year at

North Hill

FOUR SEASONS
IN A VERMONT GARDEN

Joe Eck and Wayne Winterrowd

PHOTOGRAPHS BY JOE ECK

LITTLE, BROWN AND COMPANY

Boston New York Toronto London

First Edition

Library of Congress Cataloging-in-Publication Data
Eck, Joe.
A year at North Hill : four seasons in a Vermont garden / Joe Eck and
Wayne Winterrowd ; photographs by Joe Eck. — Ist ed.
p.   cm.
ISBN 0-316-20916-3
I. Gardening — Vermont. 2. Eck, Joe — Homes and haunts — Vermont. 3. Winterrowd,
Wayne — Homes and haunts — Vermont. 4. North Hill Garden (Vt.)
I. Winterrowd, Wayne. II. Title.
SB453.2.V4E35   1995
635′.09743 — dc20   94-7791

10 9 8 7 6 5 4 3 2 I

RRD-OH

Designed by Barbara Werden

Published simultaneously in Canada by Little, Brown & Company (Canada) Limited

Printed in the United States of America

For

HELEN PRATT

"Accept . . . this speaking garden, that may inform you
in all the particulars of your store, as well as wants,
when you cannot see any of them
fresh upon the ground."

PARKINSON

Contents

Acknowledgments

OF the many people we must thank for the making of this book, those we must thank first have earned a deeper gratitude than words can pay, because their encouragement in the making of our garden has taken both emotional and material form. For both, we are deeply grateful to Mr. and Mrs. Walter J. Eck, the late Mr. William P. Winterrowd, Dane and Alice Morgan, and Martha Ronk. Precious support in what we were "up to" has come as well from Bill Heap and from Faith Sprague, who are among our very best garden visitors.

A garden may come into existence through such support, but a book, existing as it must "out there" in the world, requires something else. So we are very grateful to Christina Ward, who first saw that North Hill, having made its pattern on the ground, might also do so in print, and to Ray Roberts, who bought her

suggestion and has been encouraging its progress all along. To Jennifer Josephy at Little, Brown fell the actual work of putting our manuscript into hard covers. It was difficult work done well, for which we thank her. Our agent, Helen Pratt, we have thanked in another place.

There are people who have written books about their gardens — or about gardening — with no prior training in how to go about such work, often with great success. We would have found that quite impossible to do. And so we must express our deepest gratitude to the staff of *Horticulture* magazine — particularly Tom Cooper, its guiding light — who have trained us in how to go about the labor, and sometimes, by a casual word dropped in conversation, have saved us from some (though perhaps not all) follies we might have committed. Several passages in this book originally appeared in print within the pages of *Horticulture*, and though they have been revised for our purposes here, if readers feel occasionally that some words or perceptions are vaguely familiar, it will have been in that magazine that they first read them.

Though a book about gardening must really begin with a garden, the labor of writing it occurs elsewhere, indoors, at the desk and at the typewriter. What happens to the garden, then? In our case, without the labors of Stuart Aylin, Thomas Smith, and Anna Bolognani, the act of chronicling the garden would essentially have destroyed it. What a great luxury it has been to know that as we were writing, all the tasks crucial to the garden's life would be done, and done so well.

Finally, though we have never met her, we must extend thanks to Thalassa Crusoe, whose books, particularly *Making Things Grow Outdoors*, tremendously empowered us in the early stages of our garden's creation. Her clear message was, "I have done this. You can do it too, and here is how it is done." Such stern, bracing, and eminently practical advice was the best encouragement we could have had. We hope our book catches a shadow of her force, so it may serve, in turn, to encourage others.

A YEAR AT NORTH HILL

North Hill is located in a narrow valley in southern Vermont, on a south-facing slope that warms early in spring.
Much of the land is old-growth hardwood forest. A small stream purrs through the garden,
always companionable, like a liquid cat.

Introduction

*T*HIS is a book about gardening, and between its covers we have tried to squeeze as many things as we know about that activity. But we should perhaps say straight off that it is *primarily* a book about gardening, for, being a record of one year of our life at North Hill, other things have perforce crept in. It will quickly become apparent to any reader that gardening is at the center of our life, so much so that it seems sometimes little is left over for any other pursuit. As such, gardening is the knot we have chosen to catch up all the other threads of our existence. It has been many years since — if ever — we thought of gardening as a pastime, a sort of craft or hobby we engaged in at the odd moments left over from other activities. So in writing a book about it, and specifically a book about our own garden, we are actually writing about our life, or at least the hugest chunk of it.

We hope this book is plentifully furnished with practical advice. We hope further that it will empower new gardeners, just beginning on the path we have traveled with such satisfaction, whom we ask to remember that everyone, in this endeavor, is an amateur. We would be very glad to know that experienced gardeners could take pleasure from sharing with us all the triumphs and defeats that make the gardener's life so rich. But our greatest hope for this book is that it might serve as a sort of testimony of what gardening can be, offering — even to those who never willingly touch dirt — a window on this odd way (among so many others that are possible) of organizing a life.

Our garden is, as American gardens go, a fairly large one, comprising about five acres under intense cultivation within a larger tract of mature hardwoods — beech and maple with a sprinkling of native hemlock. It is located at the southernmost edge of Vermont, about five miles from the Massachusetts border, close enough to the midpoint between the equator and the North Pole to say that it is essentially there. Its climate – for both good and ill – is squarely within USDA Zone 4, which is to say that it routinely experiences winter lows of −20°F and may, in a bad winter, get as cold as −25°F. In most years snow is abundant and a great blessing, as it insulates the earth. Even so, freezes can still go as deep as three feet into the earth. Killing frosts come as early as the first week of September, and it is not safe to plant out tender annuals or tomatoes much before the first week of June.

If one thinks of a garden primarily in terms of its tenderest plants, such parameters do not leave much space in which to make a garden. But we have found a huge range of plants – for flower, for leaf, for twig and berry – that can make even so cold a garden as ours a pleasure twelve months in the year. Plants flourish in our cool mountain air, refreshed by heavy dews, that would perish in Boston or in other gardens farther south. In midsummer, gardeners from such places who come to visit enter a garden where the grass is emerald green and where *Meconopsis betonicifolia,* the fabled Himalayan blue poppy, may be reaching its peak of bloom. Still, our climate has imposed on us many tricks and shifts, all of which we share in this book. But we must say that, even with all the space we have at our command, it is hard to find room for all the wonderful plants we can grow.

The garden at North Hill is divided into many compartments, or rooms, each with its special growing conditions, its special character, its special pleasures. All of them are discussed in this book, usually in the chapter for the month in which they reach their peak of interest and give us the greatest satisfaction.

What isn't discussed is how we came to this spot, where we have spent the peak of our gardening life and where we presume we will remain for as long as it lasts. An introduction seems the best place to do that.

There are gardeners – we have read of them, and even know some – who inherit or buy fine established gardens of distinguished trees, splendid boundary hedges, and mature old shrubberies, with even sometimes expanses of weathered paving crusted with lichens and with moss. We do not know that we would envy them much now, though in the beginning we would have given anything for such a backdrop against which to work. Such places – if they exist in Vermont at all "for sale" – would surely have been far beyond our reach. But we did spend our first two years here attempting to find at least a good, old farmhouse around which we could fashion gardens. We knew people who lived in glorious places bought years ago at auction "for nothing," and we were renters in just such a place, into which we could have settled for life, were it only ours. So we knew what we wanted.

So, apparently, did lots of other people, all of them more flush than we. A few almost likely candidates were shown us by optimistic real estate agents. They were all equipped with "charm" and with various stages of dereliction that included sagging roofs, rotten sills, punky bricks, and vast expanses of antique linoleum, maybe with wide-plank floors beneath and maybe not. And there was always something – an abandoned trailer, an automobile graveyard – blocking our view of the distant hills. "Of course," the cheerful real estate agent would say, "you'll want to plant a few evergreens, as a screen." But a few evergreens were not what we had in mind, and we were prudent enough to know that the pleasures of serious structural repair lay far outside the range of things we really enjoyed in life. So we decided to build, and that required a new search — for just the right bit of land.

We found it above a tiny and unfashionable village (for so much of our part of Vermont *is* fashionable) on a steep wooded mountainside called North Hill. It was a chilly and daunting name, but the slope of the land was south, and we knew what that would mean in avoiding late frosts in spring and early ones in autumn. We could also see that our side of the narrow valley would catch the last rays of the sun long after the more happily named South Hill and the village below were in shadow. The parcel of land we were shown (about twenty-four acres) had never been farmed, and its wood had not been harvested for fifty years or more, resulting in splendid stands of mature trees. Finally, by consulting USDA weather records for the last thirty years, we found that if one wished to live in Vermont, this town — and especially the little piece of it we contemplated buying — was the warmest spot in the whole state.

But even with all these advantages, which were considerable, we still might not have chosen to settle here except for the stream. We call it *the* stream, for of all others in the world it has become the most important to us. Still, it is hardly more than a runlet, and in dry summers it tends to take a vacation. But mostly it tumbles through the length of our property, surfacing at the top of the garden from its subterranean course beneath a neighbor's pasture and losing itself at the other end in another neighbor's beaver swamp. The day after we met that stream, we put down the money for the land, not even having seen much of its deep woods or bothered to verify its boundaries. (Boundaries in old Vermont deeds are at best vague, anyway.)

These essential variables of hill, wood, and stream have controlled the character of the garden from its beginnings. Like so many gardeners, we had at the start a quite different notion of what the garden might be from what has in fact turned out. The land imposed its will, and in only a few cases have we thought it wise to alter what it offered us. The soils of the garden are all generally good, ranging in character from fecund bog to moist stream bank to open meadow tilth to dry, shady slopes. Each type, we have been glad to learn, provides its own precious habitat for plants. An apposition is often struck — a false one we think — between collectors of plants and makers of gardens. The first, it is smugly assumed, create "plant museums," while the second merely make pretty pictures from "plant material." Our site has very luckily spared us either excess, for its extent and its varied growing conditions have allowed us to exercise our passion for every monocot and dicot in creation and still succeed — or so we hope — in making a beautiful garden.

We have been lucky, generally. And the greatest depth of that luck has not even been in our site, fortunate as we feel to have it, or in its location within a state that, for political, ecological, and social wisdom, is bettered by none in our nation. Years of teaching in public high schools gave us brief but precious summers to work in the garden, and that was lucky, too. But our deepest luck has been in the fact that there have been two of us at this work — twice the muscle, twice the courage, twice the attention, and twice the dream. One can, of course, go it alone, and sometimes — sooner or later — one must. It has been our great good fortune, however, that we have not had to do that often. Or yet.

Still, though our deepest gratitude is not to the land, there is enough there to make measuring which is greatest an academic exercise. It is a curious thing to "own" a bit of land, as in "This is our own land; we own it." For we are, after all, only the briefest moments in its existence, even though we have worked a garden on its surface and inhabited its space for our best time on Earth. Its history is traceable before us, in the memories of our oldest neighbors and in town records and deeds. We know which Carpenters and Spragues owned it before us, and there is frequent testimony to their presence in bits of household detritus — glaucous, mud-filled medicine bottles, shards of slate gray pottery, a rusted horseshoe that caused one of them to curse, having lost it, a century ago. When such things are turned up by our shovels, or by the feet of the cows, we muse on them, and on their lesson, as we go about our work.

Sometimes, however, we find things that cannot be so easily digested in the planting of a young pine or hawthorne. Deep beneath layers of decomposed leaves, we come upon a streak of ash, dead-gray and unpenetrated by roots, the remains, we presume, of some ancient campfire. We must wonder whose. For even before our race came, this land had its uses and was trod by others than we. There is good evidence, too, that Europeans penetrated as deep within it as we are long before Columbus vaunted its discovery. Many people may have drunk from our stream, and through many generations, long before our country had a name or the shape of our continent was known.

And there are the rocks, the great boulders of granite that stud our garden, deposited here, just in this place, by glaciers advancing over eons and retreating, in glacier time, only slightly more rapidly. There's the stream, too, so fresh and new each spring — though it must be almost as old as they, cutting its way across this piece of land for an extent of time unthinkable to us, forming the gorge we now arrogantly call "the wild garden." Now we, too, have added our subtle accretions to the land, first by making a garden on it, and then by writing a book about it. It will not easily shake off either imposition, though certainly the words we have written about it will go first. But for how many centuries might there be the subtle tracery of a stone wall or path, the abundant progeny of *Impatiens glandulifera,* even naturalized stands of *Meconopsis betonicifolia?* We do not find any of those ideas terrible, even if there is no one, no gardener as we understand the word, to wonder and admire. But the thought does give us a shiver. That much we will admit.

April

❊

FOR those who live in Vermont, the certain sign that winter is past is mud. For a significant part of April, while daffodils bloom on Long Island and magnolias achieve perfection all up and down Commonwealth Avenue in Boston, mud is almost the only proof of spring's arrival here. Desperate though both plants and gardeners are to shake off winter's sleep and spring into activity, growth cannot begin until the frost is out of the ground.

The thawing of the earth after winter ought to be a quick and startling event, and for those who garden elsewhere — even elsewhere in New England — so it is. The warm March sun and the increasingly frost-free nights wake the earth, it would seem, almost in a day. But in northern New England the frost goes deep, three feet or more if the winter has been open, and the thawing takes weeks to accomplish. The earth's

unlocking begins at the surface and proceeds by inches downward. Rains and sodden, quick-melting snows fall in the night and sometimes all day long, but the hard mass of ice beneath the few inches of just-thawed soil prevents the penetration of the moisture. Mud is the result. It is sometimes so deep that parts of the garden are completely inaccessible, and people who live on more-traveled dirt roads get home only by trusting their fate to the unchurned "back way."

There is a kind of ontological fitness to the mud's preceding the greening of the earth, for both ancient myth and modern science concur that mud — sodden clay — is the mother of life and its first home. And mess though it certainly is — in the garden, in the house, on one's boots, and on the feet of the dog and cats (who *will* go in and out all day long, just like folks, to check on the arrival of spring) — the mud is still exciting, a cause for celebration. And it is not just domestic life that celebrates: in the warm, moist twilight the red-winged blackbirds signal their return with sweet piercing notes in the highest bare branches, and later in the night the chorus of spring peepers, tiny invisible frogs, reaches a cacophony pleasantly troubling to sleep. From the arrival of that sound until the end of autumn, the true gardener will sleep neither as deeply nor as long as in winter, and will be glad of it.

The first place in the garden to thaw — in fact, in some winters it never really freezes — is the bog. Watercourses are always warmer than the surrounding land, a fact we learned our first year here from a trio of fat white Emden geese we brought with us. They lived in their own small cabin by the stream, and though they had deep, warm bedding of fresh straw and protection from the wind, on the coldest days they preferred to stand with their feet in the flowing water. Their lesson has been a useful one, for we have learned that plants growing in or near flowing or percolating water may gain as much as a zone in hardiness. They are also precocious in their flowering, blooming sometimes a whole month before the same species blooms in other, dryer parts of the garden. Though many plants, like the geese, will accept and even be grateful for running water at their feet, true bog plants will also relish water when it becomes still and stagnant. Among perennial plants, it is these that present us with some of our earliest flowers.

The earliest of all, and the first true perennial to bloom here, is a plant extraordinary in all its parts. *Petasites japonicus* var. *giganteus,* the giant Japanese butterbur, initially appears as a tightly clasped golf ball–size bud resting just above the soil as soon as the snow melts. Sometimes they appear in the upper bog even in early March, impatient to get on with the business of being the first to attract the bees in their initial venture out of the hive. In the earliest warm days, even while ice still lies crusted over the rest of the garden, they unfurl into curiously fashioned nosegays, a ruff of pleated chartreuse bracts neatly surrounding a perfectly arranged cob of fuzzy little green daisies. They suggest a well-organized army, bent on occupying every inch of ground that is to their liking and exterminating all other vegetation in their path. They are our first cut flower for decoration indoors, for a single blossoming cob, cut near the ground, forms a complete arrangement in an old blue-and-white Japanese cup. As the days lengthen into early April, so do the cobs, telescoping upward to two feet, all together with a seemingly regulated uniformity. At this stage they are joined by the leaves, which unfurl into footwide pads of a fresh grass green. With amazing celerity, leaves continue to come. By the end of April and early May they stand almost six feet tall, each leaf perhaps three feet across on its own thick, juicy stalk, the leaves overlapping their neighbors like scales on a giant fish.

But it is perhaps not a plant for the small garden, or even for the large one if the gardener is faint of heart and terrified of all plants that know their business and mean to get on with it as fast as possible. To call the plant rampant is to understate the case, for it can, in boggy soil or even in two inches of standing water, cover many square feet in a year. But its advance guard is easy to eradicate when the leaves first appear, as the stolons that produce new plants lie only just below the surface and can be dug out and discarded without difficulty. (One must only be careful about where one throws the discards.) The labor is easy, and far less time-consuming than many hours of weeding the squishier parts of the garden might require later in the season. *Petasites japonicus* is infallible ground cover. Nothing grows beneath the gloom of its vast leaves — nothing at all.

The plant comes in two sizes, if you can find anyone brave enough to sell it to you. Straight *Petasites japonicus* grows to about three feet, and the variety appropriately named *giganteus* will top that at three feet more. It is the giant we favor, because the littler form is just as fast on its feet, and if one is in for it, one might as well be in for it big. But we had heard for years of a rare variegated form of the smaller version, and after seeking it in vain, we were given pieces of it last year from two different sources at once. It is one of the most beautifully variegated of all variegated plants. On young leaves a rich butter yellow mottles the fresh green, sometimes almost displacing it altogether. As the leaves age, some of the yellow fades to white, and the green intensifies. But early in the season the leaves look like pictures of nebulae taken from outer space — white and yellow clouds in a green sky. By keeping the plants in the cool greenhouse and forcing them into early growth, we produced six plants from the original two. We wonder now why we bothered to hasten things, for those six clothed a dank, moist part of the lower garden, deep in hemlock shade, with a thick blanket almost twelve feet square in their first season of liberation. Nothing else would grow there, however, and so we are content to let them spread as they please, adding great interest to a dull corner and relieving us (and presumably our heritors) of further worry about that spot.

Considering its propensity to spread, it is a good thing that *Petasites japonicus* is so winning in its very early flowers and so magnificent in its tropical-looking summer leaves. We could of course have too much of it, but not yet. Still, there are other perennials that love a bog and reward us with very early flowers, and so it must be kept somewhat in check. Many members of the primrose family are never so happy or so pretty as when they inhabit constantly moist soil or even an inch of standing water. Among the earliest of these to bloom is *Primula denticulata,* and it is also one of the loveliest. It is called the "drumstick" primrose for its three-inch, perfectly rounded cobs of flowers that open almost at ground level and extend without fading to a foot in height. In early April, a thriving colony can color a constantly moist but not sodden spot with a rich variation of shades, from bright pink through mauve and lilac to the clearest white. In the right place it is very long-lived, and displays as many as fifteen drumsticks to an established plant. Left to seed, it will produce never too many smaller plants that will bloom their second year, usually in either lavender or white. But the variety *rosea* should be sought out and introduced into a family to provide its stain of richer color and to vary the complexion of the progeny. A watery little circle of pale green leaves appears with the first flowers and enlarges, as the flowers fade, into an upright funnel, for all the world like a loose head of romaine lettuce, fresh and cool looking throughout the summer.

But the undisputed ruler of the moist humusy soil at the edge of a bog or stream is certainly the Lenten rose, *Helleborus orientalis.* Its colors are royal, ranging from a deep Phoenician purple through rose and ivory to a green-tinctured white, every color stained by deeper and lighter shades, as precious marble is. From a mature plant can come as many as thirty

For all its rawness, early April is still capable of an impressive show of flowers. Here the drumstick primrose, Primula denticulata, *blooms with* Helleborus orientalis. *Both plants are extraordinarily long-lived if sited in moist but well-drained humusy soil and will happily self-seed.*

Petasites japonicus *var.* giganteus *is the first perennial to bloom in the garden, its cobs of chartreuse daisies scattered over the damp soil of the bog. A single one makes a perfect flower arrangement in an old Japanese cup.*

stems. Crisply furled and flushed with red beneath the last retreating snow, the stems rise to perhaps two feet as the weather warms. Each stem faces outward, perfectly arranged as in a vase and topped with two or three nodding five-petaled bells an inch across. They have the modesty of true nobility, and to appreciate the cunning arrangement of pistil and stamens within, you must tip up each face to see what it keeps hidden. There, inside, are also the finest colors — paler, more translucent than without, netted and veined like rich blood vessels beneath a fine, thin skin.

For the true gardener, the pleasure of finding just the spot where a plant wants to grow is always greater than growing it in just the spot the gardener wants. Success then becomes a partnership rather than a bullying (and often a futile one) of the plant by the gardener. After years of mixed results with *Helleborus orientalis* in open places in the rhododendron border (where it ought to have thrived and would have looked good), we moved a plant, on a hunch, to a little island that rises above the back of the bog (taking care, as the best books tell us, to pull it apart into little rooted bits, and not plunk it down all in one clump). Water must percolate deep beneath that spot all season, but for two or three feet a shovel turns up only rich black loam, the product of centuries, perhaps aeons, of forest leaves blown into this low place. Other cranky plants thrive there, most notably the precious and willful Himalayan blue poppy, *Meconopsis betonicifolia.* The hellebore flourished mightily as well, without the cosseting of fertilizer and water we previously had to supply. So we moved others in, and they too seem to relish the independence they have been granted from our anxious ministrations. It is true that though we are able to enjoy their early April

flowers without distraction, we would like to see much more of the beautiful leathery, five-lobed leaves that follow, each neatly serrated along the edges and veined with an intricate design. So fine are those leaves in themselves that the willful gardener would want them as ground cover, richly clothing the soil inside a bay of shrubbery or along the front of a mixed border. We have such spots in plenty, but alas, the plant will not comply. Where it grows best for us its leaves are largely obscured by other plants. So it is a case of taking what we can and being grateful.

Located near the first flowers that reach springtime perfection in the bog are some that are actually passing over. April is such a time for beginnings that it seems a little odd to be bidding farewell to any flower. But, save for one lingerer, the witch hazels have all but finished their show. The first, *Hamamelis virginiana,* bloomed at the beginning of November, is its little pale yellow thrums studding its straw-colored branches amid dead and dying leaves. It could be considered the last blossomer of autumn or the first of spring, depending on the optimism of one's outlook. Actually, however, it is the first flower of winter — the most neglected season in cold climates — which, for all its harshness, can still yield a flower or two.

It is a feature of all witch hazels that they are crafty. Their popular name was given them by the first English colonists, who saw in the handsome vase-shaped form of the shrub a resemblance to the English hazelnut, *Corylus avellana,* and found their slender branches, often perfectly V-shaped, an excellent substitute for the divining rods they had used at home to locate sources of water. We have not tested this capacity in our plants, though we suspect they would be infallible, as water in some form is never far below ground anywhere in our part of Vermont. But we do know that the tendency of hamamelis to produce its odd strap-petaled flowers at very unlikely times is not a sign of depraved extravagance, but rather one of deep cunning.

For from an autumn so late that it might as well be winter to a spring so early that it might as well be too, on the very days that for their rare warmth tempt out the bees, the little straps of petals unfurl. In themselves they might be hardly noticeable, for though possessed up close of the elegance that is the birthright of every part of every member of this family, the flowers of all witch hazels from a distance are scarcely what you might call flowers at all. They are more like shreds of something, dull yellow or rust red, caught along the bare branches. It is the fragrance that bids one come have a closer look. As we stroll about the still-sleeping garden, our minds on problems the winter has brought — dead branches, fallen trees, major changes to be made — that fragrance taps us on the shoulder, asking us to come see. It is an unexpected presence in the garden at that time, the sharper for the sharpness of the air, and it draws us toward a closer examination of the little wiggly-wavy blossoms, which are actually rather prettier than they need to be, given the way they smell and the times they choose to flower.

After *Hamamelis virginiana*'s November blossoms come those of *H. mollis* 'Brevipetala'. In a warm corner of the garden, or with its feet in water (as we grow it), it can begin to bloom as early as Christmas. This winter, a mild one, it started on the twentieth of December and continued, thriftily curling its petals on cold days and uncurling them on warm ones, well into March. In that month others joined it — *Hamamelis* x *intermedia* 'Primavera', *H.* x *intermedia* 'Pallida', and *H.* x *intermedia* 'Jelena' — making

of March, often a hostile and blustery month (at least in its beginnings), quite a little festival on its own.

But, putting aside one's gratitude for a small flower in December or March (and a fragrant one at that), probably the best of all witch hazels is *Hamamelis* x *intermedia* 'Arnold's Promise'. It prudently waits until the very end of March or the first week of April to bloom, meaning to keep its word (as a promisor should) that lingering winter is past. The original 'Arnold's Promise', bred at Harvard University's Arnold Arboretum in 1928, stood until 1992 as a magnificent open tree behind the main administration building. From the fire escape to the third story, one could look down into its swirl of thousands upon thousands of daffodil yellow threads. In that year, however, an expansion of the building necessitated (or perhaps not) that it be chainsawed to the ground to make room for trucks and construction gear. So, though hale and in splendid maturity, it survives only in its progeny, happily numerous in many gardens.

Our own 'Arnold's Promise' plant is not situated in a place where it can ever attain the stature of its parent, though it may someday experience its parent's sad fate. It is planted near a small terrace of fieldstone, embraced by the back of the barn and lying just below the living room windows, where we can see it on inclement days and sit near it on mild ones. There, in early spring, its flowers — a quite clear yellow that makes them the best in the family — are a great joy. And its pleated leaves — cool grayish green and oval, like an old-fashioned palmetto fan — are an excellent foil for the pots of agapanthus and cannas that stand about the terrace in summer.

But in truth, things are a bit crowded around that terrace. We have tended to plant many shrubs and trees there that we like to look at during the harsh months of the year, and others we like to see at other times, at dawn and dusk when we are sitting indoors with coffee early and with wine late. (For sitting is not something one willingly does *in the* garden when it can be worked.) So, near our 'Arnold's Promise' is a splendid *Stewartia pteropetiolata* var. *koreana* (previously *S. koreana*), perhaps the most aristocratically small tree we can grow. It is beautiful in shape, branched to the ground and gracefully spired. Its older trunks and branches are mottled with cream and buff and green; its younger stems are dull red and clad with clean, oval green leaves, spangled in July with single, two-inch-wide white camellialike flowers, each centered with a boss of golden stamens. Also nearby, close to the protection of the house, are the only American hollies we have been able to grow, a seven-foot female with a smaller male planted close enough to make them like one plant. Studded with red berries among the glistening leaves beneath the window, they are never so beautiful as when dusted by a midwinter or early spring snow. For high spring and early summer, there is a *Rhododendron yakushimanum* 'Mist Maiden' that Allen Haskell gave us twenty years ago, when this form was still quite rare. Its time is June, long after the 'Arnold's Promise' has been forgotten and other nearby plants have assumed somber tints of green. There are several willows also, but by then they too will have given over their vivid orange or yellow stems to the pruning shears and resumed a vigorous but less showy growth.

Certainly things are crowded. And someone, years from now, will have to make some choices, for the 'Arnold's Promise' promises to grow quite large, to twenty feet in height and half that in breadth. The rhododendron will not be happy beneath its shade, and the stewartia will bump heads with it. The hollies will probably do well enough in the increasing gloom, but they will grow thinner of branch and fewer of berry, which in a holly is not the point. So someone will have to choose which of these wonderful plants will stay, and which will go. We are a little sorry to have inflicted such agony on a future owner of our garden. But for the moment — which is to say probably our time in it — the composition looks just fine.

Among the plants that grow around this little terrace, however, is at least one that will not require an agonizing decision from us or anyone, even though it ranks with the choicest of early-flowering shrubs. For *Daphne mezereum*, like all its tribe, is not long-lived. Many theories have been propounded to explain why a plant, in full and flourishing growth, will suddenly decline and perish. Age seems to have nothing to do with it, and though the soil in which it grows is often blamed, we have tried and lost it in many soils, all different, ranging from heavy clay to open woodland humus, wet and dry, sweet and sour. One reads that the flowers must never be cut, for fear of introducing a deadly pathogen; but the oldest specimen we know belongs to a gardener who routinely shears it like a privet. It is a mystery.

But brief though its life often is (seven to ten years), *Daphne mezereum* is very beautiful and quite unlike any other hardy flowering shrub in its appearance. Fortunately it grows fairly fast, producing from seed a chubby bush two feet tall in three or four years, with many fleshy-looking stems ascending from the base. For reasons it knows better than we, some individuals will increase in height to as much as five feet, while others will spread out and fatten at three. But at whatever height, each of its stems

Many forms of willow make brilliantly colored winter twigs, especially when cut back hard (pollarded) each spring. Severed from the plants, the trimmings quickly lose their vivid hues and can be used for staking in the perennial garden. Nevertheless, they should be left in the sun for a week or two, for if they are inserted in the damp ground while fresh, every one will take root.

is covered up and down in late March and early April with thickly clustered, waxy four-pointed stars that smell of honeysuckle.

Despite its perfume, many gardeners are not fond of *Daphne mezereum,* for its flowers are a difficult shade of lilac with a little too much brown in it. Actually, as with many awkward colors, it is lovely when viewed close up, and unpleasant only from a distance or in conjunction with other colors, particularly yellow. We like it quite a lot, though we take care to position it against a backdrop of evergreen foliage, far from the early yellow crocuses that bloom at the same time and near a quiet path where it can be studied close up and its wonderful fragrance enjoyed.

But if we were compelled to have only one *Daphne mezereum,* it is the white form we would choose, *alba,* which is what we have growing at the edge of the small terrace beneath the living room windows. The adjective "white" is seldom adequate alone to describe the color of any flower, and particularly those that bloom in early spring when white gains complexity from the still bare earth and the gray-brown twigs without the distraction of green. The white of *Daphne mezereum* f. *alba* might best be described as "milk white," if by milk is understood the rich cream-laden produce of well-tended Jersey cows. Because it blooms at such a cold time, the flowers of our white daphne often stay with us for two or three weeks, by which time April is well advanced and a host of other plants have come to vie with it for attention. As its flowers fade it begins to leaf out, with curious little flattened whirls atop each stem long before the nether regions of the plant produce any leaves at all. And it remains a comfortable green bush until deep in autumn when, quite without any fanfare of autumn color, it drops all its leaves to reveal dozens of fleshy berries clustered along the stems where the flowers were.

In the species form the berries are red, and in the white form they are yellow. No one has ever reported producing plants of one color from berries off the other, and that is a good thing if you only crave the white. But the berries can be stubborn to germinate if they are gathered and sown in pots. If, however, they are allowed to lie on top of the ground beneath the parent bush all winter, a surprising number — far more than one needs — will have sprouted by the following April, looking rather like the beans one sowed on blotter paper as a science experiment in grammar school. They may then be gathered up carefully and planted in pots of half peat and sand. Kept shaded and moist, by late summer each seedling will have produced a tiny, stout treelike stem topped by a tuft of leaves. Then is the time to plant them in other places in the garden they might grow, and it is good to have new generations coming on, for the old may pack off without warning, leaving you without any daphnes at all.

The little bulbs — snowdrops, scillas, crocuses, and such — began their season back in February. It is a very long one, for only in early April do they hit their peak. We are grateful for them, as must be all gardeners who endure a winter worth the name. It is not so much their precocity that causes us to treasure them, however, as the extraordinary clarity and intensity of their colors. Other flowers bloom early in the gardening year — the witch hazels, willows, *Cornus mas*, and *Petasites japonicus* — but theirs are the colors of the earth, muted rusts and browns, greenish yellow, and ocher. Only the sky can match the blues of *Chinodoxa luciliae*, *Scilla siberica*, and *Iris reticulata*, while *Iris danfordiae* and *Crocus ancyrensis* reflect the sun in tints of clear yellow and orange. And the rich creamy white of *Crocus crysanthus* 'Cream Beauty', the ice blue of *Crocus tommasinianus*, and the feathered purple of *Crocus corsicus* are the colors of the moon and stars. These purest colors of the gardening year are seen in the high bright light of the April sun, as far up in the sky as it will be in September but shining through the yet-unfurnished branches of the trees with extraordinary intensity.

All the little bulbs are easy to grow and quick to increase. They ask only to be planted in a spot where the still-brown grass, the general detritus of winter, and the mud will not spoil their beauty. Most of ours are gathered together on and around a little south-facing terrace bordered on three sides by a boxwood hedge and on the fourth by the wall of the glassed-in winter garden. It is a "planted terrace," contrived of large old plates of weathered bluestone eked out with odds and ends of native fieldstone, granite sets, and a few old weatherproof bricks. It was laid directly on the earth, and the joints, which are rather wide, provide a home for many small plants that relish a warm stony bed or are too small to show for much in the borders or, like the little bulbs, come so early that they need a frame apart from the surrounding mud.

In the planted terrace, which enjoys the full force of the sun (stored by the pavement on chilly nights and reflected back during the day by the house walls), the little bulbs come up very early, particularly the crocuses and the charming, two-inch-tall cream-and-yellow *tarda* tulip. A deep bed of them has been planted against the foundation of the winter garden; undoubtedly more heat escapes the house there. Only a gardener would celebrate as luck that loss of heat — it speeds the crocuses on their way. And in this location it is easy to get close to their sparkling magnificence, even on a wet morning. Later in the season the bed will be planted with unusual annuals. The points of the pavement, where they will also flower, will later be overspread with thyme and will provide the best place to grow sweet alyssum (the white form for preference), which was born to gentle the hard edges of stonework with its tumbled foam and its wonderful honey-eyed fragrance in late summer.

Provided with a warm, clean place to bloom as early as they please, most of the little bulbs and all the bluest ones (chinodoxa, scilla, and muscari) ask nothing more from the gardener. But the wonderful little crocuses — such pure species as the golden *C. ancyrensis*, the ice blue *C. tommasinianus*, the white, orange-anthered *C. fleisheri*, and all the wonderful forms of the *chrysanthus* group — need a little more help. They are perfectly hardy in winters as cold as ours, which can dip to −20°F. They are not particular as to soil, accepting wet heavy clay and dry sandy loam with equal philosophy. They have no diseases and increase well but, if planted rather deep, at least six inches below ground level, never so fast as to go "blind" and require frequent division. And though they

would be pleasantly surprised by a gentle dose of vegetable-garden fertilizer just after they bloom, they are content to forage for themselves, extracting whatever the native soils might offer.

But they do have an enemy. Mice are as fond of crocuses as we are, though perhaps for less aesthetic and more primitive reasons. As soon as winter's harshness has made scarce the berries and nuts and seeds they feed on, the mice will find the crocuses; a generous clump might provide comforting meals for a whole family over a long, deep winter. And the better you are to your crocuses, the better you will be to your mice — rich humus-laden soils produce earthworms, which attract moles, whose runs become easy thoroughfares for the mice through the frozen soil. It is a lesson we learned hard, for in our first years at North Hill, when the soil was still stiff clay, we had hundreds of species of crocus in early spring. The little bulbs are always cheap, and the more we had the more we planted. Grateful for their beauty, we enriched the beds each year with composts and mulches and dug deep where we could, sometimes unintentionally scattering colonies, which then would bloom in other unlikely places. They were a joy for several springs, spreading an early carpet of yellow and cream and slaty blue and purple to initiate with grace the hard labor we then faced to make a garden.

Then one spring there were no crocuses — none, not one. The mice had found them all, and where we dug to see we found only an occasional dry papery net that had once enclosed a fat corm. As one cannot have a spring without crocuses, clearly it was necessary to come up with a system. The one we contrived has served us very well for ten years, and though it is initially some work, once it is done it remains done.

Like all gardeners, we tend to build up heaps of ugly black plastic nursery cans, which *could* be stacked neatly in the back of the barn, except for their odd variety of sizes. So they pile up, adding to their unsightliness the problem of disposing of them in an ecologically responsible manner. It is always satisfying to turn a nuisance to good account, and so we were delighted when it occurred to us that the larger cans could be put to use protecting our crocuses. In autumn, when we plant the bulbs, we excavate a hole large enough to sink a can with its rim two inches below the surface of the surrounding soil. We use the dug-out earth to fill in around the outsides of the can, reserving a little to place over the top. The rest we cart away to fill a low place or a hole somewhere. Into the can we put a moderately rich layer of compost and sand in equal portions, filling it to a level about eight inches below the surrounding soil. Onto this layer we place the crocus corms, rather thickly, bearing in mind that the deeper a bulb is planted the slower it will be to increase (and therefore will need less frequent resettings). The distance between each corm should be a little more than their own width, so a two- or three-gallon can will hold a good handful and a half. Over the corms we put more compost and sand, filling to the rim of the can. On top we place a lid of stiff galvanized wire mesh, sometimes called "hardware cloth" or, more descriptively, "rat wire." We cut this wire into squares and fold the four corners down tightly around the rim of each can. On top of this we return some of the original soil in a layer about two inches thick. The crocuses come up easily between the strands of wire and flower in fine, thick clumps. Best of all, they return each year. Our original canned plantings are now ten years old and still show no signs of deterioration.

In addition to making thrifty use of a nuisance and protecting our crocuses, this system has several other beauties. Three or even five cans may be placed side by side to create large natural-looking drifts. Grass or ground cover plants can be planted around, between, or even over the cans, to cover the soil when the crocuses have completed their growth and are dormant. If, for some reason, the crocuses are displeasing where they have been planted, the whole can may be lifted and reinstalled elsewhere in the garden. And when one goes digging in summer or in autumn, one can tell exactly where the crocuses are, without discovering them by turning a whole colony topsy-turvy and having to pick the corms out of the soil, one by one, to set them right again.

From the fading of the last crocus until the opening of the first daffodil seems an age, though it is really only a matter of two or three weeks. By the last week in April the earliest of the large daffodils, and some of the most beautiful, will have begun to spangle the borders where they grow, later to be followed by waves and waves lasting well into May. Like crocuses, daffodils were some of the first things we planted when the garden was new, and they continue to be among our favorite flowers. This may in part be because, though lovely in themselves, they seem to function as bells, ringing in the first glorious display of bloom in the garden. For though we have had flowers outdoors since February, and a long sequence of them in the winter garden throughout the darkest months, it is with the daffodils that we experience the first full rush of seemingly inexhaustible wealth, of flowers everywhere, more than we could pick or even peer at closely.

In the beginning, because we wanted lots of them, we were content to buy our daffodils

Even in a large garden, it is a good thing if individual sections can provide several seasons of interest. So the rose path is planted with many daffodils that reach full bloom just as the roses are leafing out.

cheap from cut-rate bulb catalogs that offered sturdy, old-fashioned varieties. Some of these are still among our favorites. 'Golden Harvest', for example, always lives up to its name, blooming abundantly and very early and looking like the archetypal golden daffodil in one's mind or in Wordsworth's poem. It combines prettily with 'Ice Follies', which is a warm white, flat-faced, and equally early and prolific. 'Empress of Ireland', too, has been with us from the first and still continues strong, huge of cup and perianth and the purest white of all the daffodils we grow. We'll never see 'February Gold' in February, or even in March, but we treasure its perky small yellow trumpets in April. Among pinks, though many finer and stronger-colored ones have been developed, we still grow 'Mrs. R. O. Backhouse', which has increased mightily from the handful we were given by an old gardener in North Adams, Massachusetts. A neighbor from just down the road gave us a single clump of a double, green-tinctured daffodil that has grown in Vermont for at least a century and is called 'Butter and Eggs'. And from the farmhouse we rented when we first came here we brought several bulbs of 'The Bride', a pure white form with gardenialike flowers that actually bloom in June, if at all. When it blooms, it is the most fragrant daffodil we have ever met.

Luckily it seemed that the cut-rate bulb catalogs kept pace with the development of our garden, and so we could buy, for little money, in netted bags of twenty-four or sometimes in special deals of a bushel, many other quick-multiplying varieties. So we added 'Hollywood', 'Canasta', 'Kissproof', 'Walt Disney', 'Professor Einstein', 'Thalia', and 'Salome'. When we wanted to force daffodils we selected the fattest five or six from each bag, preferably "double nosed" bulbs for extra

bloom. When they were done flowering we added them to our plantings, and not always in company with the group from which they had been detached. The result has been rather a mixed planting, though it is a happy fact about daffodils that they all seem to go well together, and it is fun to pick out an especially lovely face from the crowd.

Many of these earliest plantings are now in great need of dividing, having multiplied from a single bulb poked into a hole to a thick clump a foot or more across. It is of course true that the best time to divide is just after the bulbs have flowered, when the leaves are still vigorously green and busy making next year's blossoms, and when the questing roots can be coaxed to take hold in new soil if they are thoroughly watered in after planting. But though our old clumps have put us in possession of potentially great wealth — enough to daffodil our small world, even to the roadsides — we never seem, in the press of chores that comes with the end of the month and in May, to get to the work. We could, of course, also do it in autumn, when newly ordered bulbs are planted. But then we cannot find them, buried as they are beneath perennials and lingering annuals, sleeping comfortably. Maybe next year we will exercise a more timely discipline. We ought to, for the rewards would be very great come the following April.

We will never outgrow the cut-rate catalogs, for they are the best source of daffodils in plenty to be had cheap, and each autumn there are new varieties we want. We can be sure, also, that the forms offered are sturdy and quick to increase, else they would not be there at such a price. So, though we have lately become moderate daffodil sophisticates, we return to the catalogs each year, much as one does to a good pizza parlor or steak restaurant, for a substantial though not very refined repast. As such, however, they hardly exhaust one's appetite. The world of daffodils is really quite vast, and within it there are creatures of almost unimaginable beauty and rarity. Therefore the connoisseur of daffodils might want also to turn to the catalog of a great daffodil breeder, Grant E. Mitsch, whose work is being carried on by his daughter and son-in-law, Elise and Richard Havens at Grant E. Mitsch Novelty Daffodils, Hubbard, Oregon. Their catalog contains the newest, most breathtaking forms, sometimes at the breathtaking price of $50.00 or more for a single bulb. There are also comparative bargains, at $3.00 or $4.00 a bulb, if one can but exercise restraint. As pricey, but very choice, is the list from Oakwood Daffodils in Niles, Michigan (one can, if one is in a cheap mood, also find bargains here, at $1.50 a bulb). The best source for more select daffodils, however, may be Brent and Becky Heath's Daffodil Mart in Gloucester, Virginia, which offers many old favorites at moderate quantity rates and choicer forms one will not find in the cut-rate catalogs, all of them proven "doers" in the garden. Be aware, however, that the rarer daffodils may not in their first year show that flush of lavender or biscuit brown that cajoled dollar bills out of your pocket when you read the catalog. It takes a year or two, sometimes even three, for them to muster the distinctive display of for which they were offered. But it will come, and it will be worth the wait.

It is very easy to get hooked on daffodils. Then the great question becomes not how to pay for them (though that is always a question in gardening) but where to put them. Always a keen pleasure for the gardener is the opportunity to compare a plant one loves with another, closely related plant, and with a third, fourth, and so on. One can easily run out of room (as we have). Our main plantings exist along the rose walk and the sunnier parts of the woodland borders, and they are all crammed full of our first, sturdy purchases. But we are always dreaming of specialty gardens, preferably "walks" given over to one sort or another of a plant that is brief and splendid in its display and that comes in many forms and colors. Some of them — the delphinium walk, the peony room, the geranium border — we will never possess except in our minds, for our land will not comply and we do not have just the right places to do it. But lately, with the creation of the new vegetable garden in its own secluded meadow, with a broad allée of sophora trees leading up to it, we in fact have the place for a daffodil walk. So this autumn we will order as many more as we can afford, all of select forms, and plant them in distinct colonies of ten, or five, or three, . . . or one. The effect will be a little scanty at first, for daffodils are gregarious flowers, always looking happiest in crowds. But that may make us a little more conscientious about timely division, and eventually the effect will be splendid, just as we see it now in our minds.

For most of the year our garden lives in a quiet continuum. One day passes gently into the next almost without a seam. Plants come into their season and pass out of it often without our noting much their transitions from phase to phase — our attention is absorbed by what is coming on. But there are a few events in the garden's life that mark definitive breaks between what has been and what is to be. One is the first frost, which comes in the night at summer's end and clears the garden at a stroke of all its tender annuals, marking for sure the arrival of the long, slow autumn. Another is

The point is often made that the beauty of a garden rests not primarily in its flowers but in its structure, its pattern of stones and clipped shrubs, its division into rooms. Still, it is nice to have some flowers, too, as in this picture — looking out from the still-sleeping perennial garden to clumps of daffodils and Magnolia x loebneri 'Merrill' across the lawn.

the rainy wind that arrives sometime around the second week of October, pelting and blowing all night until it has stripped the last autumn leaves from the forest trees and changed even the volumes and shadow patterns of the garden. A third is the black frost, when arctic air dips down into the garden for the first time and turns the ground iron-hard beneath one's feet, making any attempt to protect the last tomatoes and late-blooming hardy annuals pointless, and signaling the beginning, without remission, of the long winter. All these events are exercises in subtraction — by taking from the garden, they force a more concentrated attention on what remains.

But the definitive quality of April is addition, and it is signaled by the greening of the grass. Until then frosts occur frequently, night temperatures are often in the low twenties, and on a gray, cold day flakes of snow fill the air and the crocuses close up in defeat. But sometime around the fifteenth of April — earlier in some years, later in others — the very color of the world changes, not only because the grass is suddenly green, but because green light seems to reflect off its surface onto the first pale yellow flower buds on the maples, the dull reddish leaf buds on the beeches, and the first gold of the daffodils. The shadows that fall across the lawn are thicker and fuller, and all the volumes of the garden seem somehow more substantial. The cold arctic air, as sterile as a mathematical formula, no longer dips into southern Vermont. Warm rains fall from the south, sometimes two or three days on end. And though one has begun to search for signs of spring almost since January, and to receive them, like postcards sent on a long voyage to home, it is with the greening of the grass that spring has, finally, certainly arrived.

May

THE month of May is for us rather like an engaging but unruly puppy or a turbulent teenager, full of beauty and charm but also full of wayward tricks and excess born simply from an overwhelming joy in life. Of course we are fond of it, though it tries us sorely; it may be at once the most beautiful and the most difficult month of our gardening year. For by May, the long, long season of mud is over, and quickening growth is everywhere. We can stop anxiously scratching the bare twigs of the tenderest shrubs to see if a hint of life promises that they have endured the winter for another season of growth. The great forest trees that cover 90 percent of Vermont and that form the structure of our garden send out their first tentative puffs of yellow-green bloom, followed immediately by tender leaves, also more gold than green, making a sort of aureate smoke across the mountain faces. Frost is less and less likely as the month advances, making even the setting out of tomatoes a reasonable bet. And even the most frost-sensitive plants in the garden — the variegated Japanese knotweed, the *Kirengeshoma palmata*, the toad lilies — hazard lusty growth above ground. From experience, however, we know not to entirely trust to their judgment, for frost is a theoretical possibility well into the month. (Once, on the twelfth of May, snow came in the night like a gratuitous insult.) So a stack of burlap and old sheets is kept ready against the event, even though the garden is bursting with tender new growth.

But if the finest plants in the garden come to life in May, so does everything else, from seeds promiscuously scattered about by a prodigal Nature. Last year's tender and beautiful puffs of chartreuse on the maples, ashes, beeches, and birches have fulfilled their

In May, not only is the ground rich with flowers, but even the trees overhead are rich with blooms. Apples and crab apples give the finest display, as is shown here by a young tree of Malus floribunda *in the perennial garden. But even the Montmorency cherry in the background offers beautiful flowers, the better for their promise of such good pies in summer.*

promise, and joined by grasses, field weeds, and the overwhelming progeny of the native jewel weed, *Impatiens capensis,* they carpet the garden with their young. Actually, the effect of this juvenile wave of life is quite pretty, a froth of green knitting together the bare spaces between perennials and shrubs and blending into their crowns. But the rank and smothering growth that soon follows is quite another thing, and must not be allowed to occur. So if we are glad that winter is finally over, from this point on we are locked in a struggle with Nature over whose garden this in fact is.

For at its crudest level, gardening is about control. It is the human attempt to force Nature into patterns and shapes she would never fashion on her own, and may in fact abhor. Her concern is to scatter life wherever she can, letting it all contend for space, light, air, food, and water, until the strong overtop the weak. It is a form of weeding, too, and we may borrow its ruthless logic in the garden when we seek to cover the ground with soothing and weed-smothering carpets of green such as the serviceable and sturdy periwinkle or the much-scorned pachysandra, or even choicer but still thuggish plants like the giant Japanese butterbur, *Petasites japonicus* var. *giganteus.* For the most part, however, the gardener battles to sustain a more fragile and delicate life, one suited to its place only so long as something better suited does not come along to crowd it out. And nothing is so apparent in May as the number of plants — the huge number — that have been waiting in the wings to crowd others out. So in May we weed.

Weeding can be, if you are allowed to settle quietly down to it, an extraordinarily tranquilizing garden chore. You become intimately acquainted with the earth you have been given to garden, with its special advantages and needs.

You come to know the plants around which you work, not just the full splendor of their bloom, as masses of color, but the special charms of their newly emerged shoots and burgeoning leaves and even — when you must divide or reset — their roots. You can look behind with satisfaction at newly cleaned and fluffed earth, and ahead (not too far ahead — not, certainly, at the enormity of the whole task) with the power of ambition to the part you will surely get through before lunch, or the two o'clock appointment at the vet, or twilight. At its best, weeding produces a synchrony of mind and hand, and all the senses, which is peace. It may take an hour to come or, if the phone has been ringing constantly, half the morning. But when it does finally come, true gardeners understand why, despite everything, they garden. It is for this that we welcome the weeds of May in all their abundance, and do not resent the hours of labor they require of us. It would in fact be pleasant if weeding, in this busy month, were all we had to do.

But May is the foundation for all the beauty we hope to achieve in the garden throughout the summer and the long autumn, and the work that is completed now will pay far greater dividends than if it is undertaken later. Prodigious things may be done in April — the moving of large shrubs and trees, the dividing and resetting of perennials, the opening and clearing of soil for new sections of the garden. The work of May is finer, more fiddly work, preparatory not so much for the garden of next year or ten years hence as for the garden that is about to be at its peak. Pruning is a major task, though it's not the massive sort that shapes the apple trees and large flowering shrubs, for that must always be done in late winter or very early spring. May pruning consists rather of snipping out dead twigs, bush by bush, patiently and laboriously.

The first to receive attention are the antique shrub roses and their modern counterparts, for they wait until May to tell you which stems they intend to fill with life and flowers, which they have sacrificed, and which they have deferred to your wisdom for a decision. There are no better indicators of how severe a winter has been than the antique shrub roses, for in some years they will need merely a gentle snip here and there, and in others whole canes will have to be removed to the ground. But a thorough grooming, light or heavy, will always be required. So gardeners who plant shrub roses with the hope that they will ask little in return for their heavily scented blooms — single, double, or cabbage — are in for a great disappointment. Certainly the hardiest ones, including the hybrid rugosas, gallicas, and albas, in many varieties, will survive the coldest climates and bloom. But their blossoms will be scant, often on unvigorous shoots disfigured with thorny dead twigs. The kind of romantic abundance gardeners crave from these plants — like most romantic things — takes a great deal of work, and now is the time to do it. Scratchy and tedious work it is, too, checking each cane for deadwood and cutting each one back to a vigorous shoot. A prick or two is inevitable, and the severed twigs and canes must be carefully bundled or put into a basket, or bits of them will remain on the ground all summer, an affliction to bare feet and weeding hands. But like other forms of gardening maintenance, such pruning is a good way to come to know each shrub, to see if it needs feeding or perhaps to tie a wayward cane to a stake for better balance or so it will arch, or not arch, over a companion plant or the path.

Feeding the garden is also a major priority in May. It consists of two sorts, organic and inorganic. As we move through the garden in this month, any bare patch of soil that can later be planted with the annuals and perennials waiting in the cold frames — and especially those patches that are heavy and wet, poor even for weeds — catch our eye. Actually they nag at our eyes, asking for a bucket or two of pasture muck, the rich black compost left in areas where the cows have fed and bedded for the winter. So in spare moments the buckets are hauled and the soil turned in to wait for what will come. Also in May, almost every area of the garden except those sections planted with conifers or ericaceous shrubs (which should have been fed in April with evergreen food) receive their portion of vegetable-garden fertilizer. We use 5-10-10, which is both gentle and cheap and is relatively low in nitrogen (for the cows tend to that part) but heavier in phosphorus and potassium. We spread it around the crowns of virtually every perennial and deciduous shrub in the garden, with the sort of generous sprinkle with which one would apply rock salt to a kosher chicken. For we have become convinced, as unfashionable as the conviction is at present, that most of our failures with plants are the result of inadequate feeding. As American soils go, ours is among the best, consisting of a century of woodland humus over rich water-retentive clay. And every section of the garden gets a sustaining coat of pasture muck from the cows. But the kind of layered abundance of bloom and leaf we aim for, according to that magic formula of "depth, density, and diversity," results in a very crowded garden, one that must be artificially supported by chemical fertilizer. We are also sure that proper feeding increases resistance to insects, disease, and wind, and even in many cases to severe winters. So in May we visit each plant to apply a dose just when it is most full of life and the will to live.

Certain rich hues are acceptable in May as they would be at no other time, as with the deciduous 'Jane Abbott' hybrid azaleas. Their strong pink is echoed by a drift of Geranium cinereum *'Ballerina' at their feet and softened by the ice blues of* Phlox divaricata.

It is a major labor, and one that we never neglect.

Heavy as the work of May is apt to be, we try nevertheless to notice the beauty around us while we are at it. This requires a bit of conscious effort, for the time we like the best — when the garden is under our control, when one can move through it with pleasure and not so much with the sense of this crucial task to do or that — is still some way before us. Still, even beneath the press of tasks calling out to be done we practice the discipline of looking up or down, to the left or right, near at hand or to the other side of the valley, to try to take in what May offers, so much of which passes quickly and will not come again for another year. The big things — the flowering of the apples, crab apples, magnolias, and cherries, the electric vividness of the deciduous azaleas — are hard not to see. Seeing, however — really seeing — is much closer to a spiritual state than to an activity, and is very different from what one might designate as "noticing." You know you are really seeing when you are able to take in the complexity and beauty of all the ephemeral plants that bloom close to the earth — sometimes, it seems, for five minutes only, and usually when your back is turned. So we force ourselves to stand and stare at the Japanese hylomecon, a sheet of four-petaled golden poppies hardly six inches high, or at the tiny columbines of the epimediums, soon to be covered over by their beautiful newly emerging leaves. The clear blue cups of *Jeffersonia dubia* are easy to miss; sometimes they are noticeable only as a few shattered petals at the base of the plant. The double form of bloodroot lasts longer than the single — as most double flowers do — because they are sterile, having given up their reproductive structures for extra petals. But

one wonders, looking at the elegant simplicity of the single form for the three or four days it lasts, whether that is necessarily an improvement. At some point, especially in the garden, one comes to the realization that the intensity of pleasure and the length of its duration are not necessarily interdependent. If it were not so, one would be stuck with marigolds. So it is just for the transitoriness of most May plants — aptly called "ephemerals" — that we treasure them. In a garden as large as ours, it is therefore lucky that there are two of us, one to say "Go look at the *Jeffersonia;* it's in bloom," even if the other answers, as is usual, "I have."

Not every part of the garden, of course, is for May bloom only. The heather bed along the drive is dull and dingy at this season, barely recovered from the early spring shearing that ensures its long life. The perennial garden — our best show of color in high summer — is a mere collection of green tufts of foliage, waiting for their food. And the rose path is garnished by unsightly clumps of ripening daffodil foliage surmounted by the gaunt budded sticks of the roses, pruned or not depending on how efficient we have been. We know people whose gardens are primarily for May, a bath of glorious bloom with no unsightliness apparent. But we have planted our garden for a season of pleasure that will last from the first thawing of the earth until November locks it up again. At all times of the year some parts rest while others vaunt their show, and the great trick, we think, is to arrange plants according to their seasonal peak, so that at any time of the year one part of the garden is at its best while other parts have finished or are preparing for their finest display.

Emphatically at its peak by the middle of May is the rock garden, set mostly with alpine

Only the toughest plants can be expected to thrive across the face of a planted wall, and none is more reliable than Phlox subulata. *All our plants were taken from the thin turf of the local cemetery. A really close shearing after flowering keeps them compact and healthy.*

plants from high elevations. They are typically quite tiny plants, hardly six inches in height and sometimes barely an inch wide, though when really happy many of them can spread into ground-hovering mats as much as a foot across (or, in the case of *Androsace sarmentosa* and some of the phlox, a yard or two). Native to the bleak mountaintops of the world, high above the sheltering tree line, they have evolved to flower in the first few weeks after the snows depart, completing their growing, flowering, and seed-setting work before the quickly returning snows of autumn. This means that for a month or so in high spring – May in southern Vermont, though often July where they are native – they will carpet the ground with jewels, mostly in shades of white, pale and deep pink, and clearest blue. So in May, despite how busy we may be with chores in other parts of the garden, the rock garden is the place we most want to visit. Luckily for us it lies directly in the path between the lower greenhouse, where tools, fertilizers, and plants waiting to be bedded out are kept, and the house and upper reaches of the garden above.

When we first began our gardens here, we had not intended to have a section devoted to rock plants. Our first love, and still our deepest, are woody plants, flowering shrubs, and trees. Perhaps because our new garden required larger plants simply to cover the ground and structure it, or perhaps because we were younger then, we had little interest in the beginning in such tiny, briefly flowering things. But a life in gardening – like, we suppose, a life in anything else – leads one finer and finer degrees of discrimination; the things that were too subtle to notice in the beginning have become sources of intense pleasure in the end. Still, we might not yet have reached that point except for a happy accident, one of so many

that has enlarged the scope of our garden and our pleasure in it.

There is no flat land in our mountain garden, not even so much as three square feet (unless we have made it that way). A sloping terrain is at once a great advantage and a great challenge to a gardener. It is an advantage because changes in elevation offer the precious qualities of variety and surprise and distinctive habitats, from dry sloping banks to damp shady bogs. But it is a challenge, because even gardeners who are young and fit would rather move through a garden with more attention to its plantings than to the effort of climbing up it. So access must be contrived to seem as logical and effortless as possible. It is always good, too, in steeply sloping gardens, to have a place to rest, to stand still and look about. And of course, buildings generally require a flat pad on which to be built and a bit of level land before and behind.

Seven years ago, when we converted the upper greenhouse into a winter garden, it became apparent that we would need another one, a working greenhouse – neat and pretty if possible, but mostly a place to store tender plants, to start seeds, to fiddle with green things throughout the winter, and, crucially, to store all the garden paraphernalia that was rapidly accumulating about us. To achieve the flat land that such a structure would require, we had a bulldozer cut across the lower slope of the garden, a slope that had been, when it was the second of our four vegetable gardens, gentle enough that a hike up it was no great strain on wind or muscle. But to get the fill he needed, the bulldozer operator was required to make deep cuts, producing a precipitous slope in the heavy wet clay. The work was done in July, our driest month, but water nevertheless oozed out of the ugly yellow

Having been assured that many cranky alpines would thrive in coarse, gravelly sand, we filled our planted wall with "bank run." Daphne cneorum *var.* pygmaea *thrives on such a lean diet, bearing its richly fragrant flowers at nose level on top of the wall.*

With a name longer than the plant is wide or tall, Campanula tridentata x saxifraga *grows on the top of the planted wall. Far showier, and also choice in its way, is a sheet of lavender-gray* Phlox subulata *found in the cemetery among hard magentas and strident pinks.*

earth and collected in a narrow pool at the base of the slope. "Gawd!" said our bulldozer operator, a neighbor from up the road, "you got a really major water problem here. You're going to need drainage tiles all through this." "Oh, no," we said, standing there bemused with rapture as dirty water cut little rivers down the slope. "It's perfect. It's great!"

This was not the first time we perplexed our neighbors over what we were up to, nor certainly the last. Few people would find much sense in a permanently wet slope ending in a stagnant, mosquito-breeding pool. But to us it was the ideal situation for an alpine garden, one such as rock gardeners dream about and sometimes contrive at horrific expense with underground watering devices. For by sheer good fortune we had uncovered a true moraine, in which water percolates through the soil continuously, just as it does on the high mountain slopes where so many rock plants are native. And the stagnant pool at the base would provide the perfect habitat for bog plants like the beautiful native lotus; the variegated form of *Acorus calamus, Iris laevigata* 'Variegata'; and the great banded and frosted rushes. With the addition of a few ditch minnows, mosquitoes would not even be a problem. So we felt that our site had once again presented us with a great gift. All that our steep and gooey slope needed to become the perfect rock garden — in our eyes at least — was the addition of a few large rocks, some soil amendment, a gravel mulch, and lots of plants.

We were lucky again in acquiring the rocks. For our mystified bulldozer operator had for years stored gigantic boulders — some as big as Volkswagens — in a waste place up the road. They were the detritus of his labors, irritating obstacles in the pouring of new cement basements and now clutter on his land. And they

were free. So, on his bemused invitation, we took some white school chalk up to this graveyard of stones to X and number any we liked. There were all sizes and sorts, white and yellow marble, cold slate and crumbly shale, and wonderful thick plates of aged granite. His opinion was that we should take the marble, because "It'll show up better among the plants"; but we of course chalked the granite, choosing flat, oblongish stones as big as we thought could be moved. Our plan was to build a series of outcroppings that would mimic, as closely as possible, the native ones we had studied. With great patience on his part and nervous exactitude on ours, we laid natural-seeming terraces across the slope, burying at least a third of each stone in the earth to suggest that it was part of the living bedrock, exposed by erosion but retaining sustaining pockets of soil in the crevices.

Most bulldozer operators are quite sensitive people with a practiced awareness of how the earth behaves; it is their business to study it closely, and they can become quite enthusiastic about such a project once they understand what you want to see. A bulldozer is also both a huge and a thrifty luxury, for as mounds of earth are scooped out and enormous rocks put into place, one cannot but think of the hours and hours of frustrating and sweaty labor saved by not having to do the work by hand. Still, the labor is always fraught with tensions, and you must be clear in your own head about the vision you intend to turn into reality, and give clear instructions. ("No, tilt it; tilt it just so." "But the last one you wanted perfectly level!" "Right; tilt this one.") And if things do not seem just right, you must be prepared to hurt feelings and increase frustrations by having everything torn up to start all over again. If you are the slightest bit foggy in your vision, it is far better to serve coffee, or whatever, to the operator while you fret out the problem alone. Clashes in aesthetic judgment are also inevitable. ("This egg-shaped one — why don't we stand it upright?" "No, bury it so just the top shows, just *barely*.") But sculpting the earth and putting in major stonework is a tremendous pleasure, as close as the average home owner is likely to get to the feelings of William Randolph Hearst when his towering live oaks arrived at San Simeon by barge and railway flatbed. One is laying the foundation for a pleasure that will last for as long as one has to garden in one's place, far longer (one hopes) than the memory of the tensions involved or even the bill that must be paid.

When the stonework in our rock garden was completed, we were left with a space about 120 feet across and equally as deep, roughly bowl-shaped, with three gentle terraces cut into the slope and an S-shaped path leading from the lawn above to the greenhouse below. We also had a great deal of ugly wet clay. All through the spring and into the early summer, when the work was finally finished, we had been accumulating plants, treasures ordered from nurseries that specialize in alpine plants, and others dug and divided from other places in the garden. Because we were impatient to clothe the ground, or perhaps because we were guided by a deeper wisdom, we spent little time preparing the soil. We did not lace it with compost and peat to achieve the devil's-food-cake-like consistency rock gardeners usually want. Rather, we worked in a little Pro-Mix to lighten each planting hole and popped in a tiny specimen, hoping for the best. We finished the whole surface with a two-inch mulch of pea stone, both to unify the space and to suppress weeds.

The results have been surprising. Gentians of all sorts thrive there and even self-seed,

auricula primroses grow to the size of cabbages, and many choice plants thought to be too tender for our climate survive and flourish. We cannot recommend our practice with authority, for all sites are particular in their needs, and ours has the inestimable benefits of fresh mountain air, cool nights, and evenly spaced rainfalls. Also, water percolates through it continually from above. But we have come to feel that heavy clay, if it is not of the plasticine sort that adds pounds to one's boots as one works, is a rich medium for cultivating plants, particularly alpine plants. All that is necessary is that it be lightened somewhat for questing roots, and that it be kept evenly moist. So many of these plants seem to relish it, particularly if they are given a dressing of granular fertilizer rich in phosphorus and potassium. (For it must always be remembered that though these plants have little available nitrogen in the soils to which they are native, and do not wish it, they usually enjoy a mineral-rich medium, provided from decomposing rock and particles of sand.) Whatever the source of our luck, the plants in the rock garden thrive, and it has asked little attention from us beyond perpetual weeding (for weeds thrive there too) and has given us much pleasure.

Gardeners who become interested in the fascinating world of rock and alpine plants cannot do better than to acquire a copy of the late H. Lincoln Foster's book on that subject, *Rock Gardening* (Houghton Mifflin, 1968; reprint edition Timber Press, 1982). It remains the classic in its field, remarkable both for its erudition and for its grace and wit. Every page of it should be read, though initially the novice is apt to be overwhelmed by the huge range of plants discussed, which includes many much-neglected American natives. One can also join one of the many chapters of The American Rock Garden Society, where in monthly meetings one will see slide presentations by authorities on specific groups of plants. Even better, one will come in contact with some of the best gardeners in North America, always generous with their knowledge. Better still, there are usually sales of plants after each meeting, to be had cheap and often with cultural advice from their donors. The American Rock Garden Society also offers an extensive seed list annually to its members, the best and surest way to acquire many of the plants one has learned about and come to long to grow.

What is or is not an alpine or rock garden plant has always been a subject of hot debate, especially in a society that is very well organized and jealous of its particular interests. We are hardly purists in this regard, preferring to think that a sturdy border perennial or even a common annual, if it looks good there, belongs in our rock garden. So learned visitors sometimes survey a planting of which we are very proud and murmur acidly, "Very pretty, but of course *not* a rock garden plant!" We have our share of fussy gentians, tiny rosetted androsaces, and saxifrages, whose half-inch wheels of leaf are frosted by the lime they extract from the earth to make protective shells for themselves. Primroses of all sorts flourish, as do fragrant dianthus in many forms. But there are also irises, particularly the small ones with the species *pumilla* in their ancestry, ranging in color from white to many blues, watery or deep, and pale or strong peach to orange. Most interesting of all in this group are the ones that are an odd whitish green or greenish blue, such as 'Ice Cube', 'Green Spot', and 'Funny Blue'. There is one for which we do not have a name, but which is the color of a

sky threatening bad weather. We call it, aptly but utterly without authority, 'Tornado'. These shorter bearded irises seem less prone to all the disfiguring fungal diseases that spoil the effects of their taller relatives, and when they do go "off," somehow their untidiness is more tolerable with lots of rock and pea stone about than it would be in the border. And as our garden is windy, particularly in late May when irises tend to bloom, their fragile, iridescent flowers are less likely, being closer to the ground, to create an effect of discarded Kleenex lodged among their leaves.

Alliums, too, are great favorites with us, for all of them seem to flourish mightily in stiff clay soils. There is not one that we do not think pretty, including even the common culinary onion; the fantastically goose-necked garlic; grassy chives with their pretty flowers of mauve, pink, or white; and the Egyptian onion, with fat bulblets atop its hollow stalks instead of flowers. So far these more familiar members of the onion clan have found their place in the vegetable garden. But others, the so-called ornamental onions, grow in the rock garden and contribute to it not only their splendid flowers, but also a few grassy accents among the tufts and ground-hugging mats of the other rock garden plants. Some, such as *Allium cernuum*, with its abundant down-hanging bells of a curious grape sherbet color, blend beautifully with the silver-leaved plants around them. Others, like the tiny *Allium caeruleum*, had better be studied alone; its little six-inch shaving-brush-like leaves and its rich blue flowers can get lost among taller subjects. *Allium flavum*, graceful from the time it first emerges to the point in mid July when its minaret-shaped buds open into pale yellow bells, is welcome wherever it pops up — or almost anywhere, for it *can* pop up in the midst

It is surprising that Primula auricula *flourishes in the heavy earth of our rock garden, for such plants are generally assumed to want open, free-draining soil. Our finest specimens are still cultured in hand-thrown English clay pots for late-winter display, but those that are not of the first distinction find happy homes among the rocks, where they make a cheering show.*

of a rare kabschia saxifrage, or worse, in a drift of irises. Then the little bulbs must be dug out patiently with an old casing knife, and if they have thought to crouch for protection under an iris rhizome, it must be lifted to get at them. For it is true of most alliums that when they are really happy they will seed all over the place, just as the dreadful wild garlic does in pastures, tainting the milk of the cows. So if one grows these plants, it is a good idea to deadhead them after they bloom and before their quickly maturing grains of seed fall to ground. Otherwise one will quickly end up with an allium garden, pretty perhaps, in its way, but irritating if one had something else in mind.

It is not these plants, however, that cause sniffs from the rock garden purists, for their great charm breaks down all barriers. But planted among them — and among other plants deemed acceptable by the rigid of mind — we are apt to allow two or three Scots thistles, *Onopordum acanthium,* to develop from furry, two-foot-wide rosettes into towers of spiny silver eight feet tall. Clad top to bottom in fierce prickles, they are topped in high summer with magenta thistles and the promise of a thousand children in the next generation. We have also found many border asters useful for autumn color, particularly the low-growing forms of *Aster dumosus* and *Aster novi-belgii.* And we have discovered that the greatest problems with asters — mildew and mites — are less severe in the airier and more spacious rock garden. Into our rock garden we also drop tender plants for summer display, such as peach red diascias with their little monkey faces; *Phygelius capensis;* the "Cape" fuchsia, with panicles of inch-long bells, orange in the species, yellow in the 'Moonraker' variety; and one *Corokia cotoneaster* plant, a mass of tarnished silver wire

with a few pathetic, tiny spoon-shaped leaves sprinkled here and there.

We also encourage a few self-seeded annuals, even those whose abundant progeny can become a dreadful nuisance. Among them, our favorite is most certainly *Argemone grandiflora,* which has silver acanthuslike leaves and is topped from late June to early October with three-inch-wide white poppies, ghostly and beautiful. Of all of these plants that come up, only perhaps 3 percent can be left; but one will have to weed anyway, and so why not "weeds" that can be wonderful, at least in the very few one chooses to leave behind? But we also do not hesitate, surveying the flats of annuals we have on hand in May, to poke in drifts of some for which we have no other place, or that we think will do well in the rock garden and provide beauty in the summer and autumn when so many rock gardens look rather dull. So if we have a six-pack or two of *Salvia farinacea* left over, we will try to find a bit of bare ground to make a drift. *Salvia coccinea* has only recently become available in garden centers, and the airy scarlet flowers of the species — or better, the peach-colored ones of the 'Brenthurst' and 'Bright Eyes' varieties — are perfect in the rock garden. *Nolana paradoxa,* the "Chilean Bellflower," will open its morning-glory-like flowers of pale blue all summer along the paths, and even a few sweet alyssums (*Lobularia maritima*) left over from bedding elsewhere can be tucked here and there for mats of tiny blossoms — white, soft pink, or purple and deliciously scented of honey — all summer long and into the autumn.

Some biennials also find their place in the rock garden. They are generally a neglected class of plants, for gardeners find in them the frustrations they associate with annuals — lots of fiddling for a brief show — extended over a

two-year period (the first year of which produces, of course, no show at all). In most garden spots, it is hard to nurse the first year's
tuft of leaves because conditions are often too
crowded. In the rock garden, however, off to
the edges, there is always a bit of room. Sometimes, too, a few seedlings will show up toward
the middle, at the edge of a path (where the
best seedlings always occur), promising just
the right amount of height and bulk to prevent the overly fussy look too many rock gardens have. Our favorite in such a site is
Verbascum blattaria, which has basal leaves of a
dark crinkled green, over which towers an elegant candelabra of blossom rods, each flower a
pale primrose yellow with a dull purple spot in
its center.

All this is to say that a rock garden may be
most wonderful not as a rock garden per se, in
the sense generally understood by the strictest
members of The American Rock Garden
Society. Even when quite small, gardens gain
distinction — and their owners gain experience,
knowledge, and pleasure — when they are sub-
divided into separate habitats, each with its

own special character and its own cultural
requirements. To cultivate many alpine plants,
one does not need a rock garden. Any open
airy place exposed to the full force of the sun,
sloping a bit if possible, not too rich in nitrogen but with an abundant mineral content, and
mulched with gravel or sand for beauty and for
water and heat retention — any such place will
do. Nor will one necessarily want, given such a
place, to group only the tiniest plants close to
the path or at the edges, despite their indisputable charm. Other plants also relish such
conditions, and may grow better there than
anywhere else in the garden, surviving temperatures they are not supposed to endure and even
self-seeding. Perhaps, lacking major rocks or
outcroppings, one will end up with an effect
closer to a high mountain meadow than to a
scree, or even to the sort of abandoned vacant
lot through which one cut as a child, not
because it was really the shorter way to school,
but for the marvel of the wildflowers that
grew there abundantly. Such an effect may not
be a rock garden, but that will not be a bad
thing at all.

June

*J*UNE in Vermont is other people's May. What are almost everywhere else thought of as May's flowers — lilacs, azaleas, tulips, and rhododendrons — do not bloom here until we are within sight of the solstice. Visitors to our garden from other places experience in this month a curious time lapse, rather like the unsettling sensation of a momentary return of youth. For the flowers they have bid farewell for another year in their own gardens reach their peak here in June, spring keeping company with summer. The geographical location of Vermont, halfway between the equator and the North Pole, both delays spring and hastens autumn. So if our winters are long and our springs tardy, the reward is a summer rich with the borrowed glory of two other seasons.

Even in Vermont not all tulips wait until June to bloom. We plant the earliest ones here and there about the garden, particularly in the rock garden, where the species sorts — mostly short of stature and precocious of bloom — thrive for years in the heavy, mouse-free clay, opening their jewel-like blooms even when winter is hardly over. Pretty as they are, they are still little things, lacking the stately grandeur of the later-flowering Darwins, cottage tulips, and lily-flowered forms, and so they should be studied for themselves and not as precursors to the great tulip show. *Tulipa batalinii* always delights us on its own terms, with six-inch-tall cups of sulphur yellow tinged with apricot. *T. humilis pulchella violacea* is the color of a lipstick no longer worn by anybody, not pink or purple or red, but all of those colors blended into an even hue and set off by a black stain in the center. *T. saxatilis bakeri* 'Lilac Wonder' is a softer, gentler color, pale washed pink with a deeper stripe down each petal and

Though many small-species tulips bloom early in the spring, the stateliest ones wait until the end of May and the beginning of June to flower. We like their pointillistic effect in the perennial garden, rising above the still-increasing growth of the perennials. Planted deep — eight inches or more — most tulips will persist for many years.

a pool of clear yellow in the center; and *T. dasystemon* 'Tarda' – unaccountably named, because it comes so early – is a bouquet of as many as six open flowers on one stem, yellow and white like correctly scrambled eggs.

It seems a rule among plants, though one certainly broken by many, that the tiniest bloom early, as if they knew better than to compete with grander garden relatives. So these little tulips, which are always cheap and so can be planted in generous drifts, get the business of flowering over with long before their stately cousins are at it. But the real tulip show, what one might even call the tulip splash, waits until mild days and cool but no longer cold nights hold sway. Then it seems to us that we cannot have too many of them, for their elegance of form, their waxen sheen, and the lusciousness of their colors stir strange feelings, far deeper than the mere appreciation of a flower. "Tulipomania," the madness that swept northern Europe in the seventeenth century, seems to us, if not entirely sensible, at least understandable. We plant tulips by the hundreds – a thousand is not too many. But keen as we are for them, we are still particular about how we plant them, and where.

We could, of course, spread tulips all over the garden, in bays of shrubbery, along the rose path among the last daffodils, across the slopes of the wild garden in pockets still sunny enough to flower them. But there is, it seems to us, an essential formality, a high civilization to the major tulips. So we plant them in the perennial garden, our only formal space, and one that has, in early June, little more in the way of distractions than the cool, tidy growth of emerging perennials. The short domes of pretty geranium foliage, the emerging shoots of platycodon (still looking like diminutive asparagus), even the rich crinkled rhubarblike

leaves of *Crambe cordifolia* and the bland new growth of border phlox and bee balm – all clothe the shanks of the tulips and provide an attractive foil to their gorgeous chalices of bloom. Tulips ought never to be planted too thickly together – certainly never in the gobs of undifferentiated bloom one sees in the great Dutch display gardens, admired by so many, or in public parks. Rather, they should be spaced so that each bloom rises distinct from its neighbor, the whole planting dancing pointillistically over the garden or like the vivid dots of enlivening color in a somber painting by Corot.

Many gardeners neglect to plant tulips because the ten or fifteen cents one pays for each bulb seems costly for the return of a single flower. Given the beauty of a tulip, we would not be motivated by such thrifty attitudes. Lacking other funds, we would put by the irritating change one accumulates – the pennies, nickels, and dimes – just for an annual tulip fund. But contrary to popular belief, most tulips can be coaxed into a decent perenniality by planting them deep, a minimum of eight inches and as much as twelve, in the rather stiff soil that underlies the humus-rich top layer of the garden. Deep planting prevents the bulbs from fragmenting into nonflowering bulblets (for any bulb will reproduce more freely the shallower it is planted) and mice, voles, and other creatures that relish tulips may not burrow so deep. Depredations can also be lessened by planting the bulbs late, at the end of September or even in early October, and never using bone meal or any organic fertilizer, which will attract skunks and raccoons.

Planted this way our first tulips persisted for five years, turning to clumps and producing abundant flowers, albeit of varying sizes (which in itself is nice in its way). But we became bored with the effect — a mix of practically every color available — and so we dug them out in early July and gave them to a friend, whose meadow they now grace. We replanted the perennial garden with a limited range of pale pink, red, and cream, thinking that as tulip bulbs are cheap, they afford opportunities for the gardener to play at various color schemes and effects, much as annuals do.

That second planting was very nice for two flowering seasons, but now we are prepared to play again. So those bulbs too have been removed to our friend's meadow, and late this autumn we will replant the perennial garden with alternating drifts of only two colors, the nearly black 'Queen of the Night' and the ice white 'Maureen'. The great trick here will be to feather each drift barely into the next, so that waves of white give way at the edges to waves of black and back to white again. We cannot say if this scheme will be effective, for it exists at present only in our minds, where so many garden schemes seem dandy until they get onto the ground. But if it does not work we can try again with even bolder or more subtle effects. Drifts composed entirely of viridiflora tulips — each orange, red, yellow, or white flower marked with stripes of leaf green — might be the next scheme to try. Viridiflora tulips are not much grown except by committed tulip maniacs, for their flowers look strange in combination with other, more vivid colors. They are generally called, with an air of dismissal, "artistic." But planted alone their effect would be weird and wonderful, like a faded old botanical print.

To us tulips are rather like camellias, making up in other ways for the one quality they lack, which is fragrance. But the June garden is never lacking in fragrance, for lilacs grown throughout our garden in several species and many hybrids provide it in abundance. Lilacs are the most old-fashioned of country shrubs, growing round every farmstead and village dooryard in New England, sometimes the only apparent ornamental concession against stark housefronts and the edges of hard-worked fields. Indeed, many an abandoned farm, burned down to the cellar hole of carefully stacked fieldstone, is apparent only from a hoary lilac or two, flourishing still in neglect. In such places one might expect to find only the common lilac or perhaps its equally venerable white counterpart. But in fact many of these old plants are fancier specimens, hybrids of the "French" lilacs bred in vast numbers by the firm of Victor Lemoine et fils between 1876 and 1927. At one time 450 of these lilacs were said to exist; they may still, for a happy lilac is forever. Some of these old plants might show paler or deeper tints of lilac deepening to blue or purple; others will be double, their heavy heads hanging down like bunches of grapes. It is interesting to ponder how such horticultural sophistication came to appear in this one plant in a region that had little money or patience for mere ornament. But in early June lilacs are everywhere in Vermont, at high school graduations, at weddings and church suppers, and on everyone's kitchen table. One presumes that it has been so for a long, long time.

But if lilacs appear in the most modest of gardens, and often are the lone survivors where such gardens once were, they are not to be scorned by the most sophisticated gardeners. For their fragrance is incomparable, and though they bloom briefly — two weeks out of the year — their muscular trunks develop rapidly and become covered with patches of gray pigment and even with lichens, giving an air of settled maturity to comparatively young gardens. For the best effect young lilacs should

We often envy gardeners in warmer climates for their ability to grow camellias outdoors, or palms and cycads. In June, however, we may be envied in turn for our colonies of Meconopsis betonicifolia, *the fabled Himalayan blue poppy, which thrives in our deep, humusy soils, relishing our cool nights and evenly spaced rainfall.*

be limited to three or so main trunks and never be allowed to grow up into a thicket of many stems and suckers. Each of the main trunks might be bent outward with string and a peg in the ground for a more graceful eventual effect, such as a strong trunk under which one must stoop a bit to enter the garden gate. Though many gardeners allow a few suckers to develop into young trunks in the center of the shrub and then cut out the older ones when the new have reached flowering age, we so much like the effect of the thickened old trunks that we prefer to top-prune to keep them vigorous, cutting out about a third of the upper growth of each shrub just after flowering. With that treatment the old stems will continue to produce vigorous new growth, though not all of it will flower the first year after pruning. The only other attention lilacs require, assuming they were planted in well-prepared ground and are growing well, is a thick layer of fireplace ash about their roots in early spring or, lacking that substance, a dose of lime. For all lilacs require a sweet, limey soil to flourish, and so should never be grown near acid-loving plants such as rhododendrons. Borers, too, can be a problem in some gardens, making their presence known by the thriftless growth of a shrub and by small holes and trickles of sawdust around its trunks. It is doubtful that poking a wire or a straightened paper clip into the holes on the chance of impaling a borer will do much good to the plant, though it may do some good to the soul of an angered gardener. The chemicals sold for borer control are not pleasant things, though one may be driven to their careful use by sheer frustration. Gardeners who shy away from all chemicals must take pale comfort from the fact that borers will never kill a lilac outright, only its older trunks; new trunks will quickly

spring from the base of the plant, and will, for several years, be unattractive possibilities for tunneling.

It is *Syringa vulgaris,* called the "common" lilac for its ubiquity though never for its effect, that is most treasured in gardens. Less commonly grown and less powerfully fragrant (though powerful in every other way) are the hybrid lilacs developed by Miss Isabella Preston in Ottawa in the early twenties. By crossing *Syringa villosa* and *S. reflexa* (both extremely cold-tolerant and both worth growing on their own) she produced a race of hybrids of remarkable size, both in their eight-inch-long panicles of flowers and in the shrubs themselves. They can quickly attain fifteen or twenty feet in height with thick elephantine branches. They will grow naturally into dense, twiggy shrubs aiming at being trees, but we like them best when their arborescent ambitions are encouraged by removing weak and secondary growths to reveal the thick gray trunks. They are called, appropriately, "Preston" lilacs, and of the many forms available, we are most fond of 'Nocturne' and 'Agnes Smith'. 'Nocturne' blooms in a deep, rich purple with extraordinary abundance — our fifteen-year-old plant has produced over a thousand panicles, more or less, this season. (That is of course an estimate, though not an exaggeration; because it grows in the perennial garden, where all must look fresh in July, we patiently removed each spent flower head, perched atop a stepladder. So we know.) 'Agnes Smith' is less prodigal with its flowers (a blessing, as it happens), but they are of a haunting and rare color, pale pink in bud and white when open, but prettiest in between when pink and white shade together. It is a taller plant than 'Nocturne', reaching twenty feet or so. Embowered in flowers it is distinctly bosomy, a word we never fail to apply to it in full bloom, with a blush and an apology to Agnes Smith, whoever she was. All the Preston lilacs bloom later than the regular *vulgaris* species, never commencing until the second week of June. They are therefore invaluable, not only in themselves but as an extension of the lilac season.

Isabella Preston is one of many gardeners, both amateur and professional, who have endowed gardens with splendid plant forms previously unknown. Any gardener will be familiar with other examples of this gentle philanthropy, such as *Daphne* x *burkwoodii* 'Carol Mackie', with its silver-edged leaves and clouds of fragrant pink flowers, first recognized by Mrs. Carolyn Brett, whose maiden name it bears. Northern gardeners whose gardens are too cold to grow the native American holly, *Ilex opaca,* much less its glamorous English relative, *Ilex aquifolium,* must be forever grateful to Mrs. F. Leighton Meserve, who crossed the super-hardy Japanese holly, *Ilex rugosa,* with English holly. This produced a whole race of handsome and hardy plants, the best of which are perhaps 'Blue Prince', a pollinating male, and the abundantly berried 'Blue Princess' and 'Blue Angel'. Mrs. Meserve received a citation from the American Horticultural Society for her achievement, and her name is commemorated forever in the taxonomic names of her creations, all known as varieties of *Ilex x meserveae.* And no gardener who loves rhododendrons can be ignorant of the achievement of Dr. David Leach, who has spent a lifetime crossing and recrossing species and hybrids of rhododendrons. He has produced a race of sumptuously flowered plants in yellow, peach, and ivory, as well as more traditional rhododendron colors — all bred to thrive in northern gardens.

In any collection of plants one will find several that were originally singled out of an undistinguished swarm by the attentive eye of some gardener, passed on to friends, and propagated eventually by commercial sources for even wider distribution. Sometimes we know why they are called by people's names, as, for example, *Eryngium giganteum,* which is called 'Miss Wilmott's Ghost' because the legendary Ellen Wilmott used to sprinkle its seeds in other people's gardens to remind them of her. But who was Mrs. Moon, and was it she who first grew the fine pulmonaria that bears her name, with its silver-splattered leaves? Can anyone now tell who Miss Mellish was, though the perennial sunflower named after her, a form of *Helianthus* x *multiflorus,* has graced garbage cans and out-of-the-way places in gardens for fifty years and more? These are questions the curious gardener asks, and sometimes one stumbles on the answer in some old or new garden book. Most often not, however, and a plant with a curious name remains a part of the unrecorded history of gardening.

No such oblivion attends the most glamorous of all June-blooming shrubs, however, the hybrid azaleas now known, for convenience, as the "Exbury" azaleas. Their development has been documented from the first, beginning in 1820 in Ghent, Belgium, where several hardy American species were crossed with the European yellow-flowered *Rhododendron luteum.* The result was a group of shrubs that possessed remarkable vigor, abundant though small flowers, sometimes good fragrance, and usually brilliant autumn color. Best of all, these first crosses were extremely hardy, able to survive winter lows of at least $-20°F$ without bud loss or dieback. Among the Ghent crosses, few are now still grown except in very old gardens, though one or two — most

Our perennial garden once included a good bit of yellow, but it is now limited to plants that bloom in shades of pink, rose, mauve, blue, and white. Though such a limited range of color makes it even more difficult to ensure a full season of abundant flowers, the results have been much more satisfying.

double-flowered yellow 'Narcissiflora' — have never been bettered. Mostly the Ghent hybrids contributed their already mingled blood to a second tier of plants, made by crossing them with two Asian species, the larger-flowered but tender Chinese *Rhododendron molle* and the hardier, vividly colored *R. japonicum.* These crosses were undertaken beginning in 1850 at the venerable firm of Waterer at Knap Hill, producing plants with larger, richer flowers than the Ghent hybrids.

But it was in 1920 that these already excellent garden plants were used as the foundation for a new race that is opulently, even outrageously, glamorous while still possessing the hardiness and vigor of the first crosses. In that year Lionel de Rothschild acquired the Knap Hill stock. With tremendous enterprise and unlimited wealth, he created at his Hampshire estate hundreds of hybrids, ruthlessly selected, but with enough left over to furnish the largest garden almost by themselves. These plants flower in huge trusses, from white and ivory to pale and deep yellow, scarlet, orange, and near red, so abundant that the rest of the plant, which may be as tall as fifteen feet, seems completely smothered. Most are stocky, muscular, multistemmed shrubs that will, fairly quickly, create great tiered masses in the landscape. They are rich in flower, satisfying in leaf, are sometimes colored scarlet or maroon in autumn, and are always arresting in winter when nothing remains but their scaffold of gray trunks and branches. No cold garden, even a very small one, should be without at least one Exbury azalea, which can, with good culturing and careful training, almost do duty as a small, multistemmed tree.

There is a vividness to many Exbury azaleas that makes them sometimes more satisfying out of flower than in. To put the matter more clearly, a hybrid like 'Gibraltar' — vigorous, wide, perhaps ten feet across and as high, loaded in June with huge trusses of vibrant, burning orange — has a tropical magnificence worth staring at, even visually bathing in. Sometimes, however, beauty of a particularly assertive sort robs all around it of value; one's eyes widen, one stares to winking and is sated, and there is nothing more worth looking at for a while. Because of this somewhat dizzying effect we have passed over the Exburys that are red, scarlet, or chrome yellow in favor of plants more subtly colored — the ice whites, suave ivories, pale peaches and apricots, clear cherry reds, and fine butter yellows. But even with the exercise of this restraint, we like the Exburys we do grow to be planted by themselves, set apart in their own space where, in their moment of glory, they won't possess quite so overwhelming an edge in competing with other blooming plants.

Indeed, there are several essentially manmade plants — delphiniums, bearded irises, and tea roses come quickest to mind — that may always look their best when separated off from any companions, grown for their brief moment of splendor and then taken for granted. If we had a larger garden than we do, and an out-of-the-way corner leading perhaps to a garden shed or an old springhouse, and if the ground were perfectly level (always necessary for the best formal effects), we might well have an Exbury walk. It would need to be hedged on either side with evergreens to form a soothing background, and down the middle there should be a stone path, rather wide, say four feet. On either side could be planted the most vivid Exbury azaleas available, evenly spaced in a totally self-conscious pattern and moving in a carefully orchestrated sequence from the deepest reds to scarlets,

Vines trained on posts often provide an essential note of verticality in a mixed shrubbery. One of the best vines for this purpose is Lonicera x brownii *'Dropmore Scarlet', which blooms from June until October. Placed before it is the silver dome of a single specimen of* Artemesia *'Powis Castle' trained as a four-foot standard.*

orange-yellows, strong clear yellows, pale primroses, and finally ivories with a yellow blotch. (Only the pure whites would be excluded, but of all Exburys, they are easiest to use elsewhere in the garden.) In its season of bloom the Exbury walk would be the only place in the garden to be, a glorious experience; out of season it would be simply a well-tended walk, a double line of graceful dark green bushes mulched heavily against weeds, serene and lovely when one strayed that way. Gardeners are of course always dreaming of special gardens with special effects, and no harm and possibly a great deal of good will come from keeping these imaginary gardens in one's mind. For who knows what accidents — a mature tree blown down, a children's play yard outgrown, a bit of land acquired when the neighbor's house goes up for sale, maybe even a forced relocation — will make of them a valuable fund on which one can draw for new gardens, new pleasures.

But as we so far lack the right space for this fantasy Exbury walk, we have achieved something of the same effect by grouping our plants in the border that curves around the front lawn, providing privacy from the road. There they make up the first tier of tall woody plants that one sees when standing on the grass. They are backed by a second tier, taller still, composed of small multistemmed flowering trees — really like giant shrubs in effect — which include the graceful Sargent crab apple, *Malus sargentii;* the double-flowered cherry, *Prunus* x *subhirtella* 'Hally Jolivette'; and a Washington thorn, *Crataegus phaenopyrum,* which has brilliant scarlet berries in autumn. Behind these are evergreen trees, *Pinus resinosa, Picea pungens,* and *Picea omorika,* selected to provide screening from the road in winter and a quiet backdrop at all seasons. Though none of these

plants are in rows, but are rather staggered in a spontaneous outline, they achieve the requisite sense of depth by being in three layers, the minimum perhaps for any border that satisfies, whether herbaceous or shrubby. The small flowering trees provide abundant blooms in their space, but they were selected for May flowering, just before the Exbury azaleas take fire. There is no effect of overplus, as there would be if all bloomed simultaneously.

Nor are there any herbaceous plants around the azaleas that would compete (probably unsuccessfully) with their flowers. Instead the foreground of the border is planted primarily with hostas, which will have pretty mauve or white flowers in midsummer but at "Exbury time" present only soothing mounds of fresh green, chartreuse, powdery blue, or variegated green-and-yellow or green-and-white foliage. We have also planted *Kirengeshoma palmata* in the border, in a deep bay made by three of the azaleas, where it relishes the light shade they cast and only its vinelike leaves and graceful arching growth are apparent in June. (In August, when the stage belongs to it alone, it produces elegant ivory shuttlecock-shaped flowers.) A drift of *Astilbe chinensis* var. *pumila* hugs a strip along the front of the border. Only a low ferny carpet in June, by the end of August they are topped with foot-high architectural spires of strong pink veering toward magenta, and are best seen by themselves. Beneath all these herbaceous plants are collections of crocus species, each planted in its own submerged plastic nursery can and covered with hardware cloth against the depredations of bulb-hungry varmints. They are splendid in their brief season in early April, and then vanish, overtopped by hostas and astilbes and replaced in vividness by the azaleas in June.

It is around the summer solstice that the azaleas hit their peak here in Vermont. The date marks a decided shift in the garden's character and in the lives of those who live within it. The days are as long now as they can be. The sky grows light by half past four in the morning, and there is a lingering glow until as late as ten at night. These are perfect conditions for an after-supper ramble, when the fading light flatters shrubs hardly noticed in daytime and obscures yellowing leaves, spent flowers, and the many weeds that escape us despite our vigilance. Frost is so much a memory that it hardly seems possible, though the evenings are cool enough for a fire in the kitchen and at least one wool blanket must remain on the beds. Windows and doors can be left open day and night, admitting the evening cool and sometimes curious, scarcely identifiable night sounds — the eerie shriek or mournful hoot of night birds or the chorus of half-grown coyote pups celebrating something good brought home to them.

Those open windows bring inside not only the sounds of the night garden but also its smells, for nothing so characterizes the flowers of early summer as their scent. There are three scents we particularly associate with June: the smell of peonies, roses, and freshly cut hay. Between the first and the last lies only about three weeks, but those weeks are the summation of our work, the apotheosis of summer, and the realized dream of a country life.

The most fragrant peonies are the great old-fashioned doubles such as 'Sarah Bernhardt' (1906), 'Duchesse de Nemours' (1856), and, best of all, 'Festiva Maxima' (1851), which must bear the sublimest name ever given to a flower. There are beautiful modern hybrids of herbaceous peonies; the loveliest of

all are the single and semidouble forms with paper-thin petals of white, shell pink, or coral surrounding a great boss of golden stamens. Sadly, however, these beautiful recent creations often lack scent, or bear only the slightest memory of it, and so cannot compete in our affections with the great cold-cream-scented globes of the older forms.

It is for their flowers, scented or not, that peonies are chiefly grown, and in their season they are queens of the June garden. But peonies are rare things among perennials, offering beauty from the first appearance of their copper-colored shoots until autumn burnishes them with tints of butter yellow, ripe-pear brown, and maroon. Throughout late summer they have the carriage and dignity of shrubs, their broad, leathery, dark green leaves providing weight and substance to more fiddly perennials long after their spent flowers have been cut away. Planted well, in a deep, wide hole rich enough with compost to support a plant that will live fifty years and more, the only care they seem to require is careful staking, particularly if they are the rich fin-de-siècle forms we like the best. For the blooms of those plants are so large and heavily packed with petals that even the morning's dew will draggle them in the dirt. Peony hoops — one of the best of Scotland's many gifts to gardeners — work well with all but the heaviest double peonies, though the round circles of galvanized wire must be inserted early and each one propped up with its three legs inserted deep into the soil. But 'Festiva Maxima', with which all peonies must compete for honor, must unfortunately have each of its huge white flowers marked with a maroon stain and staked individually to thin bamboo rods. They can be arranged in such a way, however, that each flower assumes a most

If a garden is to be thought of as a series of rooms, some of them must be hallways, satisfying passages from here to there. Our favorite is the rose path, planted with old-fashioned varieties such as the corseted 'Henri Martin' and with peonies, perennials, and grasses.

graceful carriage, seeming, by a suspension of disbelief familiar to gardeners, as if it weren't staked at all. For this purpose we use our own bamboo stakes, harvested each autumn from a large clump of *Phyllostachys aureosulcata* growing in borrowed warmth from the foundation of the glassed-in winter garden. It takes over an hour to stake one plant, and we never resent the trouble, though all but the peony hoop that will support the foliage for the rest of the season must be removed in ten or twenty days.

Though we use peonies at regular intervals in the perennial garden, we set the best of them on both sides of the rose path, over its whole length, alternating with globes of English boxwood. Both provide weight and order to the tangle of antique roses that grow behind them. The roses flower right after the peonies; in some years the two overlap, mingling their fragrance and their beauty in a way that cannot but recall the heavy opulence of France at the end of the last century. There is not a rose in our garden that isn't fragrant. The very idea of a scentless rose steals away half the reason for growing roses at all. So we pass over the hybrid teas, where too often perfection of bud and flower form has been sought at the expense of fragrance. It costs us little to do this, for hybrid tea roses are not reliably hardy in our climate, even with the protection of unsightly rose cones made of white plastic foam or mounds of compost. Besides, there is a somewhat smug angularity to a tea rose which — in our climate at least — always lacks the loose abandon of the old shrub roses. So those are the ones we grow, all from the hardiest families — the hybrid rugosas, albas, gallicas, and damasks. Even among these we limit our choices to the most fragrant forms. There are enough of them, even after such rigorous selection, to furnish a garden much larger than

ours (for which we are very glad, as we have an almost unlimited appetite for them and seldom let an October pass without adding another dozen or so). We scan the rose dictionaries, of which there are so many now, and when a head shot showing a rose in its most flattering light catches our attention, with the notation that it is an alba, gallica, or damask (and better, that it is fragrant), we know that it is time to widen a border. In some ways the beds that lie just beyond the kitchen door and the French doors off the living room have been shaped and expanded just to provide a place for more roses. For though many other plants grow there out of rose season — perennials rare or common and annuals in their bright profusion — in June it must seem to visitors that we grow little else but roses. It seems so to us.

One pays, of course, quite a lot for a rose. For though there is no flowering shrub richer in its beauty and its evocation of other places and times than a rose, it must be said that out of bloom they are at best undistinguished plants, and at worst positive afflictions on the beauty of the garden. In some ways the tea roses forbidden to us (and perhaps out of the logic of sour grapes, scorned) have an advantage here. For though in climates where they grow really well we have seen them successfully integrated into wonderful garden schemes, generally they are given a place of their own, where regimented rows and neat paths lend them, out of flower, at least the ordered logic of a vegetable plot. We have found, however, that we can have all the roses we want and still create beautiful garden pictures throughout the year, by combining our roses with other plants that will either enhance them while they are in flower or be quite absent until they have finished blooming and need all the help they can get.

Though for the most part they only bloom once, we prefer antique shrub and species roses to modern hybrids for their good health, their abundance of flowers, and the way they make of late June a sort of festival of roses. This selection at the edge of the planted terrace is on its own roots, which means that several varieties have suckered and interwoven to form a varied mass of blooms.

There is no season of the gardening year when boxwoods are not invaluable for structure, though in a cold garden they will not grow without effort. These cushions of English box must be covered with clumsy wooden crates each November in order to exclude all light and wind. But even in June, when there is so much else to look at, their quiet dignity repays the effort they require.

Nothing is more useful for this purpose than English boxwood, which can — either trimmed or untrimmed as one wishes — organize almost anything, even a patch of weeds. There is an ancient association, also, between boxwood and roses, dating back at least to Roman times and perhaps beyond. No gardener needs to be told that though we are constantly trying new combinations, new plants just discovered or new forms of old ones, there are combinations that will always please, in part because they *have* pleased for as far back in history as we can go; thus they have become a part of the collective memory prepared for all gardeners, even those yet unborn. So our main plantings of roses always have the rhythm of boxwoods to hold them together, a quiet foil in rose season and a powerful organizing principle when June and its roses are both over. Peonies, too, are always good for this, for a peony out of flower is a peony still, in ways as valuable as when it was rich with bloom. And among the roses, boxwoods, and peonies are a host of other plants, many chosen for transitory blossoms that come in July or August or even September to help the roses out when they are only a tangle of stems, disfigured — though we hope not — by black spot and the depredations of Japanese beetles. We will talk of those later, in their best time, for at present the garden is racing to its highest point, and the simple appreciation of the splendors it is unfolding is a full-time occupation, never mind getting them down on paper.

Nepeta tuberosa is a wonderful plant, its spikes of purple lasting all summer. It is tender for us, but its tubers can be dug and stored as one would a dahlia. Tender also is the coral-colored Agastache barberi *'Apricot', the wrong color for this garden, but so lovely that we let it be.*

July

*T*HE temperament that makes up all serious gardeners must have a large component of melancholy. For however glorious the garden's display might be, the true gardener seems always to look behind with regret at what has passed and ahead with longing at what is to come. To be squarely anchored in the moment, to savor just what lies before one and want nothing more — this must be a great bliss for those who possess the ability. Certainly it is true, even for the most brooding of gardeners, that the conjunction of a perfect day, a good stint at weeding, and perhaps some unlooked-for success with a difficult plant can make one feel, for a little time, that the garden is, just as it is, enough. Alas, though it may be otherwise for many gardeners, for us such moments are fleeting, and no more at our command than a perfect night's rest, the return of love, or that lift of the heart one experiences at

the brief recapture — through a fragrance, a bar of music, an old book with one's name in it — of the sensations of youth.

Generally we move through our garden at the height of our splendid but brief summer with a strong sense that it is all so transitory, that it goes by so fast, leaving us with hardly a chance to catch our breath before it is gone. By a leap of faith not too hard to bring off, we trust that the garden will be here next year, even richer with beauty, even fuller of pleasure. A slightly harder leap assures us, somewhat, that we will be here too, to make it happen and to glory in our success. The hardest leap of all is to believe that the garden might endure after us, for a time at least, giving pleasure to someone else, who might work on its canvas a whole new range of beauty we have not even dreamed of. For most of that we will simply have to wait to see.

Those gardeners whose main interest is in keeping their places trim and tidy, with perhaps a few flowers for color or to cut for the table, may be mystified by our line of thinking, if they have not been totally mystified by the efforts we expend on the garden itself. They are gardeners too, of course, and we hope that some of the experience we have offered, and perhaps a new plant or two we have discussed, will be useful to them. But it must by now be abundantly apparent that gardening is the controlling focus of our lives, that we live by its seasons, both physically and spiritually. Gardeners of our stripe will not be mystified as to why, at this season of perfection, we turn to serious thoughts. For July is one of the great hinges of the gardening year — perhaps the greatest. There are others, for in gardening the relationship between past and future comes into focus more clearly than it seems to in other pursuits of life. The two other periods that most clearly mark transitions for the gardener are April and September. They tend to be mostly unmixed in character: April brings the awareness that all that one wishes to achieve still lies ahead, while September brings a sort of tranquillity, a sense that the garden — still lovely, certainly — has been as much as one had a right to expect, and maybe more. But between April's youthful optimism and September's mature acceptance comes July; characterized both by longing and by hope, it constitutes a sort of horticultural midlife crisis.

Shame on us, perhaps, for being so confused by the beauty of July. For the weather then is lovely, perhaps the loveliest of the year for those who crave warmth. There is a predictability to the brightness of the sun that one experiences in no other season, one faultless day breaking after another. There is real

heat, the kind that puts an end to garden chores (for us, at least, who are not used to it) and offers a quiet, restorative day at the river. Rain still falls, but it occurs late in the day or when we are sleeping, the earth's risen moisture returning to it as thunderstorms crashing against the mountains. Best of all, we wake some mornings to find that a cloud has settled into the garden, trapped against our hillside until the sun's rays dissipate it in milky streams, leaving the garden wet with its moisture and every spider web silvered over.

The garden, too, is richer with flowers than it has been before or will be again. Much of the perfection of June remains with us, for cool nights cause the blooms of roses, geraniums, verbascums, and dianthus to linger. The flowers of high summer, the platycodons, mondardas, border phlox, and thistly eryngiums, will just be showing color, and Joe Pye weed will be purpling the roadsides and the garden by the end of the month. Even those flowers planted for their autumn bloom will count for something, not as bloom but as a promise. The native asters have just branched into flowering stems, and *Aster laterifolius* 'Horizontalis' has assumed the substantiality, almost, of boxwood. *Sedum telephium purpureum* 'Autumn Joy', planted in every garden but still indispensable, will have attained its full height, its waxy celadon leaves surmounted by pale florets like broccoli past its prime. Much lies before and, really, not too much behind.

But still we note, and sadly, that the sunrise, though usually glorious, comes a little later each morning. By the adjustment of an internal clock we always find curious, we tend to sleep a little later in the morning, rising not at half past four or five, but at six, or seven. As the month advances, darkness may catch us still at dinner, and the magical twilight rambles of

In the narrow mountain valley in which we live, it often happens that we wake to find a cloud settled
in the garden, dissipating with the first light of morning and promising a fine, clear day.
Never is the perennial garden more glamorous.

June are replaced by moonlit walks instead. We begin to read again, not garden books and certainly not catalogs, though those offering bulbs have begun to arrive and are carefully put aside. There's a little more music on the stereo in the evening. We go to bed a little earlier.

Still, on a moonlit night in July, nothing would keep us from rambling around the garden after supper. For in July the garden is rich with plants that are fragrant only at night, most of them white, eerie lanterns in the dark. Though the night-scented phlox, *Zaluzianskya capensis,* will begin to open its flowers around five, thereby somewhat redeeming its grassy anonymity, it is not until it is truly dark that its fragrance will begin to creep in the kitchen door. Though we have never quite dominated its impossible Latin name (commemorating a Polish physician, Adam Zaluziansky von Zaluzian), we like it so much that we have planted it everywhere. Its six or eight inches of tumbled, narrow-leaved growth takes little room and never competes with sturdier, more permanent plants. A large pot of it also sits just outside the kitchen on the terrace, and the smell of it, rather like a raspberry tart with almond crust, comes like dessert at the end of dinner, replacing the sweets we no longer eat.

Along the rose path we have also planted flowering tobaccos — the four-foot-tall Jasmine tobacco, *Nicotiana alata,* and the shorter but no less fragrant *N. suaveolens.* Both are disheveled by day, their white blooms hanging limp in the sunlight. But at dusk they raise their trumpets up to view, and they fill the night air with smells that are as delicious to people as they are to the moths they are really trying to attract. Farther along this path grow other flowers that scent the night. *Mirabilis jalapa,* the old-fashioned four-o'clock, opens its buds late in the afternoon, not precisely at four o'clock

but according to its (perhaps more accurate) sense of when that should be. Its sweet, lemony fragrance intensifies as darkness falls. At the top of the walk grow perhaps the best, certainly the most dramatic, of these night-scented treasures, two *Datura meteloides* plants. Their foot-long trumpets on sprawling four-foot bushes recall the poisonous splendor of Dr. Rappacini's garden in Hawthorne's tale. Perhaps their beauty would seem less sinister if the flowers were pure white, as they are in a related species, *Datura metel,* the jimsonweed of the southwestern United States. But on *D. meteloides,* each bloom is flushed with an unearthly violet like some chemical phosphorescence beneath its skin.

All these plants are annuals, or at least are usually grown as annuals, though *Datura meteloides* is in fact perennial and can be cut back at frost time, lifted, potted, and stored in a cool place until it is wakened in April. Treated this way, our *D. meteloides* plants have lived over four seasons, becoming larger each year and offering earlier blooms than seed-grown plants. But a significant part of the beauty of our garden in July, and later, is provided by true annuals, and on that subject we wish to spend a bit of time.

Annuals are technically plants that complete their entire life cycle, from seed through vegetative growth and flowering and back to seed again, in a single growing season, usually not longer than three or four months. Actually, however, many plants commonly grown as annuals are really tender perennials, capable of blooming in one season from seed, but also able to regenerate for many seasons in warmer gardens (and in colder gardens if one is willing to make the necessary effort) from roots, crowns, and stems. They are all plants that gardeners tend to begin with early and return to late, for a

Of all the sections of our garden, it is the room devoted to perennials that we try to keep fullest of flowers. Still, we never forget the beauty of plants still waiting to bloom, or of those whose structure is more important than any flower they might produce. Sedum telephium purpureum *is valuable at any time during the growing season for its celadon leaves, its broccolilike buds and, later, its red plush flowers. And though we appreciate the white thistles on* Echinops spaerocephalus, *it is its form that earns it its place.*

Datura metel *and* D. meteloides *are similar in character, the first bearing pure white flowers and the second, flowers flushed with lavender. Though they are tender perennials, they are best grown as annuals. They produce rank, sprawling growth and huge night-scenting trumpets throughout high summer until frost.*

row or two of bright marigolds or zinnias is often where one's love of plants begins, and rare forms of salvia and precious or barely known species like zaluzianskya or alonsoa tend to grace the most established gardens. So, for that matter, do marigolds and zinnias, though they may be forms like *Tagetes signata pumila* 'Lemon Gem', whose lacy leaves and small flowers possess a refinement far removed from the great heavy mops David Burpee loved; or *Zinnia angustifolia*, with thin narrow leaves and immaculate single flowers in yellow, white, or pink; or maybe *Zinnia peruviana*, its half-inch daisies of burnt pinkish orange too subtle to recommend it much to any park foreman in charge of bedding schemes.

Gardeners who lie between the rank novice and the sophisticated plantsman may tend, however, to turn away from annuals. The ten or so species that make up the primary trade of many garden centers — petunias, marigolds, zinnias, impatiens, *Salvia splendens, Salvia farinacea,* and the like — are depressingly overused, often in ways that rob them of the real beauty they possess. Annuals may also seem to steal attention from more serious garden matters, like creating quiet frames of evergreens and deciduous shrubs or cultivating perennials (which represent true wealth to the gardener because they may be expected to live from season to season and may be divided for even fuller and more beautiful effects). Annuals are transitory, by definition, and the time and space they require may seem too high a price for their brief season of glory.

For many years we shared this attitude, and we are not sorry, for the first requirement in creating a garden is to cultivate, in Graham Stuart Thomas's words, "suitable permanencies." The wise gardener, faced with an undeveloped plot, will begin from the edges and work inward, planting shrubs and trees to create a frame for the garden and perhaps to separate it off from the visual distractions and the flurry of the world that lies beyond. He will see first to its structuring plants, the hedges, bays of shrubbery, and small trees planted along borders yet to be. He will cultivate ground covers and perennial plants, perhaps initially in a nursery off in the corner of the yard or in unused rows on the edges of the vegetable garden. He will lay down the paths of the garden, probably following the irrefutable logic of feet that have worn away the grass in their passage from here to there. He will contrive terraces and seating areas, usually near the house as transition to the garden, close to the kitchen door for outside dining or near the pool for quiet sunning. If his site is hilly, he will need to terrace and bank the soil, perhaps laying in retaining walls or bits of rockery where it is very steep. All this is a lot of work, leaving little time (or money) for annuals, which do not assist in the steady development of the garden. But when all that work is done, when the garden begins to achieve an air of settled maturity and inevitability, he may find himself turning to annuals, all plants that cannot by themselves make a garden and that provide pleasures relatively brief in their duration.

So it was for us, but now, strolling through our garden in July, we think it would be a very poor thing indeed without true annuals and those plants usually grown as annuals. From the beginning of our history as gardeners, and long before we had fully absorbed the wisdom of Gertrude Jekyll, Vita Sackville-West, and other clever garden writers, we thought of our garden as a series of rooms, each with its own special character and its own distinct collection of plants. We began, as people generally

The bank along the side of the barn is clothed by a very hardy English ivy, Hedera helix 'Baltica'. *The annual Himalayan impatiens,* Impatiens glandulifera — *a glamorous plant that grows to eight feet and is full of flowers throughout July and August — self-seeds into the bank. Roughly 3 percent of those that come up may be allowed to stay, the rest laboriously weeded out. But they are worth the trouble.*

do, with a perennial garden, placing it in a clearly defined rectangular space bordered by our yew hedge on the house side and by stone walls on the other three, built (rather clumsily — we have gotten better at it) from stones unearthed as the garden developed. We followed it, logically, with the rose path on the other side of the hedge, first just a narrow strip of roses against the hedge and later, when the flat stones were laid for the path, a border on the lawn side as well, too meager at first but expanded to a satisfying width of twenty feet as our passion for old roses increased and we needed the space to plant them. Having worked our way almost to the top of our property, it seemed reasonable to continue across the back, through the sheltering woodland and down to the stream, where the bog lies, and up the other side, across the hillside that slants down to the bog. Then we carved the rhododendron border out of the woods below the drive, leading to the lower greenhouse and the rock garden that serendipitously resulted from its construction. All these sections of the garden are special habitats — sunny and fertile; deeply shaded; fresh with running water or stagnant where it collects into seeps; dry, gravelly, and windswept; bosky with dappled shade — each demanding its own special plants, each providing its own special season of beauty.

But it must be apparent that we are very greedy (as plantsmen if not otherwise). There are sections of the garden, such as the heather bank, that still produce only one season of beauty and then rest quietly until a full year has passed and they take on beauty again. Most of the garden, however, is asked to do double or triple duty, to be glorious in its special season and then present more interest, and yet more still, for as long as we can manage.

Herrick's wisdom that we must gather rosebuds while we may is not for us; we want to gather them, or a suitable substitute, throughout early and midsummer, into August, and through the long autumn until winter finally comes to say "Enough." So in every section of the garden suitable to them (the heather bank emphatically is not), we plant annuals, never in a way that asks them to be the only interest in the spot, but in association with other plants, with shrubs and perennials that will lend them weight and make them seem what they are best at seeming — bright, joyful, spontaneous accidents against the enduring fabric of the garden.

We try many experiments with annuals; some we discard after a season while others come to be permanent effects in the garden, replanted each year or allowed to reseed because they are perfect where they are and cannot be bettered. For example, no more satisfactory choice for the front of the house has occurred to us (for we have tried and failed to think of one) than *Nicotiana langsdorfii.* It is planted beneath the tall *Ilex verticillata* plants that screen the windows, and its tiny bells on arching four-foot stems produce a sort of pale green rain over the low boxwood hedge that makes up the front of that border. Happily, the nicotiana is shallow-rooted enough, as are most annual plants, that it does not disturb the sheets of *Scilla siberica* that make a carpet of blue there in April. Happily, too, it accepts the wide range of growing conditions that obtain there, from dappled shade to full sun, growing uniformly throughout and so presenting a consistent show across the whole face of the house. Most happily, the effect it creates is beautiful but very quiet, as seems best to us in front of a house that is surrounded by so many gardens so full of color.

Alliums of all sorts thrive in the heavy soil of the rock garden. But it is a self-seeded annual,
Argemone grandiflora, *a Mexican prickly poppy far from its arid desert home, that
provides the greatest interest from late June until frost.*

Another effect we have never felt we could improve upon is a planting of *Salvia viridis* (syn. *Salvia horminum*) in front of the hedge of *Berberis thunbergii* 'Rosy Glow' that hugs the sunny foundation of the winter garden. The bed that both these species occupy is twenty feet long and four feet wide, coped along the edge of the planted terrace with old Belgian granite blocks. Between the hedge and the coping is a collection of autumn crocuses, *Crocus speciosus,* that provide our last show of flower color from late October until past Thanksgiving. But they are dormant in summer, leaving only a strip of gravelly bed that could not be planted with deep-rooted perennials without strangling the crocuses. A planting of *Salvia viridis* is perfect there, not only because it cohabits so well with the crocuses, but also because the color of its flower bracts — a true Tyrian purple in the form we grow, called 'Cambridge Blue' — consorts magnificently with the pink-and-burgundy-splashed foliage of the berberis. One can have *Salvia viridis* in other colors, a soft romantic pink or an odd and beautiful greenish white. But the effect of the blue is rather like a botanical echo of the best and oldest glass in Chartres Cathedral, and as it has given us intense pleasure for five summers now, we see no need to change it.

Nor do we wish to change — assuming we could — the effect created by the self-seeded annuals that occupy certain other sections of the garden. To the timorous gardener a self-seeded annual is a terrifying thing, for unless he is terribly vigilant in maintaining his garden, he may find that he has simply introduced yet another noxious and persistent weed to make his life difficult. So it is with the stately *Impatiens glandulifera,* which reaches eight feet in the moist, shady places it loves. Above its wide-bladed tropical leaves are panicles of cunningly fashioned pouched flowers, each an inch across and colored pinkish white, shell pink, or burgundy. Our plants occupy a difficult site, the shaded ivy bank beside the barn, which slopes steeply down to the stream. By July they have created a sort of hedge beside the cobblestone walk there, person-high and richly topped with flowers. At least, the ones we allow to remain have done that, for the rest — hundreds and hundreds of them — we patiently weed out in barrowfuls as we struggle uneasily for footholds in the ivy. Still, impatiens are not bad to have as a weed, if one is to have weeds, for they sprout in only one late spring wave, and they are fat and defenseless, easy and satisfying to pull. Despite our warnings, however, almost every gardener who visits in mid to late summer admires the plant and wants some. ("It will take over your garden," we admonished one visitor, who replied, after our own heart, "Could I be so fortunate?") So when the seed is ripe we take paper bags and explode some into their bottoms, for impatiens are "touch-me-nots," which shoot their seeds great distances on the merest contact, with little pops and a tiny, electric-seeming shock. Those gardeners who take home these bags of seeds (which must, incidentally, be exposed to freezing temperatures or they will never sprout) may bless or curse us, according to the sort of gardener they are. But that is the way with so many desirable plants and the people who beg them.

Almost as aggressive, equally beautiful, and avidly requested by gardeners who see it in bloom is *Argemone grandiflora,* the Mexican prickly poppy. It is native to the southwestern deserts of North America, but it has seemed to find a happy home in our rock garden. It is a marvelous plant, its spiny glaucous green leaves veined in silver, with four-inch flat poppies of chalk white lasting from late June until quite heavy frosts appear. It makes of the rock garden, whose alpine plants are best in May, a whole new event throughout the summer. But it too will produce sheets and sheets of tiny plantlets, requiring rigorous thinning if the ones that remain are to develop into handsome two-root-tall bushes with abundant flowers. (And the survivors must be carefully chosen so as not to murder the tiny rock garden plants that principally grow there.) Self-seeding, or an early seeding from a packet onto cold ground, is the only way to have argemone if one wants it, for like many members of the poppy family it is entirely unwilling to be transplanted. For us, however, its annual reappearance is a great honor, despite the work it requires, for who would have thought it could be so at home here in the cool wet mountains of Vermont, so far from its native place?

There are many other annuals that will reappear in a garden, even a cold one, once they have grown happily for a season, though few are as aggressive as *Impatiens glandulifera* or *Argemone grandiflora*. The little sweet alyssum, *Lobularia maritima*, once it has been tucked along a path or its seeds sprinkled among withering daffodils, will always come back, usually near where one first planted it, though often in unexpected and perfect places it has chosen for itself. English daisies, *Bellis perennis*, will sooner or later get back into the mown lawn they love, reverting from heavy hybridized pom-poms to tiny single stars against the grass, opening on sunny days between mowings all summer long. We once planted *Hibiscus trionum* 'Sunny Day', and though we liked its three-inch cups of primrose yellow, each centered with a dark mahogany throat, we did not like it so much as to plant it again. But it has planted itself ever since, appearing here and there as if to shyly ask for a second chance at our affections. Any nicotiana will also usually return, whether a pure species like *N. sylvestris, N. langsdorfii*, or *N. alata;* a handsome reversion from the stocky, ungraceful "bedding" nicotianas; or a wonderful chance hybrid, as happened in our garden with a spontaneous cross between *N. langsdorfii* and *N. alata.* This hybrid is a stately plant, five feet tall with abundant lime green bells that are larger and flatter than those of *N. langsdorfii* but not, sadly, fragrant like *N. alata.* A first generation cross of any plant cannot be expected to produce stable seed, however, so we carry it over each year by taking root cuttings in autumn, stubby four-inch sections of thick white root that we bury in damp sand and keep cool but not freezing until small plantlets appear in April. Potted on, they make substantial plants quickly, flowering long before any of the seed-grown nicotianas have made their first buds.

Among all the annuals we grow, however, we most treasure those with sufficiently light and airy growth that they may be tucked among perennials for an additional tier of flowers with no fear of overcrowding. *Ammi majus,* for example, is planted all through the perennial garden in May, wherever five or so inches of bare ground show between the developing crowns of platycodons, veronicas, phlox, sedums, and the like. It grows quickly, with hardly five leaves per plant but many light green stems that weave upward and outward to the light and are topped, from late May into July, with fragile wheels of white flower lighter than, but closely resembling, Queen Anne's lace (*Daucus carota*). All across the front of the perennial garden's borders we also scatter the seed of *Nigella damascena* 'Love in a Mist', choosing always the fine, dark blue double form called 'Miss Jekyll's Blue'. The leaves of

Though the perennial garden is devoted primarily to permanent plants, annuals increase its interest and contribute a necessary lightness. Particularly valuable are those that may be planted in tight spaces, such as Ammi majus, which never crowds its neighbors and produces in early and midsummer its delicate Queen Anne's lace.

nigella are always pretty, hardly more than tiny threads coalesced into a green haze. Above them are oddly crafted ragged-robin-like flowers, each in a ruff of green filaments, which are later followed by funny, puffy seeds, presumably the "Devil in the Bush" (the other common name for this plant). Nigella is so light and fine that it will never crowd out other plants; rather, it may itself be shouldered about, pushed forward over the stone borders of the bed or squeezed into a green crevice between two burgeoning perennials. Those are always especially nice effects, creating just the sort of tumbled effulgence and romantic abandon we love in a garden.

The third of our favorites for tucking into bare spots in the garden is *Verbena bonariensis,* though it is actually not an annual but a true perennial. It is capable of over-wintering in gardens warmer than ours and producing many slender four-foot stems from a single crown. We would not, however, like it better if it behaved that way for us; what we treasure is the form it assumes as a first year plant from seed or from cuttings. Grown that way it has a juvenile lissomeness, each single stem branched into an airy candelabra and topped with tiny, vibrant violet flowers packed tight into flowering heads. There are really plants that dance, and *Verbena bonariensis* dances all along the rose path, brightening up the canes of the shrub roses that have long since ceased to flower. It continues its display from late June until late September. It is pretty always but perhaps most handsome — as so many purple, violet, and magenta flowers are — when the soft autumn hazes and the turning leaves give them an added glow. After severe frosts the single plants may be dug, cut back hard, and potted, to be stored in cool conditions until they may be brought into vigorous

growth in April and bedded out again in May. We take only a few stock plants, perhaps three or four, and root their first young spring growth in sand for as many plants as we want. That way we have the grace we crave from *Verbena bonariensis,* with each young plant tucked into a hollow among the roses to rise above them.

If we are fond of annuals, we are ardent about biennials, a group of plants avoided by many gardeners for the difficulties they pose. Biennials usually require a whole year of growth before they send up blooms. But as a consequence they achieve a stature that few annuals can realize, at least without running the risk of being gawky. To attain all their potential, however, they really should be planted wherever one wants them to flower and left there for most of their two-year life. This can mean a long wait for their stunning effect, and a painful sense of absence once it is over. Luckily our garden is sufficiently large that we can allow our favorite biennials two or three homes, thereby securing flowers from them in their second year of life, if not always in the same places, at least somewhere.

All is not blank during the alternate years, however, for many biennials form rosettes of leaves that are by themselves very attractive. The great Scots thistle, for example, *Onorpordum acanthium,* is a whirl of broad, prickly gray leaves that can be as much as three feet across, an apt prelude to the seven-foot stem it will grow in its second year. *Meconopsis regia* also forms an opulent rosette, not prickly like the thistle, but downed with hair that shades from silver to gold. Though we like its broad yellow poppies, which open a few at a time on five-foot stems, we would gladly grow it for its first-year rosettes alone. (We do, in fact, always try to have an abundant population of young

Biennials are even more neglected than annuals by many gardeners, because they seem to carry the double curse of being not permanent and not quick. Still, some of the finest plants of the July garden are biennials, including Onopordum acanthium, *the Scots thistle. Here it grows before the shrub rose 'Stanwell's Perpetual' with the gentle* Tanacetum niveum *(also a biennial) at its feet.*

plants coming along, just for their leaves.) The downy leaves of *Verbascum bombyciferum* are neither thorny nor hairy, but so like silver velvet that one wants to stroke them. It may be, with this plant, that we actually do prefer the first year's growth. In its second year it will throw upward a narrow silver spire, downy like the leaves and starred throughout July and well into August with mothlike inch-wide flowers of a pretty clear yellow. But the spire will fall over (not always gracefully) from the weight of the developing seed, and what was silver will very soon become tarnished and rusty looking. It is then, generally, that we remove the mature plants, even in full flower, and replace them with fresh young rosettes out of pots.

Biennials with only moderately interesting foliage seem always to compensate with spectacular flowers. Such is certainly the case with *Michauxia tchihatchewii.* Its improbable name, around which there is no shortcut, comes from two botanists, one eighteenth-century French, the other nineteenth-century Russian. But somehow that impossible series of syllables seems to fit a plant that is in flower so distinctly complicated. In its second year it produces many-branched stems up to three feet tall, each stem laden with large, campanula-like buds that open into blooms that are equal parts backswept white petals and green, forward-thrusting pistol. The whole assemblage is as frankly sexual as an orchid, looking far more appropriate to a steamy tropical jungle than to the place from which it actually comes, the arid, gravelly plains of Asia Minor. Such an origin suits it perfectly for Vermont, and for our rock garden. Experienced gardeners may know this splendid biennial very well, but it was utterly new to us, one more curiously neglected plant that we could not imagine anyone failing to want to grow once they had seen

it. We have been told that wherever it thrives, it will certainly set abundant seed and show up the following year all over. What luck if this is so, for it will be one more glorious "weed" to treasure.

But until 1985, no gardener in America or Europe, however experienced, would have known *Angelica gigas,* for that was the year of its discovery in South Korea. In less than ten years it has swept through gardens, passing rapidly as seed or young plants from one gardener to another in a fantastically spread-out pyramid like a chain letter or a family tree. It is the last of the great biennials to flower, waiting until mid-August to fully unfold its beet red umbels atop their eight-foot stems. The unfolding begins in July, as the stems elongate and the plump, rounded buds thrust out from the leaf axils like the leg of a dancer moving slowly from *passé* to *developé.* Few plants grow with such balletic grace.

Neither annuals nor biennials can by themselves make a garden; they must always depend on more permanent structures to give them value. They are still, however, terribly valuable components of the summer garden, brightening the edge of a path, weaving in and out of perennial plants, establishing themselves thickly in a bay of shrubbery in such a way as to look as if they themselves chose just the spot where they would thrive best. So, at planting-out time in May, we bring home flats and flats of them, grown to perfection by a local garden center from seed we have ordered, saved ourselves, or received from other gardeners. Finding the right places to poke them all in — some where they have grown before, others in any area that promises later to be a little dull or where the demise or relocation of a shrub or perennial has freed up a bit of unused ground — is a wonderful sort of garden play.

More than any other group of plants, annuals and biennials keep the garden fresh and colorful throughout July and into that period ruefully called by other gardeners "the August slump." More important even than that, however, is that they allow endless experiments with color, texture, and plant associations, causing us to grow as gardeners and renewing our interest in sections of the garden that would otherwise be at times unremarkable. So we spread them about wherever we can, choosing always the rare and more unusual forms, glad that we have outgrown the feeling that such plants have little place in an established garden.

More correctly, we plant them *almost* wherever we can, for there are still some sections of the garden where annuals and biennials feel inappropriate to us. The heather collection is one, for heathers are somehow rather uncompanionable plants, always looking best against others of their own kind, with perhaps a stern dwarf conifer or ground juniper — nothing more — for additional texture. There is also a section of the garden whose character is so wild and assertive that annuals and biennials have never seemed appropriate there. It fills the gorge carved out of the hillside by the little stream that falls across the length of our land. The land is quite steep there from the scouring action of the glaciers and the huge granite boulders they left behind. Folding down from the cobbled path and ivy bank on the side of the barn, it rises up again to a fieldstone path that traverses the hillside and connects the area to other sections of the garden. The earth is deep and fecund with the accumulation of aeons' worth of fallen leaves, half burying the huge rocks that must once have lain on the surface. Even in very dry periods it is always moist, and there are places where water seeps

out of its slopes, attempting to make its way to the stream at the bottom. Though we have planted some small trees to provide an understory to the great maples and beeches that rise above, most of the area enjoys full sun or at least half a day of it. As there is a clear view of it from above on both sides, but no easy access down its slopes to the stream, it has been planted with great-leaved, tropical-looking herbaceous plants that relish damp ground. At the top is a large colony of *Petasites japonicus* var. *giganteus,* a plant we love — despite its terrifying rampancy — because of its dark green sails of leaf, three feet wide, borne singly on stalks as tall or even taller. A little farther down is an old clump of *Darmera peltata,* which after fifteen years has grown to the size of a small automobile. Smaller but still imposing are several rodgersias, the best of which are *Rodgersia aesculifolia* and *R. pinata* 'Superba,' their hugeness curiously dwarfed by the even larger plants around them. In seep spots and the wetter places are the native and the Asiatic lysichitons, glamorous plants despite their common name, "skunk cabbage." Asian primroses and astilbes grow in the room that is left, crowded now a bit by bamboos; the elegant four-foot-tall *Sasa veitchii* with its curious, beautifully marginated leaves in autumn; and the taller, noninvasive but still hefty *Sinarundinaria nitida* and *S. murielae,* both of which have wide fountains of growth. There are plenty of flowers here, provided by *Primula japonica,* happily self-seeding and producing its candelabras of cherry red flowers in early June, by the astilbes in drifts of white and pale and deep pink, and, at the end of the season, by the almost magenta *Astilbe chinensis* and *A. taquetii* 'Superba'. By summer's end the marsh forget-me-not, *Myosotis palustris,* will have come of itself so thickly as almost to choke off the stream,

Though the gardens of ecological purists may contain only native species, most gardens are an assemblage of plants from all over the globe. Here, in the upper sections of our bog, is such a gathering, made up of the round-leaved California native Darmera peltata; *the single white and double yellow forms of the marsh marigold,* Caltha palustris; *the French fleur-de-lis,* Iris pseudacorus; *and a hybrid of two Himalayan primroses,* Primula Bulleyana *and* P. Beesianum.

turning it into a floral cascade of china blue flowers. Here and there are some fat ligularias, 'Othello' and 'Desdemona', with cobs of chrome yellow blossoms above their circular maroon leaves; the more slender *Ligularia przewalskii,* with sharp spires of yellow; and *L. tangutica,* with finely cut leaves and shorter spires of dull white. A spreading bush of *Hydrangea paniculata* 'Grandiflora Compacta' snuggles against a boulder as large as it is, producing greenish white cobs of flower in July that turn to fresh white in August and burnished copper in September.

But the real point of this garden is its luxurious leaves, foliage in vast fleshy magnificence, relieved by native ferns and exotic grasses. The combination of the site and the plants established there has created – in our eyes at least – an effect not unlike the deep river gorges of China where Wilson and Forrest and lately Roy Lancaster have searched for botanical treasures. Those who round the corner by the plank bridge over the bog always catch their breath in surprise – including us, who know the site so well. For wherever one thinks one might be, Vermont in summer is the last place suggested by the tropical luxuriance of the plants growing there. One expects, somehow, a flash of fire-colored plumage from a rare tropical bird, or, as in the old Episcopalian hymn, a place "where apes swing to and fro."

To us the effect is magical, though we have had visitors for whom it is simply baffling. "Why," they ask, or simply wonder to themselves if they are polite (any gardener quickly gets to be good at reading the minds of other gardeners), *"why* have you planted these things here, in Vermont, which is so pretty as it is, so peaceful and restrained, so much itself?" The answer to that question is actually rather complex, hardly exhausted by the fact that we love

plants – all plants – and are burningly curious to see how they will grow and look (in the gardener's all-encompassing monosyllable, how they will "do"). The act of gardening is freighted with many impulses; one of the most important is the wish to contrive, just on the spot one has been given to garden, other places and other experiences. A garden thus becomes a diary or a memoir, or perhaps a series of postcards. It is the act of creating and re-creating experience, maybe from memories of the place one grew up in and loved as a child, or somewhere one saw once on vacation, or will see someday when one finally gets there, or even of a place one must merely dream of going to all one's life.

It has really always been so. For from the first, the creation of gardens has been fertilized and cross-fertilized in all sorts of alien soils by nostalgia, sometimes for what has been directly experienced, sometimes for what was described by grandparents or great-grandparents, and sometimes for what exists only in the collective memory of one's blood. Thus, migrant conquerors re-created their distant homelands in walled spaces with fountains, even when the sand-laden desert winds without were half a continent away, and passed down a love for such places to their descendants. With a pocketful of Asian bulbs, crusaders canceled out the memory of the gore they had bathed in. Now these plants are one of the glories of the European spring, as if they were native wildflowers. Packets of roots and slips gave the first immigrants to New England some compensation for their hard voyage, and now lilacs bloom here in every dooryard. Pioneer wives treasured their pots of scarlet geraniums in the backs of covered wagons and grew cuttings behind tiny, frost-covered panes until they burst free as weeds in

The upper bog was our despair until we realized what a splendid habitat for plants it could be, once passage across its squishy ground was secured by a plank walkway. Moisture-loving grasses particularly have flourished here, such as the golden sedge, Carex stricta 'Aurea'; *the arching, variegated* Spartina pectinata; *and the eight-foot-tall* Miscanthus floridulus.

California, the bane of a friend of ours there who hates them. Chinese girls with painfully bound feet grew sacred lilies on high windowsills in San Francisco, from which they personally never escaped, though the bulb is now naturalized everywhere there, blooming magnificently in the dead of winter. Lordly bewigged governors re-created in Williamsburg, Virginia, the formal boxwood gardens of their English youth, and George Washington, though living in a new world, worked his ground always as if it were in England. Even in our small town there is a foreign bean, brought here by a Polish immigrant whose mother sowed it in his jacket so he would not starve in the new land. It is called the "Mike" bean, after his name (or more probably the name his Yankee neighbors called him, their closest approximation to his mouthful of identifying syllables). It is a good bean — fat, fleshy, cream-and-brown speckled, a fine keeper when dried. We all sow it.

But if gardens exist in memory, they also exist in desire. Just as fertilizing as nostalgia is longing for gardens one didn't grow up in, never saw, will never visit. Probably the first step after the most abject needs for survival are met is to grow something pretty, just because it is pretty and for no practical reason. The next, perhaps, is to pursue an act of imaginative re-creation, of the past or future or simply a place in one's mind where one would like to be, or to have been, or to be going. This is all just to say that gardening is one of the most complex acts that humanity is given to indulging in. But, of course, anyone who has read this far into our book will know that much already.

August

AUGUST is one of the quietest months in the garden, matched in some ways only by the deepest winter months. But whereas in those months Nature seems bound in a deep sleep, in August she appears to be merely in a daydream, or perhaps a gentle doze. The songbirds no longer sing, their essential business of finding a mate and raising a brood of young long since over. The weeds, so vexatiously abundant from May until July, have by now all germinated and been removed, save an occasional canny survivor of the native jewelweed, *Impatiens capensis* (our worst weed, perhaps, but very beautiful when its vibrant pouched flowers of orange or speckled pink apologetically appear in the heart of a thorny shrub rose). For the most part the borders that have been cleared of weeds remain that way, requiring only a cosmetic fluff, like vacuuming, when visitors are

due. What is in flower now – the late-season perennials, the annuals and tender plants dropped in for emphasis – hold their flowers for weeks on end, replacing the ephemeral glory of cherries, peonies, roses, and poppies with a sturdy persistence we almost come to take for granted. In the vegetable garden, where bare earth once stood between the rows, there are now lush, full leaves and opulent produce. We wake a little later each day, as the sun rises a minute later than the day before. But that bit of extra sleep, unthinkable in June, is now an accessible luxury, for the tasks that demanded our time in early summer are all done, and those the garden now demands – deadheading, staking, snipping back wayward growth, fertilizing and rearranging potted plants grown for extra color – can all be done in a comparatively leisurely way. In August we wander through a magic kingdom, marveling at how

By August the vegetable garden is rich with produce, its unruly tumble organized by formal paths and the rectangular frame of the split-locust fence. We'll never see more than one artichoke per plant, and that only in a hot, dry year; still it is a bet worth making, for a freshly harvested artichoke is quite a different creature from the mummy bought in the store.

full the garden has grown and imagining only with difficulty that it will soon be past. August is a time of abundance, and it causes us to know, for a time, what we have been working so hard to achieve.

But abundance in any garden is not just for the eye, or at least it ought not to be. It is also for the palate. We are convinced that any garden, however small, ought to offer something good for the table, to remind us that the art of cultivation, so powerfully aesthetic, is also still a residual necessity of our animal existence, motivated by the hope of being well fed. So, early in the life of the garden we planted a series of antique apples at the back of what is now the perennial garden, and the conjunction of their weighted branches with the flowers at their feet conveys to us a sense of complete satisfaction. The first to bear fruit is 'Yellow Transparent'; its apples ripen this month. The last is 'Cox's Orange Pippin', its vivid scarlet fruit keeping company with the late purple asters of October. Between the two is a steady three-month supply of fruit, and hardly a day passes that apples are not eaten here, either out of hand as we work the garden, or in pies, or simply baked with a few raisins, some nuts, and a dribble of rich cream. For that three months (and after, until Thanksgiving, for 'Cox's Orange Pippin' is an excellent keeper) we do not tire of them. Like all the rest of the garden, apples provide a seasonal delight. We are therefore never tempted by the unblemished, waxed sorts the market provides throughout late winter and into spring and even high summer. It's an unthinkable resource — we have schooled ourselves to always eat what is in season, and to preserve, in equal proportions, both the spiritual and nutritional value of what we grow.

There is, of course, always much more at harvest time than we can possibly consume. It is a lucky thing, therefore, that the relatively slow pace of our garden chores in late summer and early autumn allows time for peeling apples and baking them down into sauce to can for the winter, for stewing purple plums into jams (and better, into a runny conserve for plum chicken), for putting up ripe tomatoes for pasta sauces later, and for preparing green tomato pickle according to Joe's grandmother McIver's unimprovable recipe. These are all fruits, of course, and their preservation seems an appropriate thing to do at this season and well into autumn.

But we are inundated with vegetables also, and these we do not preserve, for a canned vegetable is a poor shadow of itself. We could freeze them, of course; for a while we did, just as we used to dry flowers for winter arrangements. Prepared with care, frozen vegetables can be excellent in flavor, appearance, and nutritional value; but we have come to feel that they rob us of all the little festivals of summer, when the first tiny beans are in, when the broccoli is tight and prime, when the corn ripens and the zucchini is still novel enough to be treated with imagination. So though each year we attempt to practice some restraint when we order vegetable seed, still we have more than we can consume. The solution we have found is to give the excess away, though it is sometimes hard to find local takers, it being a sort of proverb in Vermont that one should not leave one's car door unlocked in zucchini season, else two or three baseball bat–size zucchinis will be on the back seat. But city folk are always glad to get a package from the country in summer. And so we send off little boxes to New York or San Francisco or Los Angeles, filled with new potatoes, fresh fennel, radicchio, braids of shallots — whatever we have too much of that is choice and will stand two-day

Gardeners who refuse to grow annuals miss a great help in getting their borders through the August slump.
This four-foot, lime green nicotiana came up by itself, apparently as a spontaneous cross between two species,
Nicotiana alata *and* N. langsdorfii. *Unstable from seed, it must be carried over by root cuttings —*
worth the trouble when it is paired with a deep purple aconite.

delivery without diminishing in quality. The rest we feed to the chickens or the cows, who are always amused by our bounty, and who in turn will feed us and the garden, in so many ways.

Despite the burdens of excess, a vegetable garden has been one of the constants of our life here in Vermont. We planted our first one on rented property when we came here twenty years ago, and we have had one ever since except for a summer we spent in England, rich in other ways but bereft of our own fresh peas. For many years, until other parts of the garden were secured, the vegetable garden was a plain affair, a sort of food factory, simply a patch in which to raise the fresh produce that is one of the joys of living in the country and a compensation for the theaters, restaurants, and convenient shops one must perforce give up. We kept our vegetable garden decently neat and well tended, or as well tended as we could with other and more interesting demands upon us. But our early vegetable gardens were sometimes, it must be confessed, the poor stepchildren of the flower garden, not always an ornament to the property.

One lives by many creeds at once; not the least sustaining of them, to us, has been the belief that every part of one's life should be – if one can get to them all, if one has a little extra time, energy, or money – beautiful in themselves. A vegetable garden is such a *good* thing, in so many senses, that it ought to be beautiful too, especially as one is bound to spend so much time there, and some of it – like at day's end when one is quiet from other labor and is harvesting supper – such important time. So now that other parts of the garden have reached a satisfying maturity, we have turned to the vegetable garden, since it alone offers, in highest degree, the realization of that ancient and commanding goal that all things be useful and beautiful in equal proportion.

Our previous vegetable gardens – shabby things that they doubtless were – have been rather peripatetic presences on the property, moving here or there as advance guards to the creation of the garden itself. The first year after the house was built, we rowed up the raw but fertile clay of the backyard and grew tomatoes, beans, potatoes, and salad crops against the backdrop of the woods. We felt very much like pioneers in the wilderness, which we were in some sense, and which we quite enjoyed. The lawn that now occupies that space is a rather good one, as American lawns go, doubtless having benefited enormously from the deep cultivation of the soil, the lack of weeds, and the nitrogen-rich mulches of hay we piled around the crops. As the garden grew more civilized the vegetables moved, first to behind the yew hedge in the rectangular space currently occupied by the perennial garden, and then to below the drive, where the conifer border and the rock garden are now located. We would say to anyone faced with a new plot of earth, or even with a lawn larger than they wish to maintain, that there is no better way to come to know a particular spot than by cultivating vegetables; for in each of these cases, it was the tending of a vegetable garden that prepared the earth for other gardening effects and taught us the nature of the soil and its needs for amendment, where the prevailing winds strike with greatest force, where early and late frosts gather, and how the horizon might best be brought to earth by frames of shrubs and small trees.

From its location close to the house the vegetable garden then went for some years to a beautiful meadow at the back of the property, half a mile from the house. We justified so distant a location by the beauty of the spot, the privacy it offered, and the fact that a hike to it, uphill all the way, was of unquestionable cardiovascular benefit. Still, it really was too far away to tend properly (for whatever shape you are in, try walking that distance with a fifty-pound bag of lime on your shoulder), never mind to visit for the odd handful of parsley one needed. And so we have moved it again, to probably its final location, the back of a three-acre clearing in the woods that lies just above the house and almost, but not quite, within sight of the other gardens. There we trust it will stay, a fact we have partially ensured by surrounding it with a fence of split locust we bought from a young Vermonter who lives by the practice of the ancient craft of fence building. The rails twist and bend in a satisfyingly uneven fashion punctuated by knots and burls. Splitting them is a time-consuming and frustrating art, since at least half are spoiled when the grain runs out before the requisite eight-foot length is achieved. But the results are as countrified as can be, resonant with simple antique charm and rugged durability. It provides the perfect frame for a vegetable garden, and one on which, to maximize space, cucumbers and beans can be grown and fruits espaliered.

Though the fence and gate (also of split locust) are rustic, the vegetable garden is a more formal space than any other on the property. It is laid out in a perfect rectangle of fifty by eighty feet. There are few straight rows within it, however, the dominant pattern being established by smaller rectangles and squares. In the center of each of these is a bush or small tree, usually a currant or gooseberry. Each bed is edged with lettuce, radishes, or other salad crops, and planted in the middle with larger crops that must be rotated — potatoes, beans, broccoli, cauliflower, or cabbage.

Permanent rows for peas — marked by wire stretched between locust posts — give further structure. We have found that if the soil is kept well manured and limed, the few diseases that strike peas will not occur here. Beds of strawberries flank the main path; from the first two rise sentinels of standard *Hydrangea paniculata* 'Grandiflora', the old-fashioned "Pee-Gee" hydrangea, grown not for any culinary use that we know of, but simply because its cobs of chalk white flowers are pretty in August against the vegetables.

We know many devoted gardeners who have long since given up cultivating vegetables. We never will, and we do not find their argument convincing. It usually runs, "Why bother, when you can buy almost anything in local farmers' markets, for far less money than growing it yourselves? Why not devote all that time to shrubs and flowering plants, to rock gardening?" (or to daylilies or irises or whatever their particular passion might be). We are not convinced because for us there is a deep, elemental pleasure in growing at least some of our own food. Also, though in bean or corn season there is always plenty around to buy, and for little money, even a hiatus of an hour or two at a market stall — never mind two or three days — causes some loss of flavor. And for visitors from the city, though a farmers' market is charming, nothing compares with the pleasure of harvesting their own dinner, and nothing gets them so eagerly out of a harried cook's way as when their polite question, "Can we help?" is answered by, "Yes. You can go pick the peas and shell them." A small word of caution must be offered here: be sure they know what they are doing. For many nongardeners assume that the tomato vine or bean plant gave its all just for the one ripe fruit or pod they pick, and has no further use. Once a

Almost the first ornamental planting we established here was a collection of heathers, now knit after seventeen years into a solid carpet along the drive. In August the heather border becomes one of the most beautiful parts of the garden, though that effect is maintained by covering the plants thickly with evergreen boughs in the winter and shearing them down by a third of their height each spring.

cheery guest of ours returned to the kitchen saying, "I tried to pick some carrots, but they were all too small, so I put them back."

But if one is going to the trouble (if trouble is the word) of raising one's own vegetables, they might as well be the choicest, most flavorful, and most interesting varieties one can find. Rather than 'Katahdin' or 'Green Mountain' potatoes, excellent though they are, it is a great deal more fun (and no more work) to grow a selection of antique or heirloom varieties with wonderful shapes and names such as 'Ruby Crescent', 'Golden Banana', 'Yellow Finn', 'Lady Finger', or 'Cow Horn'. If one is going to grow tomatoes, why not grow the bright pink 'Brandywine'; the heart-shaped, yellow-and-orange-streaked 'Marvel Striped'; the weirdly pleated, almost liver-colored 'Calabash'; the chrome yellow 'Taxi'; the 'Sweet One Hundred', which almost lives up to its name; or the world's tiniest (and arguably most flavorful) tomato, the 'Currant Tomato'. Among salad greens the possibilities are legion — not just the fragile lettuces like 'Oak Leaf' that will not stand shipping, but also rarer things: arugula, miner's lettuce, golden purslane, and mache. As one always has too many beans anyway, maybe it makes sense to choose those that retain superb flavor rather than produce by the ton, such as the dark green 'Triumph de Farcy', the violet-streaked 'Marbel', the bright purple 'Royalty Purple Pod', or 'Taverna', as slender as half a pencil and suitable, if you like to do that sort of thing, for making little evenly trimmed bundles tied neatly with a ribbon of carrot. Somewhere, too, there should be room for a row of fava beans, never abundant producers but unforgettable served as a first course with bits of Italian bacon and sautéed onions. The world of unusual onions — bunching, bulbing,

and bulblet-forming, sweet and mild or tear-jerkingly pungent — is largely unexplored by most gardeners and is rich with treasures. And there are fennels, black radishes, puntarelle, radicchio, orache, scorzonera, and so on — an endless list of possibilities for exploring. Fortunately, within the last ten years small companies have sprung up like land-cress, offering unusual, exotic, and heirloom vegetables. They make possible a much more exciting vegetable garden and a much more exciting dinner table. So much so that, for us, who used to wonder too why we grew vegetables, the question now sometimes is why we grow other things, especially since we have made the vegetable garden (finally) a *real* garden, pretty and satisfying to be in.

However exotic its contents, the vegetable garden still seems — as it should — firmly anchored in its place, a small rural property in southern Vermont. That is not the case, however — or not quite the case — with the other sections of the garden. The plants we grow that are hardy but outrageously large and tropical-looking — the petasites, rodgersias, and bamboos — have by now spread themselves to their fullest extent, luxuriating in the frequent rains and sometimes muggy conditions of the month. But if in August the garden seems, more than at any other time, a garden someplace else, it is perhaps because so much of what grows here now doesn't belong to this place, and survives here only by our contrivance. The annuals, of course, are largely tender, originating in Mexico or India or Argentina or California. But in August here it is not only annuals that fill our borders with flowers. Perennials and even shrubs from just the same warm worlds give our Vermont garden a richness it could never achieve if it only contained hardy plants. So, in the perennial garden, keeping company with the last, tardy black lettuce poppies, the lavender and mauve border phlox, and the ballooned and open platycodons, are tender salvias, agastaches, and pelargoniums, and shrubby thunbergias, solanums, and agapanthus.

Of all these nonhardy blooming plants, none make a larger contribution than the salvias. There are hardy salvias, of course, but by late August most of them – the great gray-leaved *Salvia argentea*, the deep blue *Salvia x superba,* even the odd, yellow-flowered *Salvia glutinosa* — have largely finished their show for the year. But the tender ones, mostly natives of the Southwest and Mexico, do not even begin to flower until the days grow short and the evenings cool. It is a curious thing how certain groups of plants – border geraniums come immediately to mind – suddenly enjoy such a vogue that gardeners feel they must have every one. So it is, currently, with salvias, but there are so many of them that one cannot have every one, try though one might. We grow perhaps fifteen species of them, and would like to grow the rest, even though in winter it seems to us, when they cram the storage room of the lower greenhouse and make passage through it positively hazardous, that we grow already far too many.

But having carried them through the winter in pots, regrown them, and dropped them into the perennial garden, we are sure in August that we haven't quite enough, so valuable is the contribution they make. The largest we grow is easily *Salvia involucrata,* which in California gardens can become a shrub eight feet tall. And though we cut ours back to a six-inch stub each autumn when we lift and pot it, it still achieves six feet by August. Its foliage is not particularly interesting, consisting of medium green arrow-shaped leaves about four inches

long, trying for something fancy by a red central vein; but its flower panicles can be as much as three feet long and are clustered with odd, inch-long tubes with puffed cheeks and a pursed mouth, all the color of cheap pink lipstick. Planted among deep blue aconite and the silvery foliage of *Artemesia pontica* 'Powis Castle', it is very striking, looking only a little brazen.

Much more tasteful is the airy, two-foot tall *Salvia leptophylla.* Its ensign blue flowers are born sparsely on thin stems in early summer, but by August they dance by the hundreds above its delicate, grass green foliage. Like most salvias it is an amazingly quick grower, making large bushes from three-inch rooted cuttings within two months. It is the sort of plant we always treasure, for its delicacy and thinness of growth makes it suitable for planting among other things without crowding them out, thus providing a feathered effect across the front of the border and an extra ration of flowers.

Of the same shade of blue, though upright-growing and taller (to four or five feet), is the "bog" salvia, *Salvia uliginosa.* It bears a useful common name, reminding us that whereas some salvias will flourish in rather dry soil, it prefers conditions that are at least always evenly moist. Though native to Brazil, it is one of the more frost-hardy of the tender salvias, and may even over-winter in the ground in gardens a zone or two warmer than ours. The advantage its hardiness offers us is that it may be left to flower longer into the autumn than many of the salvias we grow, and we need be in no great hurry to lift its fibrous crowns for potting and winter storage.

Another salvia that has been in flower all summer, but now begins to stop us in our tracks with its richness, is *Salvia hypargeia* 'Indigo Spires'. For as fall approaches its flow-

The Korean species of angelica, Angelica gigas, *was unknown in American gardens until the mid-eighties, though it seems now to have swept through the world. A biennial that grows to eight feet tall, it prefers moist shade and rich soil, where it will self-seed in an unobtrusive way. Its only drawback is that it is pollinated by gray hornets.*

ers darken from a somewhat rusty blue to a deep purple, and its stems elongate rapidly, bending and twisting as they go. The plant tumbles under the weight of its blooms, producing new flowering shoots from the axils of each leaf. This sort of sprawling behavior in a plant can be a great nuisance earlier in the summer, but it is valuable now, since a single plant will fill a space left when a border geranium has gone shabby and been cut back or an ephemeral annual or biennial has finished its show. The display made by *Salvia hypargeia* 'Indigo Spires' continues well into autumn, becoming finer and finer and serving as a splendid companion to the asters.

If 'Indigo Spires' is lax, *Salvia confertiflora*,

however, is stately. Its habit is shrubby and firmly upright, and it will reach an easy five feet before midsummer. It is worth growing for its form and its foliage alone, for it is always attractively clad in eight-inch, broad, spear-shaped leaves, emerald green with furry purple stems. But by August its flowering stems will appear — straight as arrows, a deep orange-red from the first, and packed eventually with tiny flowers of the same color. Once a flowering stem develops, it remains in good condition for two months, which in our garden means until the plant must be cut down, lifted, and potted for the winter.

But of all the salvias we grow, the best is not really for August. Until autumn becomes at least a strong promise, *Salvia leucantha* remains only a large mound of attractive foliage — narrow, three-inch long blades of sage green, a pretty silver on the reverse. Its first blooms wait until September to appear; but we are patient with it, for once it starts to flower it will continue, growing more and more splendid until almost Christmas. What was a mound of foliage becomes a mound of flowers, six-inch spikes of clear purple mixed with silver — just the sort of color one cannot have too much of when the trees turn scarlet, yellow, and orange. Because its display lasts so long, we grow it not in the ground but in a huge clay pot, which it amply fills and which we haul into the kitchen on the coldest nights of October and back out again when the days are warm. We do not begrudge it the trouble, for in late October it is one of the last notes of splendid color we have. And when finally in November even the days are too cold for it, it is lodged in the winter garden for as long as it is attractive, and then cut back and stored dormant in the lower greenhouse.

Not all our half-hardy and tender plants are grown for the color of their flowers. Indeed, there is one we hope will never flower at all, for we have seen *Melianthus major* in bloom at Strybing Arboretum in early spring, and its foot-long panicles of brownish red flowers would be barely tolerable even without their vile smell. As a foliage plant, however, it is one of the most glamorous one can grow, forming elongated palms of fifteen toothed leaflets each, arranged oppositely until they terminate in a small trident at the end. Rarely would we call the color of anything "indescribable," for there are always words somewhere, if one can just find them, to capture a shadow at least of any tint or hue. But the leaves of *Melianthus major* elude our description, for over a celadon

background are shadows of blue and mint green. The effect comes from a thin wax overlay on the leaf. Though we try usually not to discourage fellow gardeners from touching plants, knowing that some part of the pleasure of growing plants is in how they feel to the fingers, this one really should not be touched, for its complexion is fragile and easily spoiled. Native to South Africa, *Melianthus major* is one of the tenderest plants we grow, and so it must be lifted and potted before the first frost. It cannot be stored as a dormant stool, as can the tender salvias, for the growth it continues to make in a cool greenhouse through the winter will be the basis for its summer display. Bother that it is, we will always want to grow it; we take comfort from the fact that in all but the warmest gardens in England it must be managed in just the way we do it. It is worth the trouble, anywhere.

Whether another plant we have grown this year for foliage will be worth the trouble is a question still very much in doubt. Late in the spring we were given a single seedling of *Gunnera manicata*, only two months old then but already well past infant cuteness and on the way to brawny gianthood. *Gunnera manicata* is the largest-leaved perennial that may be grown in temperate gardens. Its rough, bristly stems emerge from a central crown to reach eight feet in height, each terminating in a single richly crinkled leaf, wedge-shaped and sometimes as much as ten feet across. Though native to the humus-rich valleys of southern Brazil, the actual hardiness of *Gunnera manicata* is in some question. A single specimen startlingly reappears each year in Frank Cabot's garden in Cold Spring, New York, after waiting out the winter in an elaborate shelter made of a large plywood box filled with strawy litter. Ours is still in a pot, a very large pot, which the plant's five feet of growth and relatively modest leaves (only three feet across) are already distinctly straining. It has been a great joy, however, as a plant to stick about, here and there, and certainly one of the plants visitors are sure to ask about. We'd keep it in a pot forever if we thought we could, allowing it to go dormant in autumn and cold-storing it for the winter. But there is a limit to the size pot we can handle, and after one season of growth it appears to be demanding one the size of a refrigerator. So perhaps we too will dig a vast pit, fill it with the richest soil we have, let our gunnera grow to full size, and then, when it is dormant, cover it with several bales of hay and its own little plywood house. We have done more for less. Or perhaps we will enjoy it for a season or two and then go on to other experiments with tender plants, there being so many to try.

The last group of plants that make our Vermont garden seem distinctly exotic in August are tender vines. Perhaps it is true of all vines that when they are growing lushly, no matter how far north the garden, the effect they create is faintly reminiscent of the Tarzan movies one saw as a child. People in the South more or less expect vines, accustomed as they are to ropy tangles of smilax and muscadine in the woods, to strangling waves of *Lonicera japonica,* and to kudzu that makes full-grown forest trees look like the elephant in the belly of the Little Prince's serpent. We have few vines in our part of New England, either native or introduced. So anything we grow that ascends by clinging adds a different dimension to our gardening. We see in horizontal tiers, and vines are vertical in their growth; we like them for that, as they make possible one more kind of garden picture, one more effect to pile on top of another.

So we grow hardy, woody vines on any

permanent supports we have. The climbing hydrangea, *Hydrangea anomala* ssp. *petiolaris,* scrambles up the trunks of maple and beech trees. The porcelain berry, *Ampelopsis glandulosa* var. *brevipedunculata,* clothes the front of the barn, and the hardiest of the English ivies, *Hedera helix* 'Baltica', climbs across the bank beside it, providing a brief but happy home for the Himalayan jewelweed, *Impatiens glandulifera.* Concord grape vines wrap around the pergola built over the main bridge across the stream, causing its heavy, post-and-beam frame to look less and less like a building frame to which someone forgot to add walls and a roof. (We anticipate with pleasure the day we can sit on a bench there and look up at thick, sunlit leafage and clusters of grapes, with perhaps a cherub or two come down to steal the fruit, for then we will feel like a Renaissance pope in his bath.) There are trellises against the sides of the house, woodshed, and lower greenhouse, on which we grow common but wonderful things. There is a planting of Hall's honeysuckle, *Lonicera japonica* 'Halliana', pretty all summer with its white tubes fading to antique ivory, and the most fragrant of all honeysuckles – a splendid plant if one can control its wayward ways. We have trained a multiflora rose up the side of the shed – the convenient, easily pruned form called 'Inermis', which is thornless. It is used as understock for grafting many roses, and it is scorned by many gardeners when it appears as an unwanted sucker at the base of a treasured hybrid tea or shrub rose. But in very northern gardens it is the only rose that will form thick-muscled trunks if it is made to climb, and though its flowers are a little dowdy, its fragrance is the best "old rose." On the lower greenhouse trellis is an *Akebia quinata,* which Allen Lacy has said possesses all the charm of

Outbuildings such as barns and sheds are always more beautiful when softened by vines. One of the best is
Ampelopsis glandulosa *var.* brevipedunculata, *whose pea-size fruits turn first to pale lilac, then yellow,*
then cobalt blue. It must be pruned hard in early spring and tied in to eyebolts or nails; otherwise it will make
a wad of congested stems and probably come down in a summer rainstorm.

poison ivy. (We have no poison ivy in our part of Vermont, though it too — putting aside its liabilities — is a beautiful vine, and we have heard there is a variegated form, quite suitable for making standards.) But *Akebia quinata,* if kept *very* hard-pruned, gives plenty of pretty five-fingered leaves without making a haystack of itself, and its bruised-grape-colored flowers in late spring and early summer are odd and very wonderful. For those to whom that color looks strange and morbid widow-y, there is also a white-flowered form, with paler, apple green leaves, and even a variegated form, happily much less rampant. In the perennial garden is a standard made of the incomparable *Lonicera brownii* 'Dropmore Scarlet'. Trained to a white cedar post, it provides the only acceptable variation from the color scheme of pink, purple, and white that rules there. The beautiful white hardy sweet pea, *Lathyrus latifolius* 'Weisse Perle', is trained that way, too, for a vertical accent, and provides its familiar flowers (alas, not fragrant) from mid July through the end of August.

And there are permanent vines in pots, such as the tropical *Lonicera hildebrandiana,* a sort of beefed-up Hall's honeysuckle with similar white flowers fading to ivory, though they are almost six inches long and the vine is clad with rich, shiny evergreen leaves. The potato vine, *Solanum jasminoides,* has been with us for six years, producing its clouds of scented potato flowers in abundance just when the weather gets unbearably hot; we cut it back to a woody scaffold at first frost and store it through the winter. And though no wisteria grows in the ground here, their buds not being winter-hardy, we have a venerable standard made of a white one, in a huge and heavy old square clay pot that stands on the back terrace for emphasis; this we store under a cover for the winter.

But it is the tender vines we grow in the ground — annuals mostly — that make our garden seem so distinctly tropical in August. For though a woody vine, being so long-lived, needs firm support, a tender one can be planted almost anywhere for a single season's effect and repeated in years to come if it pleases. Thus *Tropaeolum peregrinum,* the "Canary Bird" creeper — first cousin to the familiar garden nasturtiums — can be set at the base of a yew hedge or made to scramble over a spring-blooming shrub such as a flowering quince or mock orange. Its wayward celadon green stems and funny palms of leaves are pretty in themselves, and its little yellow-winged flowers provide a second season of interest to shrubs that might be dull in mid-summer. We will never see, in our northern garden, the puffy, heart-shaped seeds that give cardiospermum its name, but its leaves, something like a recut version of poison ivy, are lovely when they weave in and out of the taller bamboos, among which we set them each year. *Cobaea scandens,* the "Cup and Saucer" vine, will throw its tendriled stems about any support, and so, though its Canterbury Bell–like flowers in blue or white occur only scarcely for us in autumn, its lusty growth ekes out the grape vines we are still waiting for on the pergola.

But for the quickest cover, we love the Japanese hop, *Humulus japonicus,* which will grow from a finger-size plant in early June to one that covers twenty square feet of wall in August, sheeting it from top to bottom with palms of seven leaflets, all marbled beautifully with white. We grow its perennial relative, too, the golden form of the beer hop, *Humulus lupulus* 'Aureus'; but while it becomes rusty and bug-eaten by late July, the annual Japanese species stays fresh at least until the end of August, and is our leaf of first choice to lay over a large ironstone platter on which cold hors d'oeuvres are piled. At the very end of summer it too will begin to produce cobs of flowers and seeds, not at all showy but a promise of more hop vines next year.

For quick cover, also, nothing can beat morning glories. They are plants one somehow expects to see on dewy high-summer mornings in country gardens, though they are just as lovely in dank city lots, where they seem to happily naturalize in sour soils. For years we grew the familiar old form called 'Heavenly Blue', its limpid, fragile flowers heavenly indeed if one is up early enough to see them before the sun strikes. Lately, though we still admire it in other people's gardens and may someday grow it again, it has been crowded out of our affections by the species form, *Ipomoeae purpurea,* which grows even more lustily and spangles itself top to bottom with deep-purple flowers, smaller than those of 'Heavenly Blue' but produced in greater profusion. We set a whole row of it against the gray sides of the barn and tie neat strings down from the roof, hoping that by season's end the vines will reach the top. By the end of August they are usually halfway up, giving us grounds for optimism. With a lucky delay of early September frost they may make it the whole twenty-five feet to the top, creating – just briefly – the picture we want to see.

Even vegetable vines are grown in the ornamental garden for quick and amusing effects. Pumpkins climb along the stone walls, threatening to engulf the clematis they were planted to set off and resting their improbably large fruits on the top. We have not yet grown a five-hundred-pounder on a pile of rotted manure, but we like the French variety called 'Rouge vif d'Etampes' because it looks just like Cinderella's coach before and after the ball, and the ghostly white 'Lunette', which surely makes the eeriest of jack-o'-lanterns. (When we harvest them, we always remember a Danish friend who could never be convinced that they are not called "Pump Kings.") Though we have never found just the right place in the flower garden for the glorious old posy or scarlet runner beans, we plant them on the fences of the vegetable garden, just for their vibrant orange flowers against the weathered wood and not for their coarse and hairy (though quite edible) beans. Cucumbers are trained there too, for they are the most elegant of vegetable vines, their black-green leaves barely concealing the dangling fruits we cannot possibly keep up with. And lately we have been planting gourds there too, for their strange, night-scented white flowers, though never in our cool garden do we hope to see a warted globe, a Turk's turban, a dinosaur, or anything suitable for making bowls and birdhouses.

But it is not just the vines – scrambling, scandent, twining, or weaving here and there – and not just the annuals and tender perennials – improbably leafed and flowered, strangely scented – that make the garden in August seem so tropical, so elsewhere. It is also the rain. Gardeners in any climate must become connoisseurs of rain, either because they want it or they don't. Each season brings its own sort, from the pelting ones of late March that drum on the roof in the night and unlock the earth, melting away the last snow and assuring one that winter is over (or almost), to the misty ones in September, fine and brief and cool, followed by halcyon skies and the sweetest days we can know on earth. July is always a dry month in the Northeast, one clear day following another, a good time to be out of the garden and at the beach or the river. By mid August, however, steamy tropical systems move

Vines enrich the August garden, causing it to look almost
tropical. Here a species morning glory, the almost-black
Ipomoea purpurea, *attempts to make its way to the top
of the barn roof before frost. A few late flowers are still
left on* Agapanthus nutans 'Peter Pan', *a conveniently
dwarfed form perfect in size for the wall it
occupies each summer.*

꙯

Though the golden hop, Humulus lupulus 'Aureus',
*becomes shabby in warmer gardens by August, it stays
fresh throughout the summer for us, providing wonderful
leaves to garnish a platter of cold meats. Arching across the
door to offer its fragrance is one of the curious and
powerfully perfumed night-scenting pelargoniums.*

꙯

in, making for days that are hot and humid and nights that are worse. One sleeps uneasily. Even early in the morning there is the promise of heat in the day, and thundershowers are predictable many afternoons and evenings. Often rain will fall for a whole day, warm enough that one can go about one's chores in it with little protection, even (in the privater parts of the garden) with none at all.

But such days are oppressive to the gardener, for the garden looks rusty and dull. It is too damp to cut the grass, which grows yellow and fat in the heat, not the tight emerald green lawns should be. Moisture-laden plants obscure the paths and arch over them, making necessary passages a quandary between two shower baths. Anything one has to haul away will be twice as heavy sodden as dry. Naps are no good at all, for one wakes tireder than before. An evening fire, so cheering generally, is out of the question. Flies and fleas multiply madly. One has no appetite, but still gains a pound or two from sheer sodden inactivity.

Yet however trying it may be for the gardener, the steamy tropical weather of mid August causes the garden to burgeon. The sort of tightening rest that came with the clear, dry days of July is followed by an explosion of leaf and flower and fruit. Tomatoes ripen, first by hesitant ones and twos, then by tens, then hundreds, rolling on the ground in their abundance. Beans elongate by inches daily, and though one might pick every morning, working up and down the rows with care, still a few escape to become appendixes on the vine. Cannas produce their improbably tropical flowers overnight, crude pink and orange and subtle peach and coral. The daturas are a nightly festival, especially if one picks a mature, tightly furled bud just at twilight to watch it stretch itself into a circle as dinner progresses. Brug-

mansias, their shrubby cousins, dangle their angel's trumpets — a foot long each and chalk white, cream, or evaporated-milk yellow — in a steady succession, all sinfully fragrant. Even figs — from our two trees in pots, one variegated and one dull purple — may be teased by the weather into ripening. We are, for the moment, living in the tropics. We feel the need of a pet monkey.

But as the month ends a switch seems to turn off. The hot, humid weather ends suddenly, and again there is rain to signal the change. Cool weather blows down from Canada, and one wakes in the night to an insistent need for an extra blanket. The early morning is not hot and hazy-gold but clear and argentine. Then the earliest asters open their stars of blue, goldenrod begins to fluff the fields and roadsides with gold, and one begins, some morning or another, to try to remember exactly where one put away the bulb catalogs. A few bulbs have actually begun to bloom in the garden. The first — never quite as precocious as it might seem, for September is tomorrow — is the tiny autumn snowflake, *Leucojum autumnale*, its minute bells of white appearing in late August even in the pots we have stored dry over the summer and forgot to reawaken with a watering. How — how in the world — does it know that autumn is coming, is almost here? In the planted walls, also, the autumn scilla, *Scilla autumnalis*, begins to appear, looking (as so many autumn-blooming bulbs do) so improbably like its spring-blooming counterpart. Maybe, if one searches, there will be a colchicum or two in the conifer border, an early promise of their purple waves in September and early October. So, we think, autumn is beginning, our longest, most favorite season of the year. We are ready.

September

WHEREVER one lives one learns to savor the special delights each season brings. For the passage of time, such a source of terror under certain circumstances, is also a great delight, offering, like pearls on the string of life, a steady sequence of causes for celebration, festivals great or small. In Vermont every month — even dreadful March — brings its own pleasures. But of the twelve, two rank as most beautiful, most clearly a cause to take joy from life. One is July, when the days are hot and clear but the nights are generally cool enough to sleep well. Then the long labors of the spring and early summer begin to pay their dividends, in the rich mature leafage of the shrubs and trees, the first full flush of summer perennials, and the lusty growth and flowering of annuals and tender plants. The other is September, which of all the months of the year offers the greatfullness of flower, along with that most precious commodity for gardeners, enough leisure to appreciate it.

Like July, the weather of the first half of September is of an intoxicating fineness, like wine in the blood. But while July's weather is golden, September's is silver, the light slanting low, far more flattering to the garden. There is a poignancy in that light, for the beauty it reveals is a terribly brief thing. Its very clarity promises imminent frost, the end of many garden pictures, and the beginning of hysterical activity — first to protect the tenderest things for a little while longer, and then to take them up if they are to be saved for another season. The end of the month begins October's work of planting bulbs, composting unthrifty patches in the borders, clearing the vegetable garden, cleaning the greenhouse, and preparing to put the garden to sleep. September's

Monkshoods are a continuous presence in the perennial garden from July to September, beginning with Aconitum smithii *'Spark's Variety' and ending with* A. carmichaelii, *pictured here. Though the vibrant blue most aconites offer is valuable at any season, it is particularly wonderful in autumn.*

Colchicum speciosum *'Album' is never as vigorous as the purple form, and its blossoms are smaller and much more fragile. It therefore should probably not be asked to compete with the straight species but should be given a place all to itself where its quiet beauty can shine without challenge.*

pleasures may last only half the month or for its full term of thirty days and even longer, depending on the behavior of those great weather forces that control the gardener's life; but whether they last briefly or long, it is always a magical month.

There is something dreamlike about September, for like a dream it folds contrasts into itself without a seam, being the last month of summer and the first of autumn all at once. Like a dream, too, it is full of surprises, moments in which one says, "Oh, there that is again. I had forgotten. I remember." Spring never catches us that way, thrilling though it is when it finally comes. We anticipate it too thoroughly, prowling around from the first thaws of March to see what is emerging. Even in late January we check on the witch hazels daily, and we know to the smallest reasonable fraction the expansion of the buds on *Viburnum x bodnantense.* By the time the first daffodils bloom we have followed their progress for weeks, gently pulling apart the emerging leaves to see what buds there are. Spring is the long-awaited season that never comes too soon, like a lover home from a long voyage, whose arrival is prefigured endlessly in anticipation. We mark its progress by inches as it comes.

But we always catch the first glimpse of autumn over our shoulder, while we are still bending to the tasks of summer. The first great surprise is a colchicum. The handsome foliage of these bulbs, called rank by some, disappears by mid July, and unless the clumps are clearly marked one is apt to forget exactly where they are. But suddenly, in earliest September, the first bud appears from nowhere, pale but already holding in its substance its eventual richness of mauve and purple. From that first bud, which shows when we are not about to be done with summer, to the last, a

survivor even of autumn, there will be waves and waves of them, as if there were no limit to their capacity to enpurple the conifer border where they grow.

The true perennials of autumn also catch us by surprise, for we are still summer-minded when they appear, and in our cold garden they always appear so much earlier than we expect. Like the colchicums, they also go on much longer than we anticipate, reminding us that autumn is a long, long season and not the brief moment between summer and winter we usually think it is. Few of the flowers of high summer remain with us for so long a time as do the asters, chrysanthemums, boltonias, and late aconites; though one thinks of summer as the time of greatest plenitude in the garden, that distinction really belongs to autumn, between which and the great show of spring, summer is in fact the entr'acte.

Abundance is a feature of almost all the flowers that bloom in September. There are many of them, and usually each one has so much to give. Never sparing in their gifts, the most characteristic ones are covered — smothered, in fact — in abundance. And because of the cooler nights, the flowers of September last. They last not only at their peak but even as they decline. Autumn is the only season in the garden when fading flowers are attractive, quite simply because they do not fade; rather they become burnished, and their colors — straw brown or freckled purple — enhance the younger blossoms still coming on.

It is odd to think that dishevelment is one of the most pleasing characteristics of autumn flowers. At any other season of the year untidiness is a blemish. One tries to pick off the spent flowers of daffodils so they will not mar the show to come, and nothing is quite so depressing as a bedraggled peony past its prime. Many a quiet rest in the summer garden is spoiled by the sight of an unstaked plant burying its head in a neighbor's foliage. From mid September through the rest of autumn, however, a certain tumble seems, strangely, to add to the beauty of the whole. It may be that the gardener has simply learned to relax (or is too tired to care). However it is, the garden in autumn has a quality of abandon, almost of carelessness, that is one of its chief charms.

In the autumn garden, also, there seem never to be clashes of color. The manipulation of color harmonies is one of the proudest accomplishments of the really good gardener; gardening often becomes not just the ability to grow a plant well (that goes without saying) but to grow it in conjunction with others that flatter and magnify its beauty. Somehow, however, everything seems curiously to go well together in the autumn garden. This is not, of course, to say that one cannot create wonderful effects with careful color combinations in autumn; but it is also true that one need not much fear a dreadful mistake. Colors that are difficult to use well at other seasons suddenly become stars. True red, perhaps the most uncompromising of all colors, accords without quarrel with mauves, pinks, purples, and yellows. The dreaded magenta, the most maligned of all colors in the garden, contributes a note of great suavity when the scarlets and russets of autumn leaves fall near it. Other violent colors, too, have their place in autumn, as one sees in the popularity of the tall aster 'Andenken an Alma Potschke', whose cerise brilliance would be called belligerent at any other season but which, in the September garden, is always very fine.

Though perennial plants that reach their peak in September are abundant, the asters are the backbone of the garden at this season.

Rightly valued are many cultivars of the native American asters, *Aster novae-angliae* and *A. novi-belgii*, whose seeds were collected by the first colonial botanists and sent home to England. Their splendid tardiness of bloom earned them their very English name; the Feast of Saint Michael and All Angels occurs on the twenty-ninth of September, and so they were returned to their American homeland as "Michaelmas daisies." A casual glance at the abandoned pastures where they flourish will show that both species display a wide variation in height, bloom time, and even color. *Aster novae-angliae* is by far the more diverse, producing stems of four to six feet clad in hairy, three-inch-long narrow leaves and topped by thickly flowered corymbs of inch-wide daisy flowers. Though their color is described in botanical manuals as violet-purple, an extensive natural population will produce a range of shades from light violet through royal blue to mulberry red. Both a pale pink and a white form, though rare, also occur hereabouts. Their bloom time can be anywhere from the second week of August to the middle of September, with some forms completing their flowering before others have even begun. The wide variability of the species appears to be the result not so much of individual plants' luck in finding just the right place as an inborn genetic diversity that seems to make no two plants ever look alike. So, when they bloom, one can prospect in abandoned fields and along country roads for individuals of particularly vivid color, early or late flower, or tall or short stature. That is what we have done, and the back of the perennial garden beneath the apple trees is rich with plants we have gathered and propagated. Among them, however, are three old varieties bred abroad — for no one who has seen them would want to be without a five-foot haystack of pale, silvery 'Harrington's Pink', a three-foot-tall glistening white stand of 'Mount Everest', or a mass of vividly cerise 'Andenken an Alma Potschke'. Because all the forms of *Aster novae-angliae* we grow are rather tall, and also perhaps because they experience some shade, we find we get sturdier, more upright, and more floriferous plants if we shear them back by half in late June or early July. And as with *Aster novi-belgii,* division annually or at least every other year, and liberal fertilizing with compost and granular vegetable-garden food, both seem important in maintaining vigor and fullness of flower.

Though *Aster novi-belgii* also shows considerable variation in the wild, it seems much more uniform than *Aster novae-angliae.* Though pink and white forms are said to occur, we have never found any. Those we have seen are all more or less three feet tall, furnished with smooth dark green leaves, and topped with loose, rather ragged panicles of blue daisies. *A. novi-belgii* has been by far the readier parent of garden-worthy offspring, particularly when crossed with the similar but bushier *A. dumosus.* A bewildering range of cultivars exists, far more than we would ever have room to grow, in colors from white and pale blue to deep blue, violet, purple, and crimson. Heights vary from little flower-smothered pillows hardly a foot high and wide to giants with graceful panicles of flowers atop five-foot stems. New forms are constantly being produced, particularly in Germany where the plant is treasured, and though all have their charms, it is the older and more readily available forms that have earned their place in our garden and which only fickleness would argue for replacing. We grow 'Professor Kippenburg', a twelve-inch plant smothered in lavender-blue semidouble flowers that has remained a favorite for half a century. A little

taller, at fifteen inches, is 'Snowsprite', with semidouble flowers in clear white with yellow centers. 'Winston Churchill' is an appropriately portly plant a foot and a half tall and as wide with rich red-maroon blossoms. All these dwarf forms of *Aster novi-belgii* have proven invaluable, not only for color at the front of the perennial border but also in the rock garden, where they form neat green bushes in summer and contribute wonderful color in autumn.

Medium-size forms of *Aster novi-belgii* have been equally valuable, though we generally end up planting them in bays of shrubbery, where their thick growth suppresses weeds and their autumn flowers gain added splendor from a dark backdrop of evergreen plants. Among the three- to four-foot cultivars of *A. novi-belgii,* the best bear the names of members of the Ballard family, in whose nursery in Colwall, Malvern, England, they were extensively bred and selected during the early part of this century. 'Ernest Ballard' has rich pink, semidouble flowers on three-foot stems. 'Patricia Ballard' bears almost fully double flowers of a softer pink at the same height, and 'Marie Ballard' is taller, at four feet, with double, powder blue flowers. 'Ada Ballard' adds a shade of lavender to this impressive family group, which never looks so good as when it is planted in interlocking masses with perhaps a dusting of silver from the semidouble 'Bonningdale's White'. *Aster novi-belgii* has also produced some very tall plants, good for the back of the perennial border, though no *novi-belgii* form, in our experience, is as shade-tolerant as varieties of *Aster novae-angliae.* In full sun, however, 'Climax' is magnificent, with three-inch pale blue flowers on five-foot stems. 'The Cardinal' is almost as tall and a rich rose red, and 'White Ladies' will tower to six feet, with blossoms of fresh clear white centered with orange.

Gardeners familiar only with the florist's chrysanthemums should know about the much hardier
Dendranthema rubellum, *which returns reliably to cold gardens each year. The two forms available in
America are the pale pink 'Clara Curtis' and the pumpkin-colored
'Mary Stoker', both single daisy forms.*

Taken altogether, in species, hybrid, variety, and cultivar, *A. novae-angliae* and *A. novi-belgii* would be enough to furnish the September garden many times over. But in the matter of native asters, America has a full bank account, hardly drawn upon even by these splendid species. Throughout eastern North America, from Newfoundland to Florida and inland to Minnesota, in damp fertile meadows and dry barren ones, in mucky swamps and under the dense shade of old maple and beech forests, are dozens of neglected species of the vast aster clan waiting to be invited into the garden. Our part of New England must be a sort of aster heaven, for from August to the end of October, unmown roadsides, hedgerows, and old pastures will show as many as a dozen varieties, all of which have found a place in our garden. Few of them display the splendid coloration and impressive stature of *A. novae-angliae* and *A. novi-belgii*, but many have a winsome simplicity, an engaging wildness to them, and all possess an inborn capacity to flourish without much coddling under the conditions in which they originated and still like the best. They have therefore been invaluable to us in corners of the garden where we take them largely for granted all summer until they remind us, in September, that they are there, with flowers simple or showy but always nice.

Among these unimproved wildlings our great favorite is *Aster divaricatus,* the white wood aster. Though many native asters will accept poor soil and grow the better for being a bit undernourished, most demand at least half a day of sun and a good supply of moisture. *Aster divaricatus* is an exception, for it loves deep shade and it never looks better than when it can throw about its foam of flowers, from mid August to mid September, under established woods of beech and in sugar bushes of old maples. Those are very difficult conditions for any plant, and so, though *Aster divaricatus* is not the showiest member of its family by a great way, it is still a plant to be treasured. We found it here in abundance when we came, and we have let it creep into the shadier parts of the garden wherever it wishes, always staying our weeding hands when we see its rosettes of dark green leaves in spring and early summer. Soon we are rewarded, for by midsummer it produces seemly loose bushes a foot or so high, composed of three to five burnished purplish black stems, covered with clean foliage and many-branched at the top. Toward autumn the stems will suddenly display flattened sprays of white flowers that last almost two months, flushing to palest lilac as they age. The individual blossoms are rather ragged and incomplete-looking, as if they had been torn at by the wind or by wanton fingers; but billowing together in gentle heaps, they combine to form an attractive mass of blooms.

Perhaps the most endearing characteristic of *A. divaricatus* is its way of weaving in and out among other plants and colonizing odd corners where little else will grow. Gertrude Jekyll was perhaps the first garden writer to praise it for this characteristic; she favored growing it in the perennial border among the stiff, paddle-shaped leaves of bergenias. We like it as well among naturalized hostas, or in any spot in the woodland border it chooses for itself, in association with any perennial that grows there. For its light, wiry growth never smothers anything, and it seems capable of the closest association with other plants, poking up here and there among them as if they were all part of the same thing. Its real victory over any prejudice one might hold against a mere "weed" is when it grows beneath the shade of tall shrubs or in the inhospitable gloom of the woods, appearing, suddenly lovely and complete, where one never thought to plant it and didn't even know it grew. Then, for us, it is simply one of the very nicest things that came with the place.

Also amiably adaptive is *Aster ericoides*, though in a quite different way. For it chooses to live not in deep shade but on a dry sun-parched bank, barren of much other growth and deficient in nutrients. It is called the "heath" aster, because its delicate arching stems are covered with tiny, half-inch leaves of nearly the same size as those of the ericas, the true heaths. But the older name, *A. multiflorus* ("many flowered"), really suits it better, for though there is little that is heathlike about the plant but its leaves, it smothers its stems in early autumn with hundreds of tiny up-facing white daisies, each with a dull maroon center. The height of the plant is listed at from one to three feet, depending on whether it grows in rich or thin soil. But in the thin soil of the cemetery below our garden, we have found diminutive and perfectly formed specimens hardly four inches tall and full of flowers, suggesting that if one had a mind to do it, they could be cultured in shallow trays of soil as bonsai. This capacity to flourish in barren conditions makes *Aster ericoides* a perfect candidate for the rock garden, where we have planted it in many forms, both collected and ordered through the mail. One of the prettiest is 'Ring Dove', a thick, almost shrublike plant that covers itself with half-inch flowers of a color more rose-tan than white. Both 'Constance' and 'Monte Casino', by contrast, are delicate, almost transparent until they fill their stems with gray-white daisies, which occurs much later than with other forms, the flowers waiting until early October to appear. All forms of *A. ericoides* last well when cut, their

airy beauty a perfect complement to heavier, more showy flowers. This fact has not escaped the modern florist industry, and now one sees them even in early spring, forced by manipulations of heat and light. Pretty though they are, even then, we turn away with a shudder, for they are autumn flowers; they ought to be left to their proper season, and not made to get so hopelessly mixed up with other things.

By contrast, *Aster lateriflorus* can expect no great future as a cut flower. It is popularly called the "calico" aster, presumably because the hundreds of quarter-inch, raggedly circular flowers it bears open a dull white and fade quickly to many shades of dim lavender, suggesting a much-worn, much-washed calico frock. Each flower possesses a little bristly center that is often called crimson but is really only a dull brownish purple. The thick bunched stems it produces are all clad in minute toothed leaves that turn to tarnished copper when touched by autumn frost, just as the little flowers are fading toward purplish tan. It is a plant that might be said to have not one single good feature, but that is, when all its features are put together, entirely beautiful. Even in the thin soils of clear-cut woods here in Vermont (where it is called the "starved" aster) the thrifty little two-foot-tall bushes, smothered in faded flowers, possess a distinction. In the selected variety 'Horizontalis' — so named because the stiff-twigged branches on each stem grow horizontally, crisscrossing one another — this distinction achieves the dignity almost of boxwood. And that is how we have most effectively used it, as single, shrublike masses in the rock garden, or as congested, twiggy drifts in bays of shrubbery. We have seen it included in perennial borders, and have tried to include it in our own. Somehow, however, the shy charm of its flowers and its sublimely weedlike quality seem not to work well in such mannered and highly cultivated spaces. Like most of the smaller species of asters, to achieve its full beauty it seems to need to grow in places not too far in character from those it might naturally have chosen for itself.

There is one more species of American aster, however, that can rival even the Michaelmas daisies as a distinguished candidate for the perennial border: *Aster cordifolius.* It is called "bee weed" or "bee tongue" aster for its thin, five-inch-long, sharply toothed upper leaves, though the observer must have been close indeed who named it for this least apparent part of a bee's anatomy. Another popular name, "frost flower," is prettier, and quite apt, for it signifies not only the plant's bloom time in late September but also the curious color of its flower. To call that color simply blue is to miss some of its charm, for it is an odd blue, closer generally to gray, with perhaps — as the light shifts or as the tiny individual flowers age — flushes of ice blue and lavender in its graceful, loose panicles of hundreds of half-inch daisies. *Aster cordifolius* has always been popular with gardeners able to look past its status as a roadside weed, for it blooms quite late — from the end of September to the middle of October — it tolerates considerable shade, and it requires, from year to year, no particular attention from the gardener, not even division.

Margery Fish, called in her time "the champion of weeds," collected at East Lambrook, Somerset, England, many named forms of *Aster cordifolius,* several of which, like 'Photograph', 'Sweet Lavender', and 'Blue Star', are good shades of blue. Of all the ones she grew, it appears now that only 'Silver Spray' is still in circulation, at least in America. Each half-inch daisy is a lovely pristine white centered with

yellow. It blooms rather early for a *cordifolius* aster, reaching its peak here about the second week of September, just as the Michaelmas daisies are in fullest force. The best of the other new forms of *Aster cordifolius* now being introduced is a magnificent English variety called 'Little Carlow.' It has a profusion of clear violet blue flowers on willowy, graceful rods about four feet tall. With a bit of shade it will bloom from the second week of September well into the middle of October, even, sometimes, catching the first dusting of snow among its flowers. Of all the asters we grow, it strikes us as one of the very finest.

But asters, plentiful as they are, are not all that the September garden has to offer. Everywhere there is something in bloom or in fruit, appearing suddenly out of the late summer quietude. The great Japanese *Kirengeshoma palmata,* three feet tall and more across, has been producing scattered blooms since late August. But in early September its fat, pale yellow marbles of buds open in profusion, producing curious and beautiful flowers, unusually thick and with a waxen texture as if they had been carved of old ivory. Shaped like inch-long shuttlecocks, they spangle the dark, handsome leaves that make up the bulk of the plant; the leaves and flowers together produce a distinctly exotic look. No success can be had with *Kirengeshoma palmata,* however, unless it is located in dappled shade, more bright than gloomy, in rich soil that retains even moisture. We have planted it among hostas beneath the open branches of a mature crab apple in the front border, a site that appears to suit it to perfection. Those who wish to grow *Kirengeshoma palmata* in USDA Zones 5 and 4, however, should know that though it is perfectly root-hardy, its early-appearing asparagus-like shoots are susceptible to damage from late spring

In its effect, at least, Kirengeshoma palmata *is the most exotic plant in the border edging the front lawn. A native of Japan, it produces beautiful vinelike leaves on four-foot stems, each stem terminating in a panicle of round buds opening into thick funnels that look as if they had been carved from old ivory.*

frosts, and the full perfection of its flowers may be spoiled by unusually early fall ones. In both cases, the protection of an old sheet or blanket may be needed to get the best from it.

Our garden is rich with astilbes, most of which are gathered among the large boulders of the wild garden, along the stream, for early summer blooms and satisfying ground cover later. One of the most delightful astilbes we grow, however, is *Astilbe chinensis* var. *pumila*, which waits until early September to flower, surmounting its low, finely cut ground-hugging foliage with spires of lavender-pink flowers. Each spire is about a foot tall and rigidly upright, and though they are of a color that might not entirely please in other seasons, they

are beautiful in early autumn. When the flowers fade they leave behind their firm and satisfying architecture, gone to a warm cinnamon brown by the time the first snows fall. We have planted *Astilbe chinensis* var. *pumila* near the *Kirengeshoma palmata*, where it hugs the front of the border in a long, narrow drift of the sort that always seems so satisfying in such a spot. Beneath it — and throughout the front border — are cans of crocuses, for the astilbe will disappear in winter and will not emerge again until spring, leaving the stage clear for early crocuses and later providing cover when their wispy leaves have ripened and vanished.

In the holly court, one of the most elegant of September-blooming perennials, the Japanese anemone, *Anemone x hybrida,* reaches perfection by the end of the month. Of the many cultivars available we grow only two, the silvery pink 'Honorine Jobert' and the very tall, six-foot *Anemone x hybrida* 'Alba'. Of the two, 'Alba' is to us the more exciting, for a note of pristine white is always precious among the predominately pink, rose, mauve, and blue autumn-blooming perennials. There are plants that one feels it is an enormous privilege to grow, and this anemone is one; its three-inch wheels of flower are boldly beautiful, born on rigid, self-supporting stems. The whole plant suggests an entirely self-possessed elegance. It does not grow as well here as we wish, however. In the Los Angeles garden where we got our stock it flowers from early August well into the winter months, producing an unending succession of blooms even after the first flowers have gone to cottony seed heads. In that climate it is a rather rampant plant, spreading vigorously not only from underground stolons but also from seed. But we barely see its first beautiful flowers, for it is frost-tender, and a good bit of its bloom must wait out cold nights under three stout stakes and a bedsheet (and sometimes even that protection is to no avail). Still it is worth growing, for the brief gift it gives is an event to anticipate in late September.

In comparison with *Anemone x hybrida*'s cool elegance, the only South African resident of our garden, *Kniphofia galpinii,* is distinctly pronounced in appearance, perhaps even a little vulgar. Despite its improbable origins, it has flourished for years in the gravelly free-draining soil of the rock garden; each spring we have divided its grassy tufts, and now it forms a quite sizable drift. Throughout the summer it is not much to look at. But in September it tops its anonymous thin foliage with two-foot

pokers of vibrant orange, the color of Halloween candles or the bottom part of the candy corn that appears in shops around then. It would be an intolerable color in any other season, but in autumn it is wonderful. Our success with *Kniphofia galpinii* leads us to think that we could grow other red-hot pokers, at least in that species, which possesses some wonderful pale yellow and lime green cultivars. We will try them, certainly, when we can get the seed.

To these rarities the September garden adds a host of other flowers, some merely roadside weeds, and others squarely in the range of those cultivated plants gardeners expect to see at this season. The late-blooming aconites add a precious powder blue coloring to the general mauve and pink puffiness of the garden with their curious hooded flowers. We had no great success with them until we learned of their hunger for phosphorus, potassium, and rich, water-retentive soil; but now, with a spring dressing of 5-10-10 fertilizer and an annual late-autumn coat of pasture muck, we have them in profusion among the russet-colored plush of *Sedum telephium purpureum* 'Autumn Joy'. There are late-blooming Korean chrysanthemums in various shades of burnished copper, pink, and rose, far more persistent than florist's mums if one remembers to divide them annually and feed them well. Boltonias add their daisies, looking very like the native asters but with glaucous foliage and generally later blooms. A particular treasure is the species out of which *Boltonia asteroides latisquama* 'Snow Bank' was bred; for whereas 'Snow Bank' is an excellent garden plant, at about four feet with clouds of long-lasting flowers, the species towers to six or seven feet and so can add its grayish white blooms to the back of a deep border.

For most of September, annual plants also

continue to be good value in the garden. Some, such as the serviceable cosmos, the dramatic, great-trumpeted *Datura meteloides,* and many species of tender salvia, reach a brief but long-awaited perfection. We are always surprised by how frost-hardy some annuals – or plants generally grown as annuals – can be. Nicotianas, particularly if they are self-seeded "volunteers" from the previous year's planting, can endure quite heavy frosts, curling up at first and turning dark watery green as if all is over, but plumping up and continuing to bloom in warmer spells well into the first weeks of October. *Tweedia caerulea,* a foot-tall milkweed, seems to take new hope from the declining year, producing more of its half-inch turquoise stars, freckled with purple, now than at any other time. The soft foam of self-seeded sweet alyssum, *Lobularia maritima,* though it has been an unobtrusive presence in the garden all summer over the bulbs of disappeared daffodils, suddenly becomes quite prominent for such a gentle thing, insistently adding its honey-scented flowers to the general picture. Even pansies, poked in for spring and early summer color and ignored later, present a host of new faces under shrubs and at the edges of borders. And in pots, sheared-back lobelias show new flowers of gentian blue, asking to be saved for the winter, and the crinodonna (an interspecific cross between crinum and *Amaryllis beladonna*) suddenly rewards a whole summer of patient watering with a three-foot bloom stem crowded with pale pink, sweet-scented trumpets.

If all the flowers of September seem to us surprises, they are also great gifts; we live a whole year in expectation of what this season might bring, like children waiting for their birthday. But the greatest gifts of the September garden are not flowers, splendid though they are, but fruits and berries. One expects flowers in a garden. But in September, quite suddenly, berries and fruits that may be yellow, garnet, orange, and scarlet shine everywhere, reminding us – we always forget – that they are here. Nothing imaginable could be a finer effect of autumn, its ripeness crowned with flowers and fruit mingled all together.

And so it is, surprisingly perhaps, with many roses. No one plants roses primarily for their fruit; the best are selected rather for the opulence of their July flowers, red or pink or white and sweetly scented. What a surprise, then, to find that many roses – particularly species ones – replace their spent flowers with vividly colored fruit. *Rosa glauca* (syn. *R. rubrifolia*) may be among the best, for though its lead-purple leave and single pink flowers are wonderful, it is its clear scarlet hips that finally win it an unchallengeable place in the garden. Many of the rugosas, too, are heavy producers of large hips, tomato red and as big around as a nickel, good for jelly but better as a visual feast on the bush. *Rosa eglanteria,* the eglantine of English hedgerows, is not much noticeable for its two-inch-wide pink flowers or even for its foliage that smells of tea after a summer rain, though both are nice; its spangling of cranberry-size hips, however – all a vibrant orange – is the bonus that makes one determined to grow it. Though *Rosa moyesii* 'Geranium' has a strong claim on any sunny garden spot, with locustlike foliage and an unusual clarity in its single blood red blossoms, it is most unforgettable when it is thick with eight-foot-high arching canes hung with flagon-shaped hips of the clearest red. Even *Rosa multiflora,* a lowly grafting base for hybrid teas that has now escaped into pastures and is much cursed as a weed shrub, will show thick fringy panicles of brownish red hips after its leaves have fallen, perfect to insert into harvest

Sedum telephium *ssp.* maximum *'Atropurpureum'* would be a valuable plant even if it never bloomed,
for its deep purple foliage makes everything nearby look better. In September, however,
it does produce flowers, of a rare shade of flesh pink
that lasts throughout the month.

arrangements or even Christmas wreaths for interesting color and texture.

It is across the front of the house, however, that late September offers one of its finest gifts of fruit. There, five specimens of *Ilex verticillata*, the native sparkleberry, were established in the first year we gardened here. They have since grown as tall as the roof, providing a thick green shade before the windows in the summer months. Hidden beneath their leaves are thousands of pea-size fruits waiting for the first frosts of September to color. They do so, of course, to attract the attention of migrant birds, particularly the robins, in whose flyway we are squarely centered. Though it is pleasant to think of the seeds of so excellent a native plant disseminating far and wide from our very own garden, we have other notions for those berries. For from their first coloring, still surrounded by persistent green leaves, until late December, when the heaviest frosts have long since stripped those leaves away, we glory in the flash of crimson they provide against the weathered gray clapboards of the house. So, before September turns to October and the great migration begins, we will net these shrubs, just as we netted the strawberries in June and the cherries in July, until an early morning glance out the window shows no robins on the lawn, and we are left, for feathered companions, largely with the raucous jays. The robins may have all the crab apples they wish to speed them on their long journey, for we are not entirely hard-hearted, and in any case, the crab apples will turn mushy and dull with heavy frosts, offering no persistent beauty. But we will have the berries on the ilex a long time, to the point that, besides the somber beauty of the evergreens, they will be almost all the garden, outdoors, that we have.

What makes the difference between the gardener's summer and his autumn is the first frost, which may come in a bad year as early as the end of August, but generally holds back until September is almost spent. Even before the first frost there are signs, sure and inexorable, that autumn is on the way. The first colchicum appears, a single leaf of *Geranium macrorrhizum* takes on tints of pumpkin or scarlet, a swamp maple along the highway turns gloriously red. Because September is one of the great hinges of the gardening year, the gardener finds himself curiously double-minded, one part glorying in the continued presence of summer, the other always wary, always anticipating what is surely to come. The garden seems caught in a rich stasis of perfection as one warm day succeeds another, but still one must scan the newspapers to understand the continental weather patterns, and listen attentively to the morning weather report; for however fine the promise of the day, frost may still come by the end of the week or the beginning of next. Most especially one watches the thermometer, just in case the authorities are all wrong. (Or wrong, at least, about what the gardener cares most for, his own little patch, which might receive a kiss from winter — merely a withered squash leaf or a blackened basil plant — when all the rest of the world has been assured that frost is "not likely.")

There are two attitudes to take toward the first frost. The first is simply to welcome its arrival, letting go for the season those plants that could last awhile longer with some protection, and even giving up those that — unless they are promptly snatched from the garden — will be utterly lost. Gardeners who share this attitude generally greet the first frost with their feet up on a cushion, a book in their hands, and a sense of relaxation — even relief — in their hearts. We envy them their repose, but it is not for us. For we belong to the other school, the anxious one, that will fight with every ounce of energy we have to prolong, to protect, to save as much as ever we can. For us, and for gardeners of our stripe, it is lucky when one has plenty of advance warning, when one knows that frost is most certainly due tomorrow or the day after.

Almost always, however, we don't have that luxury. Most likely we will be returning from a trip, exhausted from a hard day's travel, to find the thermometer already below forty degrees at six in the evening and steadily dropping. Then there is nothing for it but to go to work, hauling in the pots of tender plants (how ever could there be so many?), and traveling through the garden — by flashlight if necessary — dropping over the most susceptible plants every sheet, blanket, shirt, tablecloth, and towel in the house. Frost almost always follows a period of quite fine weather, and so it is likely they will all be clean. For that night, we might well sleep on the bare ticking of the mattress, and the bathroom may be damp next morning from the absence of a shower curtain. We inevitably wonder, with all that laundry to do over, why we bother.

The answer to that question is quite simple. For after the first frost there generally occurs a period of extraordinary mellowness, not summer at all, but better, what is generally called Indian summer. Then the garden, still graced by its tender perennials and annuals and rich with autumn flowers garnished by the first glorious autumn colors, is lovelier perhaps than it has been all season and will be again until a full year has passed. For if the first frost is a

defining moment in the life of the garden and the gardener, it is not a sudden shutting down, an absolute end to what has come before. The great show of October's brilliance is just beginning, and some of the most intense pleasure a gardener can take from the garden still lies ahead.

So, of course, does a great deal of hard work. For by the end of the month or the beginning of the next, those annuals that have finally succumbed to progressively more severe waves of frost must be removed. Tender perennials that can take a touch of frost, but not the "black frost" that crusts the ground, must all be lifted, cut back, and potted. Eventually even the hardiest perennials will go shabby, needing to be cut down, their tops hauled to the compost and muck brought in to dress their beds. The greenhouse must be cleaned and made neat for all the plants that need to be kept growing, and the cold frames readied for those that will sleep out the winter there. Goldfish must be netted carefully from the barrels, tanks, and ponds where they have fattened all summer on mosquito larvae, and put in a half whiskey barrel to live on store-bought food until they can be liberated again. Bulbs have begun to arrive, and the major and joyful work of planting them all must soon begin. In the distance, but still coming closer every day, is the necessity of putting the garden finally to bed, by spreading evergreen boughs, wrapping tender conifers in burlap, and finally covering the boxwoods with their clumsy wooden covers. One knows now that all that work is soon to come. But for a time — a brief time that can actually seem endless — one relaxes in the glory of September.

October

I F we were very rich and had several houses to live in, it would be tempting to think of one having a garden planted just for autumn. It would certainly have to be in Vermont, on a quiet country road with a good view of the distant hills. In the garden and all around the house there would have to be mature trees of beech and maple for red and gold, with a sparkle of aspens (and birches, especially) for clearest yellow against chalk white trunks. We'd like an oak too, occasionally, as big and old as can be, for later color — a somber chestnut red — and for a rain of acorns and a circus for acrobatic gray squirrels. There should certainly be a generous sprinkling of conifers — hemlock and spruce and pine — to give weight to the picture and a black or smoky green contrast to the fiery splendor of the woods. If the house were in one of those narrow valleys, perched high

enough up on a hillside that clouds would catch against it in the night and show milky in the clefts of the mountains, so much the better. There should be a little village down below, complete with a white-spired church. But we would want to be above it, on a south-facing slope and high enough up that all the glorious October sun that could be had would shine on us.

The garden we would make in such a place wouldn't need to be very large — five acres or so would do. But we'd want more land of our own than that, just for a mood of expansiveness. So there would be fields to wander in, well tended and emerald green after the last haying. They would be bordered by woods to scuffle in — well managed for household fires, but not according to the professional woodsman's wisdom, for we would take the young trees and leave the old, especially a "scag" or

Like most other gardeners, we find it impossible to resist putting in some chrysanthemums where the annuals have been cleared away, a process referred to by some wit as "mummification."
Still, we prefer the simple, single forms — a little ragged if possible — to the smug, perfect doubles.

two, standing rotted trunks upright for the pileated woodpecker to work at, always invisible except for his laughing shriek. There would be old stone walls, too — bordering fields or buried in woods that were once pasture — on which we could sit, crowding a bit an angry chipmunk chattering fiercely at the human invasion.

In any garden one should always hear birds; our autumn garden would be filled with the raucous gossip of handsome black crows, discussing, like professional gourmets in a restaurant, the relative merits of the offal thrown on the compost heap. There would also be the tearing, unmellifluous cry of the blue jay, the bird of coming winter, whose flash of slaty gray looks so good against the tawny splendor of the autumn woods. Maybe, while gathering late blackberries at the edges of the fields, we would hear as well the melancholy two-note whistle of the chickadee, a sort of farewell to summer and to the place.

Somewhere, also, tucked away a bit, there would be a small vegetable garden, perhaps surrounded by old stone walls or a fence of split locust bearing espaliered apple trees. At this season it would hold all the late crops — cabbages, second-growth broccoli, carrots, leeks, late onions and shallots curing atop their rows, bitter Italian greens for savory autumn salads. If frosts had not been too heavy, there would also be a pumpkin or two for jack-o'-lanterns, not common roundish ones but the old, pleated, vivid orange sorts like 'Rouge d'Etampes'. And for the decoration of the autumn table there might be a straw yellow crookneck squash, an overgrown zucchini, a tawny cucumber, or maybe, if the summer had been warm, even a gourd or two.

And of course in the flower garden there would be lots of flowers, as many as the sea-could offer. We'd have chrysanthemums, not only the "mum" sorts that can be bought already grown and in flower at roadside stands, but also the free-flowering Korean ones and the rubellums — the biscuit-colored 'Mary Stoker' and clear pink 'Clara Curtis'. There would be asters of all sorts, not just the familiar Michaelmas daisies in white, silvery pink, and light and deep blue, but also species dug from the woods and roadsides, orphans worthy of adoption into the garden. Goldenrods would be everywhere, of course, in any neglected spot or field edge; but there might be some in the garden, too, having crept in or even been planted deliberately for their mimosalike flowers, so good for cutting. We'd have monkshoods of cobalt blue or blue and white, and as much *Sedum telephium purpureum* 'Autumn Joy' as we could crowd in, for its sturdy puffs of flower, like snippets of Turkish carpet up on stems. And there would even be bulbs — colchicum and true autumn crocuses and *Kniphofia galpinii* with its candles of Halloween orange.

All this is of course to say that if we *were* very rich, we'd choose to have our autumn garden just where it is, just as it is. Seeing that we aren't very rich, this in itself is a huge piece of good fortune, for, in the vision sketched above, one might be able to buy what nature grants, but not what the gardener contrives against it. That takes time and vigilance and love.

It is a little odd to live all the year in a region which, for two or three weeks in October, becomes one of the major tourist attractions in North America, perhaps (judging from the number of Japanese tourists in the supermarket) even the world. Roads hardly traveled become jammed with cars, slow-moving and given to sudden erratic stops. You must add a little extra to the time it takes for

The foliage season reaches its peak in southern Vermont somewhere around the tenth of October.
Then, and for about two weeks, it seems that the whole world is red and gold. There are still flowers, too,
one of the most valuable being — for contrast — the cobalt blue of Aconitum carmichaelii.

routine errands, but still your temper may be frayed. Gas must be bought early in the morning, before the motels disgorge their crowds; restaurants, such as they are around here, must be avoided; and you get used – almost – to giving directions at the front gate to people hopelessly lost but mostly having fun anyway, soaking up what they came a distance to see. What is most uncanny about living, just briefly, in the midst of such beauty is that you become oddly anxious about missing something, as if you had yourself driven all the way from Florida or Arizona. But maybe that is a natural feeling anyway, for though you find yourself repeating frequently, "I *live* here," and you have seen the woods burst into color many times (and will, you trust, see them do it many times again . . . or at least a few), still, you realize that October in Vermont *is* splendid, and its splendor is all too brief.

It is for that reason, partly, that we try so hard to prolong it. The peak of foliage season typically occurs about the second week of October, though there have been flashes since August of what it will be, in the sudden scarlet of an occasional swamp maple or the burnish of maroon on a roadside aronia or native viburnum. Color comes in waves from then on; but in the woods and on the mountainsides it is a truncated crescendo, for by the third week of October (or a little later in a good foliage year) there will come a chilly wind with pelting rains or even snow, wantonly bent on ripping every vividly colored leaf from the trees. The leaves will lie in sodden, browning heaps about the garden; later, with drier weather, they will blow and whirl about until they catch in corners and under the larger shrubs. At that point, as far as the forest trees go, the great show of autumn is over for the year. This is not to say, however, that the

autumn beauty of the garden ends when the trees have shed their garments of clear red, scarlet, russet, and orange. Those colors persist in the richly colored leaves of the garden; but for them one must look closer to the ground and at exotic shrubs and perennials.

Roses, for example, though hardly ever grown for autumn color, shine at this season. Any rose with the species *rugosa* in its blood may be expected to assume a clothing of butter yellow, deepening in the heart of the bush to chestnut brown – an almost edible combination like a ripe pear. Almost all the rugosa roses produce vivid hips as well – scarlet or tomato red – among which a few last flowers of white, cerise, or pale pink shine with double value. *Rosa glauca* (syn. *R. rubrifolia*), once stripped of its curiously lead-purple leaves, becomes a rain of vermilion hips, unfaded by heavy frosts. Many of the spinosissima roses burnish to a dull oxblood, a harmonious color against their almost-chocolate-colored hips. And the shrub rose called 'Metis' assumes at this season all the colors of autumn – scarlet, purple, burnt orange, and clear yellow – as if to prove that its soft, two-inch pale pink flowers in July are not all it has to show.

The vast rose clan, so richly endowed with beauty, is not the only family of shrubs bent on proving what it can do in the autumn color line. For though relatively modest in their other claims, berberis turn brilliant by mid October. *Berberis vulgaris,* a European native widely naturalized in New England and cursed by farmers for its spiny stems, regularly feeds bonfires in neglected pastures hereabouts. Though a common plant, and scorned, it is still an excellent choice for dry waste places and under the high shade of maples and beeches, where few other shrubs will grow. Though not much more than a "suitable

Some of the most brilliant autumn colors occur not on the
great forest trees, but on shrubs and perennials within
the garden. The royal azaleas, Rhododendron
schlippenbachii, are among the most vivid. They are,
therefore, two-season shrubs, for they will be just as
beautiful in May, hung with two-inch blossoms
of a rare, silvery pink.

❧

Those who know only the florist's cyclamen, Cyclamen
persicum, are surprised to learn that several hardy
forms exist, of which the best for us is Cyclamen
hederifolium. They are quite tiny, hardly six inches tall,
but an old corm like this, of C. hederifolium album,
will produce a long succession of flowers.

❧

permanency" in summer, with its small dark leaves on congested stems, its autumn tints are splendid and will last well into early November. When the severest frosts finally cause its leaves to drop to the ground, abundant tiny orange-red berries are revealed, too sour for the birds but the best of all fruited branches for late autumn and winter arrangements. One must wear stout gloves when picking them, for they are armed up and down with wicked prickles; but two or three fat branches, abundant with fruit, will grace an old earthenware jar from October until well past Christmas. It need not even be a jar that can hold water, for the berries – drupes, actually – will stay in good condition that long without any water at all.

Berberis thunbergii atropurpurea 'Nana', despite its clumsy name, is a far more elegant plant than *Berberis vulgaris,* forming neat three-foot domes of dull purple that last all summer, useful as foliage intensifiers and makeweights against soft blue, pink, and mauve perennials. But long after the perennials have been cut to the ground, it dresses for autumn in tints of pale rose and faded orange. Most elegant to us of all the berberis, however, is *Berberis thunbergii* 'Rose Glow'. It is capable of achieving five feet but is willing to be pruned lower. Though its finest leaf color is achieved in full sun, like all its clan it is willing to put up with truly dreadful growing conditions, even dry shady areas, and so is a useful plant for adding interest to neglected spots. But we like it so well that we have given it a better home, using twenty plants as a hedge along the foundation of the glassed-in winter garden. There, its burgundy leaves shot through with clear pink are beautiful all summer, a perfect backdrop for billows of the royal blue form of *Salvia viridis* (syn. *Salvia horminum*), called 'Cambridge Blue'. The

effect of strong blue against pink and wine red is as vivid as medieval stained glass. And when the salvias are cleared away to the compost, the berberis remain, their burgundy deepening with cool weather to a maroon ground and their pink turning almost electrically vivid. The effect lasts until quite heavy frosts wither the leaves and cause them to drop, leaving a thick congested line of spiny, cinnamon brown stems.

Though perennials are generally valued for their flowers or perhaps for the texture of their leaves in the summer garden, no one ever seems to think of them for the autumn colors of their leaves. But a few of them – actually a fair number – offer this gift, a sort of autumn encore well after the symphony of the great woodland trees is over. In October, for example, *Amsonia tabernaemontana* is a splendid mass of clear yellow leaves, not prettier certainly than the clean shrublike growth and half-inch, sky blue flowers of early summer, but still arresting, giving us the sort of overplus of beauty a good plant can sometimes provide. And though peonies are rightly valued for their great scented globes of flower in late June and their substantial heavy green weight in the border thereafter, in October their leaves can become overcast with rich color. They are generally closer to chestnut brown than to red, but their veins sometimes stand out to the ends a fine olive green, and there are occasionally tints of pink and rose scattered over the surface, a hint of what June was. Sometimes, too, for no apparent reason, an entire plant will turn rich yellow with no brown or russet in sight. And though the autumn leaves of trees and shrubs often turn papery and dull quickly when picked, peony leaves can last a surprisingly long time in water, providing the perfect foil for a few late frost-burnished roses, a handful of colchicum, or a collection of scarlet and red hips and berries. Even casually strewn across a platter of apples and concord grapes, they will last through dinner and assist the feast.

Though no one perhaps would plant peonies just for their autumn leaves, we think we might plant *Lysimachia clethroides* for no other reason. It is called the "gooseneck" loosestrife because its four-inch cobs of little white stars, born singly atop four-foot stems in high summer, are curiously twisted down and up, like geese bowing to the flock. In ancient times it was assumed to be a cure for untoward rage, a good thing if true, for the gardener may often find himself losing his temper with it. Though disease-free and never in need of staking, *Lysimachia clethroides* is a rampageous perennial with a strong preference for permanently moist soil. So we have consigned it to the wilder sections of the garden along the stream, where its determined spread is restricted by large boulders and by other, equally thuggish plants. In that remote spot their early August flowers seldom get the close attention their beauty merits. In mid October, however, *Lysimachia clethroides* puts on a show that cannot be ignored, even from a distance. For then each stem, closely packed against its neighbors, becomes a brilliant scarlet, and the leaves take on shades of crimson and dusky rose, textured above and below like suede. This is when it must be picked, to place alone in a vase — clear glass preferably — so that the fine architecture of the stems and the brilliance of their colors is apparent from top to bottom.

Though even in its season of autumn beauty one might sometimes have a little more *Lysimachia clethroides* than one needs, there can never be too much *Geranium macrorrhizum* in the garden. All true geraniums are precious to us, grown for the simplicity and beauty of their flowers, usually in rich shades of veined purple and blue but sometimes in pale or shocking pink, magenta, or even a suave gray (on *Geranium pratense* 'Mrs. Kendall Clark') or almost true black (on *G. phaeum*, the "mourning widow"). And when out of flower, a geranium's leaves are never ugly, or even homely, and almost all varieties may stop you in your tracks with a splash of crimson or carmine here or there in late autumn. But *Geranium macrorrhizum* will present you with a whole clump of vivid color, or a drift, or even — should you have so much space to give — an entire woodland.

To call any plant ground cover is a dubious compliment. It too often suggests dreary, serviceable plants that can be poked in without much care to clothe out-of-the-way parts of the garden while the busy gardener rushes past on his way to more interesting places. *Geranium macrorrhizum* really *is* good ground cover, but it will not let you move on so quickly. You will stop, first to admire its velvety apple green leaves in spring, a few of which have been held all winter beneath the snow. Each leaf is cut into seven lobes and each lobe is further cut into sevens, forming a beautifully balanced palm around the stem. Later, in early July, there will be flowers, not boldly showy but very winsome, colored pink in the species, purplish pink in 'Ingwersen's Variety', or a pink-stained white in the variety 'Spessart' — all emerging from a prominent wine red calyx. Later still come sheets and sheets of leaves, admirable both by themselves and in the way they spread out from the center of the plant to smother all the weeds around, saving the gardener a deal of work and pleasing him with their beauty. Propagating the plant is ease itself; thickened stems with their crowns of leaves may be detached from the parent plant

As the light declines and frosts become heavier, Salvia leucantha *reaches its peak of bloom, its frank magenta gaining suavity from the garden's predominant rust and red. The box of apples is from a tree of 'Cox's Orange Pippin' in the perennial garden, one of the richest-flavored and longest-keeping of the antique apples.*

and inserted in moist soil, where they will always take root.

Starting in October, however, *Geranium macrorrhizum* begins to color. First one leaf and then another displays a splash of dull red, perhaps a circular zone midway down the leaf. Soon a leaf will turn pumpkin colored, followed by another which adds for originality a margin of burning orange blended into pink. But only the older leaves assume these autumn tints, leaving the younger ones quite green to continue for the year to come. It is as if they have assigned roles, each leaf taking up its part in a carefully conducted dramatic sequence that may continue into December, making warm places in the snow. And though at every season the leaves of *Geranium macrorrhizum* are rich with a fragrant oil that smells of myrrh, it is never so strong as in the autumn — simply to pick a leaf and crush it will leave your hand perfumed for half a day.

Most plants that color in autumn do so in preparation for their farewell, retreating into bare twigs for a long winter's sleep, to greet the gardener again in spring with new shoots, fresh growth, and a new season of beauty. Some, however, linger for surprisingly long, and may — where snows do not quite cover them — provide a note of color throughout the long wintry days and even into early spring. Chief among these sturdy lingerers in our garden are the bergenias, which burnish their leaves with deep maroon in late September and hold them in good color well into April. Though they are limp on the bitterest days they are crisp on mild ones. There is no season of the year when bergenias are not valuable in the garden, for they tolerate sun and shade, flourish for many years without resetting, and produce colonies of paddle-shaped leaves sometimes a foot long and almost half as wide. Such a leaf

shape is scarce among hardy perennial plants, so bergenias provide much-needed contrast, both at the edges of a perennial border and among ferns in the woodland garden. They provide as well the perfect weight beneath the sometimes gawky stems of tall flowering shrubs, relishing the shade and mulched coolness that obtains there. Their pretty spring and early summer flowers — cobs of tightly packed florets in bright pink, rose, or white — are also always welcome, when late frosts have spared the buds. But it is when the bergenias color in late autumn that one notices and treasures them most. For the deep olive of each leaf is evenly spread with a maroon like the fine leather once called "oxblood." Several of these leaves should always be picked and brought into the house, burnished lightly with a soft cloth to bring up their sheen, as one would an apple, and placed in water. They will last the whole winter through, beautiful alone in a vase or as a supporting component in many arrangements, from Christmas holly to the luxury of a bunch of small, pale pink florist's roses in March.

October seems to belong to grasses, though they are never as vivid as other perennials. Nevertheless, in autumn even scruffy anonymous roadsides can turn glorious. Within gardens, many grasses planted for ornamental effect throughout the summer can contribute cherished gifts in autumn also — gifts of color or, when all the color is drained from them, of form, becoming a net in which the first heavy frosts are caught and on which the first snows sparkle. Of all the grasses in our garden, the best at all seasons are members of the genus *Miscanthus*. Particularly wonderful is *M. sinensis* 'Gracillimus', the "maiden grass," most graceful indeed with its five-foot upright fountains of dark, narrow leaves veined down the center with silver. Both *M. sinensis* 'Variegatus' and *M. sinensis* 'Zebrinus' create shimmering haystacks in the perennial border, the first with silver stripes down the whole surface of its leaves and the second with inch-wide yellowish white bands across them. Among *Miscanthus sinensis* varieties are also plants that will produce plumes of flower from late August well into November, even in our Zone 4 garden — the best of which is aptly named 'Silver Feather'.

But for the finest autumn color, the choice among miscanthus narrows to *M. sinensis purpurascens*, whose varietal name indicates something of what it can do in autumn. It is not the most distinguished of its clan in posture, though only by comparison with its close cousins is it in any way deficient. For it still possesses a fine figure, upright to four feet, a little more matronly than the maiden grass but furnished with wider, dark green blades a foot or more long from the stem. It is reliably hardy to at least Zone 4, and more shade-tolerant than many other miscanthus. Along a summer woodland walk it can be very beautiful contrasting with ferns or rising out of ground covers, though like any other miscanthus it is always best when placed a little forward so one can see its full architecture, from tightly bunched stems to fountains of leaves. It is in late autumn, however, that *M. sinensis purpurascens* becomes most beautiful, each blade assuming tints of dull red with here and there a streak of orange or rust or rose. It is never actually purple, as its name suggests it should be (happy thought if it were!), but it is still wonderful in its subtle autumn colors, which it maintains well into early November, later fading to a tawny sheaf of straw.

Far more dramatic in every way is *Miscanthus floridulus*, the "Giant Chinese Silver Grass," sometimes listed under the name *Miscanthus sinensis* 'Giganteus'. It is, in fact, gigantic; from a well-established clump in damp humusy soil, thirty or forty tightly packed canes will emerge come spring and grow rapidly to nine feet or so. These canes are clothed in broad blades, three feet long and an inch or more wide, that thicken at the top into graceful plumes. It is actually a hardy plant, though in our northern garden it looks like some great tropical grass unaccountably thriving far from home. At the edge of our bog garden, close to the end of the plank bridge, other tropical-looking plants join it — *Darmera peltata*, with leaves the size of dinner plates, and *Petasites japonicus* var. *giganteus*, with its vast, four-foot-wide umbrellas. The picture is one of jungle-like exuberance.

But after its lush, round-leaved companions have all been leveled by frost, *Miscanthus floridulus* begins another wonderful show. Green slowly retreats from its leaves, replaced by a color more pink than straw — a curious warm tint in the cold mists of late October and the snows of December. Wind whips through these tall pennants, causing them to look like the war banners in a Kurosawa film. Finally the leaves are stripped away, leaving the rigid canes still upright. It is then that *Miscanthus floridulus* hints that it may be not only beautiful, but useful as well, for these bare clumps yield excellent garden stakes. They lack the tremendous tensile strength of bamboo, but they are still strong enough for most perennials that need staking. They are a beautiful polished tan, so fine that they can be made into tripods for light summer vines without apology for their presence.

But it is not only on the last autumn-coloring shrubs and perennials, or even on the buff and pinkish tan of the grasses, that we must depend for flashes of color after the flaming-up of the woods is over. Late in the gardening year as it is, we still look in October for outdoor flowers. There will be plenty of time, after all — a whole winter of it — to study with moody pleasure the stark outlines of the landscape, the black-and-white elegance of bare branches against the snow. In October, even in Vermont, there will still be a precious handful or two of flowers, to be admired as one strolls about the garden on misty days or in the mellow light of sunny ones, or to pick, minding not at all their frost-inflicted blemishes and freckles, marks they bear as intrepid last survivors.

Gertrude Jekyll once observed that flowers gathered in the hand always make the most beautiful arrangements; it is especially true of the small bouquets that October offers. So one starts with a few fine leaves — of a bergenia perhaps — adding to them single blossoms culled from here and there, not forgetting some fine scarlet hips from *Rosa glauca* or an especially brilliant blade from *Miscanthus sinensis purpurascens.*

In most cases the flowers of October are far from the showiest or choicest our garden can boast in its pride. In fact some are quite common, like the winsome Johnny-jump-ups we see at this season — the few among thousands that managed to escape our weeding hands by hunkering down modestly beneath the skirts of a shrub rose or lilac bush. How glad we are at this season that they did; for their tiny faces, generally an infelicitous combination of purple and yellow, charm us now with their bravery and their uncanny skill at evasion. They are not much good for picking, for their stems are short, and even in the tiniest glass they look like scrawny kids desperately trying to chin themselves against its edge. But we are always

glad to have them when it comes time to wrap an October birthday present. The only wrapping paper we have used for years is yesterday's newspaper, and the only ribbon the baling twine the cows leave from their breakfast or supper. So a bunch of Johnny-jump-ups tucked around the "bow" adds greatly to the finished package.

It is a curiosity of so many late-autumn flowers that they are counterparts to the flowers of early spring. So it is certainly with the Johnny-jump-ups, which end our year and begin it with their greetings, being both the last and the first flowers in the garden. But others of the last autumn flowers have an uncanny resemblance and a botanical relationship to the first flowers of April. *Hamamelis virginiana*, for example, is the last or the first witch hazel to bloom, depending on your view of things. For if it is the last, there is a long gap between its autumn flowers and those of *Hamamelis x intermedia* 'Arnold's Promise', which bloomed in April; and if it is the first, then there is an equally long gap — a whole winter's worth in some years — between it and *Hamamelis mollis* 'Brevipetala', which sometimes surprises us with blooms in late December but more typically at the end of January.

Still, a flower that relishes late October is to be treasured. *Hamamelis virginiana* is not the best of the witch hazels, and our plants — four small trees planted as a grove along the drive and now interwoven into a thicket eight feet tall — are certainly not the best form of *Hamamelis virginiana*. For they bloom while still clinging to their tawny withered leaves, and one must peer close indeed to see their tiny yellow threads of flowers, and concentrate very hard to smell the flowers' magic scent beyond the smell (nice too in its way) of the dying foliage. We have seen much better plants, just

Colchicum, which begin blooming in September, continue well into October, until quite heavy frosts cut them down. To build up a large stock, annual resetting is necessary and is best done when the plants are fairly dormant.

A certain kind of frost, occurring when the air is laden with moisture and temperatures drop suddenly, glorifies everything on which it falls. The foliage of Rosa pimpinellifolia *is always pretty and clean, but laced with frost, its tidy and presentable leaves gain great elegance.*

north of Greenfield, Massachusetts, where they grow wild in the woods and the tiny flowers on naked stems create a haze of yellow in the understory of the forest. Some atavistic memory stirs in us at such a sight, and though we are not hunters, we seem to need to tread these woods, as if the sight and smell of the witch hazels might signal the smoky flash of a white-tailed deer or a gathering of wild turkeys searching the forest floor for beech mast in the early dawn. We'll have better *Hamamelis virginiana* plants someday, ones that bloom properly naked. But that is not to say that we will discard those we have, for it is a principle of our garden that nothing is thrown away. And in October, when any flower is bound to possess a certain subtlety, who minds searching a bit to find it?

Among the last flowers of October are several bulbs that have a relationship, in physical resemblance if not in botany, to the first ones of spring. Colchicums, for example, are not crocuses, though their five-petaled chalices of purple look like a more substantial version of them. Colchicums are intrepid plants, blooming in mid September and continuing until October spins to an end. They produce fresh waves of flowers throughout this season until really cold weather flattens them; they are warriors, the young and old alike, felled only by the advance of winter. Even at the end of October a few of the youngest may still be gathered up where they lie supine, brought indoors, and made to straighten up in the warmth.

Sturdier even than colchicum, though it hardly looks it, is the only of several true autumn-flowering crocuses we can grow, *Crocus speciosus*. It begins to flower in late October, and even in early December one can still find a shy lingerer in the snow. We wonder how so fragile-

looking a creature can be so strong, for it hasn't a stem, really, only a six-inch watery tube that bears aloft a flower which must be heavy for such a support, though it looks gossamer. And the color, too — a rare clear violet seldom seen except in violets, some of them, and lilacs — isn't generally thought of as the color of strength. Actually, the intensity of that color is due to a number of fine blue lines radiating outward across each sheeny, pale lilac-gray petal. Whenever a stronger color is overlaid on a lighter one, as happens with many poppies and with *Jalapa mirabilis* (four-o'clocks) as well, the effect is often a curious vibrancy. But for all the delicacy and brilliance of its violet color, to pick a few tightly closed *Crocus speciosus* buds on a frosty late-October morning and place them in water in a warm room is to get an even greater surprise. For they will then open, revealing all the complexity of their veined petals, within which stand the vivid orange stigma against the paler yellow stamens. And if one is keen of nose and closely attentive, one can catch a pronounced whiff of saffron, a reminder of the near relationship of *Crocus speciosus* to *Crocus sativus*, the priceless saffron crocus. It is, alas, impossible for us to grow, for it requires a hot baking summer soil, gritty and alkaline, to be found nowhere in Vermont. And if it's grown in a pot it requires careful annual lifting and dividing or it will run to leaf and tiny cormels in three years or less. So we stay with *Crocus speciosus*, which, on a rare warm day in late October or (more frequently) as a tight bouquet on the writing desk, presents us with flowers the likes of which we will not see again until late March.

All the flowers of autumn seem to laugh at our sense of time and make puns to frustrate our cutting up and neatly boxing the seasons so they do not become confused. No greater joker is to be found than *Galanthus reginae-olgae,* called "Queen Olga's" snowdrop. It does indeed bloom in the snow, the first snow, which generally comes about the last week of October. To anyone but a trained botanist the tiny flower it produces looks exactly like those of *Galanthus nivalis,* the familiar early spring snowdrop of which some consider it a sub-species. The effect is either unsettling or boundlessly optimistic, depending on your cast of mind. But because snow can be heavy here, even in late October, Queen Olga lives in a pot for us, blooming in the cool greenhouse from October to late November. We have heard, also, that her sense of humor does not end with an autumn look like her spring-blooming counterpart; for there is a form of *G. reginae-olgae,* subspecies (or variety) *vernalis,* that blooms in spring. We do not grow it; or rather, we assume that we do not grow it, for who but a botanist could be sure that it is not laughing at us, mixed in with the sheets of *Galanthus nivalis* that bloom along the entrance path to our garden in March?

One other flower blooms now to stitch together the fading and the approaching year, and that is *Gentiana scabra.* Gentians are a fabled race in gardens; we grow all we can, for there is no other blue among flowers that quite matches its intensity. The first to bloom for us, in the stiff wet clay of the rock garden, is *Gentiana acaulis,* covering its tufts of ever-green foliage with tubular up-facing blossoms in May, as vivid as the flash of a kingfisher's wing. It is followed by *Gentiana frigida* in July, and by *Gentiana asclepiadea* in August. Last to bloom, from the first through the last week of October, is *Gentiana scabra.* It is dear to us for that, though its terminal, tight-packed clusters of frost-faded blossoms are not the finest blue a gentian can achieve. Still, they are lovely, each

two-inch long funnel of five petals rendered more complex by overlays of wine and olive green against the blue. It is also a stately plant, rigidly upright though only three feet tall. From a central crown as many as twenty stems emerge, each furnished with five-inch-long blades, dark green in summer but at flowering time overlaid with dull maroon. And, like most gentians when they are happy, it is very long-lived. Ours have surprised us for ten years in a shady corner of the hillside along a path, pre-senting their clean growth and their gift of late flowers with no particular attention from us.

We read an article in the local paper this month titled "This Year's Garden Is History." All that we have so far said about our garden at this season indicates, we hope, that this is not so. By "garden," the writer of the article clearly meant "vegetable garden," the usual sig-nificance of that word here in Vermont. (The quaint, old-fashioned term "posy patch" is still in use for flower gardens.) Still, we had to smile, for even the vegetable garden at this sea-son is full of riches, a feast both for the eye and the table. Though the high summer abun-dance of beans and peas is gone, the potatoes have been put in cool dark quarters for winter use, and all tomatoes that showed any promise of ripening have been spread on newspapers in a corner of the upstairs hall, there are still wonderful things to harvest from the cold ground. Cabbages and brussels sprouts, in both glaucous green and burgundy red, improve in flavor with each progressive frost, as do the carrots and leeks, the last of which we will pry from the frozen ground with a col-lar of ice around their necks. And there is still a fine mixed salad to harvest of late-sown spinach, chicory, endive, and the last lettuces. All have grown a little bitter by now, requiring both a long soak in ice water to sweeten them and a dressing rather richer in anchovies, garlic, herbs, balsamic vinegar, and rock salt than the lighter one of summer.

The best salad of this season, however, is now only just ready; it consists of the Italian green puntarelle, a form of chicory that is worth all the trouble it takes, both to grow and to prepare. For here in Vermont it must be seeded in early spring, grown to as fat as it can be all summer long, and harvested only when frosts have concentrated its flavor. It can be seeded rather thickly, for only the pale stems — each about six to eight inches long — are taken, and crowded growth seems to improve their flavor. The attractive blade-shaped leaves, doubtless abundant with vitamins, may be cooked by those who like bitter greens. We throw them to the chickens, who do, and return to the kitchen with only the stems. Each stem must be split, once into halves or again into quarters, and then plunged into cold water for an hour or two. In this chilly bath the stems curl up; they are then drained, spun or patted dry, and dressed. Rare treat that it is, we eat puntarelle practically until we are sick of it, which fortunately occurs just before nighttime temperatures consistently in the low 20s make it too tough to be palatable. Then we give it up, an event analogous to giving up the dandelion greens of spring when their bitterness and the lawn have both increased enough to require a first mowing.

The last of all the crops we take — excepting, of course, the deeply buried parsnips — are the leeks, whose gray-green flags have flown unblemished throughout the end of October and into November, but whose thick white stems must finally be severed from root and leaves, wrapped individually in plastic, and piled in the bottom of the refrigerator for late autumn and winter use. From there they are taken by ones and twos and added to winter soups, or perhaps browned lightly in butter, simmered in chicken stock until it is reduced to a syrup and they are tender, dusted with hard Italian cheese, and sent under the broiler for a second or two. Prepared this way, they provide a first course as succulent as spring asparagus, which is saying much.

Even without the leeks — the last of its above-ground denizens to harvest — the vegetable garden is still beautiful. But now it depends for its beauty not on abundant herbage or the plethora of crops it has produced all summer long, but on paths, the fence, the severe outlines of the espaliered fruit trees, and the smug skeletons of the standard gooseberry and currant trees in the centers of its many squares. Beautiful also, to the gardener's eye, is its deep rich soil, cleared of withered stems and weeds and ready for the final attention the vegetable garden will require this year, a covering blanket of rich pasture muck.

November

E could never say about this somber month that it is our favorite in the garden. As the year winds down to its close, gray days occur with greater and greater frequency — not cloudy and not sunny, but simply gray. Gray is also the predominant color of the garden and the surrounding woods. Most of the fiery splendor of October has fallen, revealing the great boles of trees and the tangled architecture of deciduous shrubs, now an endless play on one monochromatic color. Leaves, faded to a papery dull rose, catch in piles and drifts, obscuring paths and collecting among the shrubs and ground covers; there they will remain, forming a sustaining mulch, or perhaps they will be whirled about the garden by gusts later in the month, to catch elsewhere. Those that gather in the corners of the lawns or lodge too thickly over fragile perennials will have to be gathered up, after the

wind has done its helpful work, to tuck around young rhododendrons and the skirts of woodland shrubs. Most, however, we let lie, pitying those gardeners whose excessive love of tidiness forces on them the tedious job of raking — or worse, the noise and noxious fumes of leaf blowers. For winter snows will reduce the fallen leaves to a fecund deep brown cover for the soil, nourishing it and saving many tedious hours of weeding in the season to come. And the leaves, which look at this season like an ecologically sound wrapping paper for the garden, clothe the earth and form a beautiful, neutral ground against which the subtle grays of trunk, branch, and stem stand forth with quiet beauty.

This is not to say that every morning and every garden effect at this season reflect only the color of a mouse's fur. For the lowering sun can still shine warmly, producing a day

Even when stripped of leaves, the shapes of deciduous shrubs — thickly congested or gaunt — and their colors —
mouse-gray, olive green, or warm straw brown — can give pleasure on a rare, sunny day in November.
Then is perhaps the best time to make plans of what to move, how
to prune, what to add. Bed lines, particularly, are apparent at this season,
in their pleasant (or not) sweeps.

that tempts one out to evaluate plantings that show their structures better for having been stripped, and to make ambitious plans for the spring — what to move and what to order. Generally, however, on such rare sunny days in November, one simply floats through the garden — mindless, suspended, waiting — scuffling in the leaves and savoring the last flashes of color, the more precious for their scarcity and the intensity with which they glow against the neutral gray backdrop. Even deep in the native woods the young beeches hold their leaves, and will all winter, fading through all the colors of expensive Japanese silk, from russet brown to the palest straw faintly tinctured with rose.

Nevertheless, and despite these occasional sunny days, for most gardeners November is the beginning of the downtime of the year. The weather turns progressively colder and more drizzly, and they retreat indoors, to long drowsy hours before the fire, to the promise of something savory simmering on the back of the stove, to correspondence unanswered, to books and magazines unread. Thoughts of the garden retreat to the pleasant memory of something one did, and will do again, but not just now, not for a while, not as long as the weather is so cold and raw. Lessons are taken from a companionable cat, who stretches languorously, curls herself into an even more compact ball on the sofa, and rests one paw beneath her chin for greater comfort.

We are not such fools for gardening that this fantasy hasn't a great hold on us, at least in the imagination. But we know that November is in some ways one of the most demanding times in the garden, presenting almost the last moment when many necessary chores must be done before the advancing winter makes them impossible. And beyond those that are obligatory for the survival of the garden are those that could be deferred until spring, but that if accomplished now are pure gain. Weeding, for example, particularly of deep-rooted grasses, is more easily done now than at any other time, and now is the only time that infestations of quack grass can be cleaned from clumps of Siberian irises or daylilies without uprooting them altogether and pulling them to bits. And the rock garden, at its prime from very early to middle spring, will be all the lovelier then for some patient attention now, even at the expense of raw and frozen fingers. November is also the best time to renew permanent mulches of wood chips or fir bark, for one can spread it over the crowns of dormant perennials and tiny spring bulbs, both for added winter protection and as a foil for their fresh spring growth and flowers, which will sparkle all the brighter against it. So we defer thoughts of winter leisure, which *will* come, and which will be the more enjoyable for the smug satisfaction of knowing that we worked as long as we could, and that the garden is ready for its last, best protection, a thick blanket of snow. So at this season the cat can do as she pleases, for she is always jumping the gun anyway. We must go out, and into the garden.

Chilly mists are the best working conditions we can hope for throughout most of November. Pelting rains and even flurries are worse, but worst of all are the hard clear days when dry arctic air sweeps down from northern Canada, clearing out the chill mists and rain to deep-freeze the garden and the gardener alike. Still, we must work until all is done; and given the weather, whatever it is, it is fortunate that the garden still presents us with so much beauty. For though all the flowers are gone by now, even the last sturdy lingerers, November is the beginning of the conifer season. It is always with sharp surprise that we realize how splendid they are. For though they are constant and permanent members of the garden, always there to provide weight and depth to other plantings, in spring, summer, and early fall they are eclipsed by the fully clothed forms of the deciduous trees and shrubs. When the last leaves fall, however, the conifers emerge in an astonishing range of colors and shapes, all thickly clad with fresh new needles. Their return to prominence is as thrilling in its way as the emerging bulbs of March or the re-leafing of the maples and beeches in May. It is the return to consciousness of something loved but almost forgotten.

North Hill is a largely informal garden, one that follows the contours of the hillside on which it sits, the plants arranged in natural drifts or tucked among taller shrubs and trees that seem, we hope, as if they had come of themselves. We would not say, even now, that we adopted this style of gardening by preference, for we could have come to love any garden we crafted onto the land, and there is still something thrilling to us about straight axes and perfectly formal and regular arrangements of plants. This bit of land, however, would never have complied with a formal scheme, folding as it does down to the stream that dominates everything and rising steadily from the bottom to the top of the garden in an incline that we have tried to tame but must still respect. It demanded natural plantings, and the style has served us well, not only by harmonizing the garden with its surroundings but also by making possible a far vaster collection of plants than any formal style could have easily accommodated. We have found, nevertheless, that the most seemingly spontaneous plantings — in their high season as romantically exuberant as one could wish — still benefit tremendously from a note of formality, brought forward as a

disciplining focal point or pushed behind as a controlling backdrop. And if individual plantings gain by this conjunction of formal and informal, so does the garden as a whole; it is knitted together with conifers and other evergreens that are half lost, as they should he, in the abundance of summer, but stand forth now, their severe and regular beauty in perfect harmony with the austerity of the season.

In November, one can see that the entire garden is in fact bordered by a mixed hedge of evergreens that forms its frame and creates a sort of wall between it and the surrounding fields and forests. The first section of this hedge was planted fifteen years ago; it existed at first mostly in our minds, the small evergreens hidden behind the much more vigorous growth of deciduous shrubs. But now the fast-growing pines from that first planting stand twenty feet tall, and even the slow-growing junipers and spruces are ten feet tall or so, enough to show, and to prove that we knew what we were doing.

Not all our initial choices were wise ones, however. The Scots pines, for example, though compact little plants when put in, have now begun to shed their lower branches, as is their habit, and will have to be replaced before we lose our privacy from the road. And the *Pinus resinosa* trees are clearly going to be too big too soon, forcing on us the choice of retaining at most two or three and felling all the rest. This is the greater pity, of course, because both species, when given space to develop well, can make magnificent specimens; still, it is never wise to reason that way, for there isn't space, and they won't be magnificent specimens, but only a liability on the garden that increases with the years. Better to have them out, without regrets, admitting that they served us well for a time, and plant in their stead evergreens that are bent on achieving a less massive maturity.

It is amazing that a flower so fragile-seeming as Crocus speciosus *can be so intrepid. For though the bitterest weather November can offer falls on it, and also the snows of early December, waves of blooms still continue to appear. Even when frozen quite dead, the flowers leave a violet shadow on the snow.*

On the other hand, a grove of the Rocky Mountain white pine, *Pinus flexilis,* has behaved with exemplary grace, the trees weaving themselves into a dense thick screen, their long flexible branches threading into one another as if they enjoyed the company of their fellows and were better off for it. *Picea omorika,* the graceful Serbian spruce, has spires tall enough to hide telephone wires; ours are also beginning to show the graceful upturned arms and pendant branchlets for which they are treasured. The Norway spruces, *Picea abies,* have bulked out into vast Christmas trees, dark and somber, never overassertive, but almost the most beautiful evergreen of winter once one comes to focus on them. And the Colorado spruce, *Picea pungens,* which one too often sees as a visually indigestible single specimen of a most assertive powder blue, has achieved a great suavity by being planted in a flattened grove along the drive, like a folded Chinese screen, with various shades of blue mixed sparingly with predominantly blue-green and sea green seedlings.

Our first evergreen plantings were put in not so much for reasons of theory, for we had not yet crystallized on our own the perception any good garden-design book would have offered – that the first step in making a garden is to define its perimeters by creating a frame. Instead, our first evergreen plantings were a response to the fact that the house is quite close to the road, positioned there not by preference, for we would have liked to build it deeper in the woods, but because our little stream – the chief reason for buying the property in the first place – could not be bridged without a considerable outlay of cash we didn't have. Actually, our builder offered us, bluntly, a choice: "For the money you have, you can either get a bridge over the stream or a brick chimney block big enough to have a fire-place in every room." We chose the chimney block, and have never been sorry, as ours is a climate in which a fire is welcome almost every night of the year. (We have further found, both here at North Hill and at other properties on which we have worked, that seldom is there no way to create a screen of plants thick enough to ensure privacy and baffle the noise of passing traffic.) So our first concern in planting our evergreens was to shield ourselves from public view. Not that the "public view" is either all that frequent or in any way hostile; our road could hardly be called well traveled, and those who come by are generally people we want to greet, by a wave or the exchange of a word or two. Nevertheless, we quickly grasped the fact that a garden, a proper garden, should possess, almost as a first principle, a sense of privacy and tranquil enclosure. Though the small evergreens we initially planted hardly provided it at first, they do now, to the disgust of our oil delivery man, who says frequently, "This place is a mess! You can't see out, you can't see in. Open it up! Show people what you got in here."

Encouraged by this clear testimony to our success, we decided to extend the conifer planting, creating a bed twenty feet wide along the road from the entrance drive to the rock garden at the base of the property. In our first years here, we thought of conifers primarily as sturdy makeweights for small deciduous trees and shrubs planted in front of them, a necessary guarantee of privacy, and a garden interest in winter. But after ten years we came to love our conifers for themselves and to think that at all seasons we could not see enough of them. And for a certain kind of gardener, also, the successful growing of any plant in at least two forms leads to a collection; with the right kind of plant, a collection leads to an absorbing passion. Conifers, once you come to love them, easily conduct you in that direction; for their forms are infinitely varied, ranging from magnificent forest giants down to tiny dwarfs hardly larger than a cantaloupe, with shapes that can be loosely or tightly conical, eccentric or even ragged, rounded, flattened, bristly, soft, weeping, or creeping along the ground. So we decided that with this new planting we would have a true conifer border, in which the shapes, forms, and colors of only this group of plants would predominate.

We have cheated a little on this original intention. Indeed, we had to cheat from the first, for at the head of the proposed border was a single plum tree, a 'Stanley's Blue Egg', planted in the garden's second year and now richly productive of fine blue plums, suitable for eating fresh and of one of the best varieties for making plum jam. Even with these claims we might have felled our tree for the sake of theory, except that its form — vase-shaped and breaking into many branches close to the ground — is a perfect complement to the predominantly conical forms of the conifers. Also, its fine polished gray limbs and froth of tiny white flowers in May — not to mention the bloomy cobalt blue of its fruits in August — enhance a planting of conifers better than anything we might have thought of, had thought been at issue.

So the plum was spared. And once the conifers were in fact planted we found that a few other deciduous plants, carefully chosen for their strong, even (sometimes) eccentric presence, improved the effect without blurring our intent. Above the plum we added a magnificent specimen of *Ulmus procera* var. *viminalis* 'Aurea', the golden English elm, given us by the Arnold Arboretum with the hope that, as all the American elms in our area had long since fallen to Dutch elm disease, it would have a chance to reach maturity. To balance the plum, at the bottom of the border we planted a tree of the antique apple called 'Pitmaston Pineapple', just where the conifers give way to the rock garden. It is small still and very slow-growing, but some day its slender branches will be crowded with tiny yellow apples (which really do taste of pineapple, for we have tried them from other trees). Finally we planted a specimen of the weeping pussy willow, *Salix caprea pendula*, not in the more familiar male form, called the "Kilmarnok" willow, but in the rarer female form, nicely called "Weeping Sally." It is trained as a standard on a six-foot-tall pole of concrete-reinforcing rod called "rebar," the best material gardeners can use for stakings that must be really permanent. From the top of this support, the willow weeps down to the ground in a graceful veil, its pendulous branches ornamented at every leaf joint in early spring with two-inch catkins of pale silvery gray.

But since the new conifer border was designed primarily to collect conifers, the predominant planting, some fifty specimens, was chosen with that in mind. Against a magnificent Norway spruce, original to the garden and now thirty feet high, we added three others to form a massive anchoring grove at the head of the drive. Below them we planted two more specimens of *Pinus flexilis*, remembering how well they had served us before; this time, however, we chose the very graceful steel-blue form called 'Pagoda'. Below them is another Norway spruce, to echo the grove, though this one adds the subtle difference of a burnish of old gold on its newest branches. Following it is yet another *Pinus flexilis* 'Pagoda', which gains an interesting value by being a little separated

So much of our garden was made on bare land, with no structure except what we imposed upon it. There were, however, some fine old trees, a few of which make an entrance to the garden. None pleases us more than this middle-aged maple by the front path, which provides a sort of gatepost. It is clothed now with an exotic hydrangea it would never have thought it would wear when it sprouted fifty years ago.

from its companions. Then there are four black pines (*Pinus nigra*) planted in a staggered row and chosen to avoid the mistake we originally made with *Pinus resinosa*, for *P. nigra* retains a compact form for many years. Its heavy black-green needles are also a wonderful counterpoise to the steely blue of *Pinus flexilis* and the finer, denser texture of the spruces. The back of the planting terminates in a grove of four *Picea omorika* trees, planted to conceal yet another telephone pole, a job this species does better than any other evergreen. For though it towers up quickly, achieving three feet of growth in a single season, it always remains narrow, scarcely more than ten or so feet through, and so can be planted rather close together, each tree seeming to embrace its neighbor with graceful arms. Because of these qualities, it has come to be indispensable to us wherever a narrow screen of greenery is needed or a single graceful spire must rise for accent (or a telephone pole must be concealed).

All the trees planted at the back of the conifer border are rapid growers and can become quite large with age. In order to maintain shapely forms and dense, full growth, all are trimmed, though with different techniques according to whether they are spruces or pines. Spruces are sheared each spring before new growth emerges. Because the idea is to maintain a natural silhouette, hand shears are used rather than hedge clippers, taking six to eight inches of terminal growth from each branch. Pines, on the other hand, are "candled," by snapping off half or a third of each branch's annual spurt of growth before it hardens and the needles form. Shears may not be used for this because they will sever the embryonic needles evenly, creating eventually an unattractive brush at the end of each growth. Thumb and forefinger are the tools of choice for candling,

but as the new growths are rich with resin it is a messy job, requiring turpentine for cleaning up one's hands. We continue this barbering of all major conifers for as long as our tallest stepladder can reach the top growth on the trees. Eventually, however, they must be let go to interlace, though the annual trimmings will have resulted in a thick, impenetrable wall between us and the road. Even now, after five or six years, they are from six to eight feet tall; if one stands just right, they present a solid, serried rank with no gaps in between.

Once this backbone of major trees was in place, we began planting the front of the border with rarer, choicer dwarf and slow-growing conifers. The range of possibilities among these plants is enormous, though most of the ones we can grow belong to the familiar genera of pine *(Pinus)*, spruce *(Picea)*, fir *(Abies)*, juniper *(Juniperus)*, hemlock *(Tsuga)*, arborvitae *(Thuja)*, and *Chamaecyparis*. All these groups are capable of fantastic variations, either as genetic mutants from seed or as witches'-brooms, anomalous congested growths occurring on branches of otherwise normal plants and propagated by alert nurserymen. Though many have been in American gardens for a century or more, and others in Japanese gardens — where they are especially treasured — for much longer, new ones are constantly being discovered, and vast books have been written on them alone. We could never hope to become specialists on the subject, which would be work for more of a lifetime than we have left. In any case, we are far too fond of all plants to specialize in anything, or to reject any plant from our garden because it is not an alpine, or an iris . . . or a conifer. So in planting the foreground of our conifer border, we simply chose what we liked from a well-stocked nursery and brought home our little plants in cans, merrily setting about the work of planting them in front of the major conifers we had already established.

Actually, however, one does not so much plant a border of dwarf conifers as one choreographs it, positioning the little plants in their cans in an at first tentative and then ever-surer way so that their forms — rounded, irregular, matted, cone-shaped, or columnar — their eventual heights, and their endless variations of needle densities and color will complement one another. Usually it is better not to place two varieties of the same genus side by side, for their subtle differences get lost in each other, causing one of them to merely look more robust, better shaped, or unaccountably stunted and bent to ground than the other. And in the matter of height, especially, one must be careful. For "dwarf," among conifers, is a relative word. "Slow-growing" is more accurate, though even there the catalogs have more than once led us astray. It seems our cool mountain garden, with its evenly spaced rainfalls throughout the year and its annual heavy blanket of snow, is a sort of conifer heaven. Specimens that the catalogs promised would increase at the rate of only three inches a year have nonetheless shot up surprisingly fast to four or five feet, though they still show, by their tighter and more congested growth, that they have not thrown off their dwarfdom under our conditions to the extent of resuming the stature of the species. (Growers of dwarf conifers are always alert for the sudden appearance of an unusually vigorous or large-needled branch on a specimen, for that will mean the plant has begun to revert to its natural form; such growths must be promptly removed at their origin, or else what was meant to be a foot-tall muffin will in a few short years become a thirty-foot forest tree.)

An unexpected vigor in some of our plants has actually not been a bad thing, however, for this self-willed behavior has saved us from an error it is far too easy to make in planting any border — arranging the shortest plants in front, the next-tallest behind, and the tallest at the back, creating an effect as regular and orderly as a set of high school bleachers. A certain irregularity in height is always an asset in any border and one from which conifers particularly benefit. For instead of sliding restlessly over uniform ranks, the eye pauses to enjoy each individual shape and texture. One must only be certain that the advancing growth of one specimen does not crowd out and distort the more timid increase of its neighbor.

It is a happy fact about dwarf conifers, however — and most other evergreen plants — that they may be moved at almost any age, given courage and muscle and a little advanced preparation in the form of root pruning a year or two before the move is to be made. With conifers careful timing is also necessary, for the work must he done either before the plant has begun its spurt of annual growth in the spring, or after the new growth has hardened into its adult state later in the summer. After mid September it is best in our climate to leave any evergreen in place until spring, so as not to expose it to the force of the winter before it has had time to build a new system of sustaining roots. But with these cautions in mind, almost any dwarf conifer can be transplanted if it threatens to outgrow its allotted space. We have already had to relocate a "dwarf" white pine (*Pinus strobus* 'Nana') that grew to a surprising eight feet in as many years and showed no sign of slowing. Despite our best digging efforts it came up from the ground essentially bare-rooted, but we planted it in almost a whole bale of wet peat and

In its summer dress of dark green, Sasa veitchii is
always pleasing. In autumn, however, when it develops a
papery margin of parchment brown around each leaf,
it becomes thrilling, one of the last and most
enduring beauties of the declining year.

ॐ

Hamamelis virginiana is hardly the showiest
of its family, its tiny yellow thrums of flowers creating
an effect that would most charitably be described as subtle.
But a flower outdoors in latest November has to be
considered precious, which is perhaps the reason it chooses
to bloom now rather than in competition with its
showier Asian relatives.

ॐ

reduced its branches by a third to bring them into balance with its meager roots. Despite this radical treatment it has never looked back, only checked and tightened its growth a bit, which is, as it happens, appreciated.

When we completed our conifer border we were immensely satisfied by it, and we showed it with pride to an eminent lady gardener of our acquaintance who is also — we know from many experiences — not slow with her judgments. "Weel," she said with her characteristic New England bluntness, "I suppose it will be very fine, someday. But it *is* very . . . masculine!" We are hardly afraid of being masculine, at least in the nicer senses of that word, and even if we were, for obvious reasons it would do us little good to fret overmuch about it. But as we assumed she meant there was something rather rigid and overly direct about our planting, we added some swirls of heathers to the feet of the conifers to gentle it a bit.

Heathers, though they can look dreadful in a perennial border or with other small shrubs, are always good companions to dwarf conifers. Though they are not conifers themselves, their small bristly leaves look somewhat like needles, and their stature, never more than two feet in height, cuts against the somewhat determined march a collection of conifers can have, relating them to the ground. The border looked immediately better by their addition, and has become even more attractive after three years. The heathers have knit together to form their own harmonious carpet at the feet of the conifers, echoing their colors of glaucous blue, bronze, gold, and dull green. But for good measure we gathered up all the autumn-blooming colchicum we had planted over the years for one grand splash of mauve during October — beautiful by itself but most beautiful when the mists of late autumn catch in the needles of the conifers and the tufts of heather, silvering them over with a million droplets. Then the picture is beyond any epithet of masculine or feminine. It is merely beautiful.

Conifers, both alone and as a backdrop for other plantings, have taught us so much that now, when new sections of the garden are developed or older ones strike us as somehow unfocused, our first question is whether the introduction of a conifer, or a grove of them, might not be the first step in creating a new planting or in improving an existing one. It is almost always so. Most often for background plants we find ourselves choosing quite familiar forms, even quite common ones, from within the families of spruce, hemlock, juniper, arborvitae, and yew. These are all known in the nursery trade as "bread and butter" plants, for they may be rowed out as cuttings and grown to a salable size quickly and without much trouble, thereby supplying nurserymen with reliable income. They are the darlings of development contractors also, for they are relatively cheap, easy to come by, and they may be plunked down against the foundations of a raw new house to give it what they call a "finished" look, though of course it rarely is. The ubiquity of these conifers in new housing developments and in front of filling stations causes many sensitive gardeners to shun them; but the very qualities that make them so treasured there also recommend them strongly to the gardener, for they are easy and quick to grow, are often amenable to shaping, and are relatively disease-free. It is a sound principle of landscape design, also, that the background to the garden, its frame, ought not to call undue attention to itself. Choicer, rarer, and more striking plants will gain by being placed against a backdrop of blander ones. So gardeners who object to common, serviceable evergreens simply because they have mistakenly been asked to do the work of feature plants might well rethink their prejudices.

For us it was a happy day when we overcame our objection to arborvitaes. We planted five large specimens, slightly varying in height in a staggered row on the side of the perennial garden against the road, in a desperate attempt to win some privacy there. We chose the form called "Nigra" (*Thuja occidentalis* 'Nigra') for its ability to assume a rich, dark color in winter, as opposed to the species and many other forms, which can turn a rather dingy and depressing yellowish green in the cold. Though the original plants were only three to five feet tall, almost immediately we achieved a sense of closure. We found also that perennials are not difficult to establish against their roots, and that some, such as the elegant bugbanes (genus *Cimicifuga*), the magnificent native American goatsbeard (*Aruncus dioicus*), and the broad-leaved *Crambe cordifolia*, with its six-foot clouds of honey-scented flowers in late June, relished the shade the arborvitaes cast and could even be tucked in bays among them, their white flowers looking all the better for a backdrop of green. And, of course, when the masses of perennials at their feet have all been cut down to the bare ground, the arborvitaes still stand splendid, making the border both a private and a beautiful place even in the dead of winter.

But though evergreens are the back curtain to the drama of our garden's flowers, we have also used them as features, placing them as carefully as sculptures and often with a similar effect. Thinking of any plant with a determined or eccentric shape as a sculpture — whether it is a columnar grass like *Miscanthus sinensis* 'Gracillimus', a mop-headed or weeping standard like *Salix caprea* "Weeping Sally," or a smug globe like many boxwoods — is always useful, for careful placement of such elements can save a planting from becoming a formless wash of romantic exuberance and rescue a group of treasured flowers from looking, even in their good season and perhaps after, like a mess. Evergreens are preeminent for this use. Most valuable to us has been the Alberta spruce, *Picea glauca albertiana* 'Conica', familiar to all gardeners as a rigid cone as definite in shape as an old-fashioned paper drinking cup. It requires no shearing to maintain this outline, and its tiny inch-long needles both look and are soft. It is slow-growing, but after fifteen years or so it can achieve eight feet from a two-foot high specimen in a can, substituting a certain portly magnificence for its original cuteness.

We began with three specimens, acquired as most of our plants have been because we liked them and not because we had a clear sense of how we might use them in the garden. One of our three original plants was about four feet tall, and the others two feet tall. After strolling around our developing garden for a while, we finally decided that their proper place was at the head of the rose border, just where the path turns and widens into a small terrace before meandering into a woodland walk. There, we reasoned, they would serve as a full stop to the rose path, signaling by their dense texture and emphatic shape a change of intent (for it is always important in a garden to find ways to indicate where one section stops and another begins).

With some courage, we planted all three plants in a rough triangle about five feet across, with the tallest at the back. Alberta spruces can be moved at any size, and for that reason they should generally be grown with lots of space around them so as not to spoil their symmetry should they need to be relocated. But we had seen somewhere an old specimen that had developed multiple leaders, and we liked the effect of several spires emerging from the same dense mass. So we forfeited the advantage of being able to someday recycle our plants, knowing that where they touched they would shade out one another's growth, and would therefore forever be one indivisible unit. After ten years it has become so, and the path, which had to turn anyway, turns around and behind a solid mass of Alberta spruce with three summits of varying heights. The spruces look as if they were there before the path was thought of and provided the reason for its turning, inevitably, at just that place. For it is a truth about paths that when they turn, they must seem to do so because some solid obstacle — a large stone, an evergreen, the bole of a tree — demands it. Otherwise one wonders why one is not allowed to go straight on and save a few steps. But only to go straight and to see everything in the garden lying directly ahead can quickly become tedious, and forfeits perhaps the greatest of all garden values, that of surprise. So, though one can make a path turn in other ways, a single large evergreen or a group of them has often been for us the most successful way. The device seems to say, "There, now, you've had quite enough of this. Turn this corner and you'll see something else wonderful."

And when a path cannot turn because it must logically go in a straight shot from here to there, an evergreen brought close to its edge can still break up its tedium, functioning as those dinner guests do whose presence makes everything better, to left and right. We have used additional Alberta spruces as single specimens to achieve this effect; we are particularly

delighted by the form called 'Sanders' Blue', which adds to the usual fineness of the spruce's form the magic of a blue sheen, not regular but occurring in puffs here and there. Where spots are shady we use fastigiate yews in broad dark columns (for Alberta spruces demand full sun to look their best), and where they are dry and difficult — such as against the boles of mature maples — we use arborvitae, in globe forms like 'Woodwardii' (the most familiar) or narrow, pencil-straight columnar forms like 'Holmstrup' and 'Unicorn'. And where there is a tangle of permanent growth, brilliant at one season but undistinguished otherwise, there is no better way to bring a sense of order and of point than with an upright, formal juniper.

We have many such plantings, but perhaps the most illustrative is a bed of antique shrub roses bordering the planted terrace across from the glassed-in winter garden. It holds our first acquisition of these wonderful shrubs, which have since spread through the garden in such a way that anyone visiting in late June — the height of rose season — would assume that we are rose specialists, growing them to the exclusion of all else. In this regard they are like many other collections we maintain, which step into an overwhelming prominence briefly and then retreat, sometimes gracefully (or at least unobtrusively), and sometimes with the determination to exact, by a measure of homeliness, a price for all they gave earlier of beauty.

This first planting of old roses is like that, for it exists in a solid mass some twenty feet broad and long, and the individual varieties — familiar old bone-hardy plants like the silver-pink 'Cuisse de Nymphe'; the quartered, double white 'Mme. Hardy', with her wonderful green eye; the old rose rugosa 'Belle Poitvine'; and the taller, wine red 'Hansa' — were all planted on their own roots or, when they were grafted, planted with the graft union three or four inches below ground so they would form their own roots and sucker freely. Though contrary to popular advice, this deep planting is a useful trick, as it will leave some tissue protected beneath the earth, from which the rose will regenerate should a particularly dreadful winter without snow cover kill it to the ground. And though in tidier plantings suckers are discouraged, in this case the result has been an interlaced tangle of rose stems, each laden in season with fragrant blossoms in pale pink, strong pink, deep purple, and white.

That is the effect "in season," and though most of these roses are fairly disease-free and present throughout the summer a loose hedge of presentable green leaves, by now, in November, they are nothing but a tangle of spiny olive green stems, less than nothing to look at. So, like many plantings of this sort, they need something to organize them and give them form. We planted two upright junipers in their midst, *Juniperus scopularum* 'Witchita Blue' and *Juniperus virginiana* 'Oxford Green', the first slightly in front of the second, with perhaps eight feet between. They served their purpose almost from the beginning, as five-foot specimens fresh from their cans; but now, after twelve years or so and at a height of fifteen feet each, they do more, their rigid columns focusing the view through the general tangle of the rose canes. We might, of course, have planted three specimens, as is almost always the gardener's instinct. But these trees have taught us the power of two, in the right place, when one specimen is staged slightly before the other. The effect is as refreshing as a dish that, just for once, does not include garlic, and there is great interest in the fact that the forms are identical but the colors subtly different. It

is a trick that works as well with plants other than conifers, as, for example, when one forgoes planting together two evergreen rhododendrons of the same color, choosing instead to place one with a strong cerise flower before another of a pale shell pink, or to slightly intermingle a deciduous *Ilex verticillata* with yellow berries with one that bears fruit of a tawny, vibrant orange.

Such pleasing effects as the conifers offer keep us going in the wan light of a late November afternoon as we pursue the necessary tasks of the garden. For if making a garden takes a practiced eye and a constant determination to improve aesthetic values, it takes even more a relentless willingness to work, even at a season when there are a hundred things one would rather be doing. Gardens are, after all, unnatural things, and if they are to succeed, the gardener must recompense the earth for what he takes from it, not only in the form of pleasure, but also in the tons and tons of spent leaves and stems that must be hauled away to leave the earth, if bare of beauty, at least tidy. So in late November we pay our debts for all the garden has given. We renew the soil.

In the vegetable garden renewal is a straightforward and a satisfying process, if also a very fatiguing one. But we are not alone in the work we must do there. Closing off one end of its rectangle are two small chicken houses with a fenced run between them. All summer long, and especially from mid October until now, the spent growth of vegetables is tossed over the fence. Usually it consists of withered stems and leaves only, but occasionally there is an overly fat zucchini spared by the frost or a bush of beans laden with pods that were too large for snapping and too immature to shell and dry. Bright feathers flurry and eager eyes search out

Some of the most beautiful flower arrangements of the gardening year occur when one must search a bit for things to put in them. Here, all the best effects of the November garden have been gathered together in an old clay pot. There are not many flowers, and such as there are have been grown in the greenhouse. But there is a wealth of interesting foliage, and of course there are berries, the most vivid of which are the down-hanging clusters of Viburnum opulus.

the best morsels, and then busy feet — blue or yellow scaled, or covered, as in dwarf Cochins (our favorite breed) with feathered boots — turn and pulverize the remains into a rich organic mass, more pleasant perhaps to think about in its benefits to the earth than to handle. It must be spread sparingly, however, and only on bare rows and empty beds, for it is potent stuff, able to give its richness slowly into the soil during the winter but too strong to come in contact with living plants.

Over this bed of enriched vegetable debris we spread a blanket of dark cow "muck," the old Vermont word for the top six or so inches of the feed lot, composed of rotted hay, cow manure, and partially decomposed autumn leaves, all churned up by the feet of the cows into a homogeneous and blessedly odorless (almost) mass. It is mild in its effects, consisting more of sustaining humus than of violent doses of nitrogen. With luck we are able to dig it by the bucketful almost until the end of November, after which the ground freezes solid and it must be not so much dug as chipped up. Usually by that time the entire vegetable garden is swathed in a deep blanket of richness, giving us tremendous satisfaction and promising abundant future crops. Like so many late-season jobs in the garden, it brings its own rewards, even aesthetic ones; for when the work has been well done and every inch of growing space has been covered over, when the beds have been heaped up and dusted with lime, when the stone paths have been swept clean and the ties renewed on the espaliered fruit trees to prevent tears through the winter, then every trip up to the vegetable garden to water and feed the chickens, to renew their warm bed of wood shavings and perhaps let them free on a cold, crisp day, brings its own intense satisfaction, different from, but certainly equal to, the intense pleasure of turning the fresh soil in spring for the first seed, or the high summer magnificence of burgeoning crops, all promising trugs of good things for the kitchen and after, in a logical rhythm, for the chickens. We are free then, spiritually as well as actually, to turn to the needs of other parts of the garden, those parts that are, as they say here in Vermont, "just for show," and to prepare them also for the steady, almost daily advance of winter.

December snows are often wet and thick, as are the snows at the other end of winter, in March. Caught in branches and berried twigs, they can be very beautiful, but also very destructive. Hollies are particularly brittle, and so, lovely as this effect is, the burden of snow must be gently shaken off.

December

THOUGH we have tied this book firmly to the calendar, using the arbitrary passage of the months as a scaffold on which to arrange our experience of the garden and to discuss its changing features, it is not by the flipping of a calendar leaf that most gardeners live. Rather, they judge the progress of the gardening year by certain events which, though certainly seasonal, do not come, as the swallows of Capistrano are said to, on a definite date (or even, necessarily, in a specific month). Though hardly convenient for easy reference, it might have made sense to arrange this book according to those events, as, for example, the night in early April when the tiny spring peepers first burst into their cacophonous song in bogs and low places hereabouts, or the day we first hear the sweet piercing note of the red-winged blackbird, high in the tip-top of the tallest tree, telling us that spring is at last a certainty.

From there we might have moved to the first mowing of the grass, to the first shucking of heavy shoes and socks to tread the ground barefoot, as it was meant to be, or to the first picking of peas, never of course adequate to our hunger but enough at least to signal the arrival of our brief but precious summer. The first sign of autumn – our longest season in Vermont – can come as early as mid August, when the light changes subtly in its fall and slant and becomes more silver than gold, and when the first swamp maples, spendthrifts of their time, suddenly turn scarlet. And what might be called hard autumn – rather than the soft Indian summer days of late asters and brilliant woodland colors – occurs when the black frost sweeps the garden clean in a night, even of its toughest annuals, and turns the ground iron-hard beneath the gardener's heel.

It is with the first really hard frosts that the signs of the year passing occur as much indoors as out. For the fire on the kitchen hearth, always a nightly ritual in summer in our cool mountain climate, becomes a daily occurrence as well. Each morning's fire is built on the ashes of its predecessor and kept going all day long, a place to warm oneself quickly before returning to the garden for yet another stint at cutting down perennials and covering the bare ground with muck. What's on the stove requires longer to cook as well, taking a whole day sometimes rather than the thirty-minute sleight of hand allowed by summer's abundance. Hearty soups and rich, wine-laced stews strengthen us for our work with their savor, and in our anticipation provide some compensation for the steadily shortening days, a progression toward the darkest part of the year that no gardener requires a calendar to judge.

And though outdoors there may be a few shy hardy blossoms to pick or admire well into late November, the first fine wave of greenhouse flowers is beginning in the glassed-in winter garden off the kitchen. First to bloom is always the sasanqua called 'Misty Moon', with five-inch single flowers dark pink as buds and silver pink when open, wonderfully scented with the smell of fresh-brewed tea and something sweeter. They are followed by the first flowers of the smaller, blood red sasanqua called 'Yuletide'. Given where it lives, it must be forgiven for jumping its season by almost a month; but in its happy concordance with 'Misty Moon' it is an example of what we mean when we say that both plants and the gardener know a truer passage of the seasons than is indicated by the ordered structuring of the year into months and days.

So, of course, do farmers. The first sure sign of winter, though it also will slide free of the calendar by a week or two and sometimes more, is unmistakable — even, we might say, irreversible. It is a telephone call from our friend Bummy Allen, whom we do not see from one autumn's end to the next, but who always calls faithfully, earlier or later according to his judgment, to ask about the "brush." That is his old Vermonter's word for the evergreen boughs we spread on the garden, for which we have a standing order of two tons toward year's end. For fifteen years, more or less, our conversation has followed a firmly set pattern: "Hi, thisus Bummy. You'll be wantin' some brush soon, I guess? I got one load t'deliver, but it's been s'wet. Guss'll have anotha by end-of-week, weather permittin'."

Bummy is a great connoisseur of brush, knowing that hemlock is worthless because it will shed its needles well before winter's end, and that white pine, though durable, is too loosely knit to provide much protection. The lusty young spruces that colonize ungrazed pasture are the best — dark green, thick, and full with needles. They must of course be removed, for they are the first wave of trees bent on reclaiming the fields for the forests. So cutting them out and stripping their trunks of clean three- to four-foot-long branches turns a bit of money for Bummy, and provides us with the material essential for protecting the garden.

Two tons of evergreen boughs — roughly six generous pickup-truck loads — seems like a lot, and, in six neat piles spaced down the property line, looks it. They are dispersed, however, with surprising quickness. By far the greatest number go to cover the shallow-rooted plants that retain their leaves all winter. Larger evergreens — spruces, pines, firs, and hemlocks — and all their endless progeny of dwarfs, are either of iron-clad hardiness to begin with, or they have root systems that penetrate well below the frost line, allowing them to replenish whatever moisture is lost through transpiration. But shallow-rooted plants with persistent leaves also continue to transpire, especially on the clear, crisp, bitter-cold days that come in January and early February. With luck they will all be buried deep in snow, nature's own protection and our best insurance against their loss. But though our garden exists in a snow belt that extends from Canada through Vermont to twenty miles south of us, we still may experience a dreaded snowless "open" winter, which has occurred of late more frequently than our old Vermont neighbors can recall from their long memories of winters past. From bitter experience we know that a host of otherwise hardy plants will essentially freeze-dry under such conditions, perishing long before the unlocking of the earth and the first spring rains.

Of the plants that we know from experience require a cover of evergreen boughs, the most fragile are the heathers. We have two generous plantings, one along the entrance drive and the other swirled among the tall and dwarf evergreens in the conifer border. Both plantings receive the full force of the west wind that whirls up from the valley below, sometimes stripping away the snow that has fallen and wreaking havoc on the exposed plants. This exposure to the winter sun and wind accounts for more failures in growing heathers where the ground freezes deep than any other cause, and so we are especially generous with brush, covering the interlaced plants so thoroughly that all sunlight and wind is excluded. In most years snow will then fall heavily and lock among the branches to complete our work; but in open years the blanket of evergreen boughs is still thick enough to minimize the damage.

A second large consignment of boughs is used to cover the rock garden that lies below the conifer border, where it is even more exposed to wind because of its acute slope. Most of the plants that grow there are in fact quite hardy, though still not proof against the desiccating sun and wind. The earth of the rock garden is of stiff clay liberally laced with sand and gravel, the type most prone to suffer another great winter problem, the heaving of plants that occurs when the top six inches or so of the earth alternately freezes and thaws. Such conditions can cause shallow-rooted plants to pop out of the ground like corks, leaving their crowns and roots exposed to winter's full force. So the entire slope, some fifty feet in extent each way, is swathed in boughs for protection.

Leftover boughs are gathered up and dropped here and there about the garden, for as long as they last, on all those plants we have learned from experience not to leave unprotected in the face of winter's cruelty. We must pay particular attention to the hellebores, the tiny hardy cyclamens, the gentians, the ground-covering bamboos and the taller ones that may be bent to ground and covered, and all the felt-leaved biennials, particularly the verbascums and foxgloves. They receive this care either because they died or were severely damaged one winter or another, or because we know from their provenance that we are asking them to survive in conditions far from the habitats to which they are best adapted. Many of the plants we cover do not positively need protection, even in our garden (and certainly not in one that experiences a less severe winter). But we take no chances, for the odd winter does come that is bare of snow and has searing temperatures below −20°F, guaranteed to eliminate from the garden all plants that are

The gardener in winter must treasure those plants that are beautiful in death, refraining from too vigorous a use of the pruning shears until he can count on fresh beauty in the spring. Here the skeletal panicles of the climbing hydrangea, Hydrangea anomala *ssp.* petiolaris, *catch the frost and manage somehow to look curiously warm.*

marginal and many that are hardy. We can remember a June without foxgloves, so we take the extra trouble.

And it is not much trouble, actually, though two tons of evergreen boughs must sound like a daunting amount to deal with. The work, however, is pleasant, the material clean and sweet smelling, and the results, when the job is complete, are very satisfying, a snug dark green blanket over portions of the garden that could only otherwise show plants in stress and bare ground crusted with frost. We wish that we could take so much pleasure in other tricks we use to shelter what is tender in the garden, but they, alas, are more difficult to put in place and far less pleasing in their appearance. After we have spread the boughs wherever they are needed we must turn to stakes and sheets of burlap, neither of which is attractive or particularly pleasant to handle. Most of them we use to build a thicket of little tents in the rhododendron garden, which looks, when we have finished, like an encampment of very small and not very tidy vagrants settled on the land.

Living where we do, we perhaps have no business growing rhododendrons at all. For except for a few stalwarts called "ironclads," most of the splendid old rhododendrons are not hardy enough for us. There are a few, chiefly hybrids with *Rhododendron catawbiense* in their genes; but they mostly bear flowers stained with magenta, pretty enough up close but dull and dirty looking from a distance. An exception, almost an indispensable one for us, is the compact, white-flowering 'Boule de Neige', bred around 1878 and still a standard among hardy rhododendrons. We also grow some beautiful pure species, the most wonderful of which perhaps is *Rhododendron yakushimanum*, low and dense to four feet tall and six

feet wide, with deep pink buds fading to white as they open. The native American *Rhododendron maximum* has also been invaluable, not so much for its flowers, which are a pale rosy white and appear in July when one doesn't need them, but for its noble stature, reaching ten feet in as many years, and its luxuriant dark green leaves, eight inches long and three across. And though many gardeners scorn it for its uncompromisingly vivid purple flowers, we treasure the May-blooming rhododendron called 'PJM' for its sturdiness, its neat full growth, and its healthy three-inch-long leaves, which are dark green in summer but turn a dull brownish maroon with cold weather.

Early in the history of our garden we planted these hardy rhododendrons, and over a dozen years they have matured to become significant features of the landscape. But, liking rhododendrons as much as we do — for their satisfying volume and the distinction their broad evergreen leaves gives to plantings of conifers, deciduous shrubs, and shade-loving perennials — we wanted others. Fortunately the recent work of rhododendron hybridizers, most notably David Leach, has created a host of new forms, with opulent trusses of flowers in yellow, peach, rose, and clear white — colors that had been almost forbidden to gardeners in climates as cold as ours. The availability of these wonderful new plants, most of which are quite hardy, put us on the way to forming a new plant collection, and to creating a new garden to house it.

We cleared a space in the woods along the stream, below the drive and across a wide sweep of lawn opposite the conifer border. The space is approximately 100 feet wide and 250 feet long, and is bisected by a six-foot-wide grass path extending its full length from the drive to the lower greenhouse. The tall trees we left in the space, chiefly mature ashes, maples, cherries, and oaks, give it a satisfying woodland structure and provide just the right amount of dappled shade for rhododendrons and a host of other woodland treasures. It gave us a place for wonderful small understory trees, such as the surprisingly hardy purple-leaved redbud, *Cercis canadensis* 'Forest Pansy'; for shade-tolerant deciduous shrubs, among the best of which may be *Heptacodium miconoides,* which blooms in September and is scented like jasmine; and for many woodland perennials and ground covers. We established there our collection of ornamental rhubarbs, relatives of the culinary sort (itself a beautiful plant for the flower garden) but entirely inedible, with three-foot-wide leaves of green or red. We planted many hostas to suppress weeds (and because we like them), either divisions of older plants in the garden or costly single ones out of pots. We added some new bamboos, and many native plants that love light shade, including the charming but neglected wood-land asters like *Aster macrophyllus* and *A. divaricatus.* Here and there were special pockets of richness and moisture where we could establish new colonies of the fabled Himalayan blue poppy, *Meconopsis betonicifolia,* or new stands of *Kirengeshoma palmata,* stingy with its best effects unless it is perfectly pleased with where you put it.

But the purpose of this part of the garden, the theory behind it and the rhythm that knits it together, was to come from rhododendrons, as many, in the best new hybrids, as we could lay hands on. Our sources, because the plants are new, were mail-order nurseries. Because of their rarity, their expense, and the cost of shipping them, we perforce had to content ourselves with quite small plants, generally only a year past the cutting stage, or barely a foot to

eighteen inches tall. Such small plants need protection, but as they are too brittle to bend them to earth and cover them with evergreen boughs, the only recourse is three wooden stakes, a piece of burlap, and a staple gun.

It is true that all woody plants gain in hardiness with each passing year, as their bark thickens and they build deep root systems that can continue to draw moisture into plant tissue throughout much of the winter. While this maturation develops, however, the gardener must supply protection, especially to any shrub or tree planted as a rooted cutting or as a one- or two-year-old grown from seed. Though plants known to be quite hardy can struggle through without this help, they are the better for receiving it. For even they, in infancy, would in the wild receive some shelter from others of their kind, from a deep litter of fallen leaves, or even from a large rock or the stump of a felled tree. So we provide all small woody plants, and certainly all rhododendrons, with a sheltering winter tent of burlap. We cannot, of course, keep up this sort of protection forever; nor, once questing roots have gone deep enough, will it always be necessary. That is a blessing, for beyond the effort it requires, the look is about as attractive as the town dump. In another year or two, most of our initial plantings of rhododendrons will be able to sustain themselves without these visible afflictions, and we will turn our attention to saving the irresistible infants we will surely add each year as new colors and forms become available.

Though the young specimens must depend on us for protection, rhododendrons do have an innate protective device of their own. Their evergreen leaves curl into progressively tighter cylinders as temperatures drop. And though each species has its own specialized response to

Never do boxwoods make a more valuable contribution to the garden than just before they must be given up.
For in our climate, English box (Buxus sempervirens) *is quite hardy only if it can be protected from sun and wind.*
So in December, this quiet, soothing rhythm of dark green must give way to a series of vast,
ugly wooden crates. It is the price to be paid.

cold, curling sooner or later, looser or tighter, there are people who claim that they can tell winter temperatures simply from how far the leaves have curled on one well-known specimen under the living room window. We admire how these plants know, from information embedded in their genes, how to best save themselves. Even so we feel, as their custodians, that we should offer some help. For the curling of the leaves of all evergreen rhododendrons in extreme cold is an attempt to expose as little leaf surface as possible to the desiccating combination of cold, wind, and sun. They will always do it, for it is a mechanism triggered by atmospheric cold and nothing more. By using antidesiccant sprays, however, gardeners can help them achieve the goal for which the mechanism is designed, namely the prevention of the loss of vital fluids.

Antidesiccant sprays are simply soluble plastics that coat the leaves with a transparent film that retards transpiration through the winter months. We apply the first dose as late in the year as possible, usually during what our instincts tell us is the last warm spell we can expect, which occurs sometime in late November or early December. Antidesiccant sprays must be applied when temperatures are above 40°F, but as they are water soluble they should not be put on when autumn rains can be expected to wash them away. The substance is mixed with water and applied with a backpack sprayer in the proportions recommended by the manufacturer. It isn't hard work, and once the liquid dries, all broad-leaved evergreens, particularly hollies, shine with the polish it leaves behind. With luck we will be able to make another application during that curious period called the January thaw, though we cannot rely upon it each year for the requisite 40°F temperature. But even our initial treat-

ment seems enough to add a crucial margin of protection to our broad-leaved evergreens, of which the rhododendrons form the greatest number.

There is one preparation for the winter – the last – about which we always grieve a little. A major component of our garden is English boxwood (*Buxus sempervirens*), fifteen old plants are set rhythmically along the length of the rose path. As the autumn advances they seem to step forward, emerging from the tangle of now-naked rose canes and the bare earth that once was clothed in peony foliage and other old-fashioned perennials. Though they are vital elements at every season, from late autumn until early spring they are the dominant structure in that section of the garden, their rich dark globes affirming in an almost formal way the endurance of the garden in the midst of what has been. We are not much given to garden jealousy, for though the climate in which our garden is located exacts its price and imposes its special labors, it nevertheless offers beauty enough for us. Still we do deeply envy those gardeners whose climate allows them to enjoy boxwood all through the winter. We have enough of somber dignity from them, especially on damp frosty mornings when each tiny leaf is whiskered with rime, to know that if we could, we would glory in their beauty all winter long.

The English boxwoods in our garden are actually the hardiest of their kind, all children of a venerable planting in Marblehead, Massachusetts, that has itself known at least fifty rigorous winters. So, as English boxwoods go, they had already proven their toughness when they were brought to us seventeen years ago as a basket of trimmings. Until they were large enough to put in place they were grown in the shelter of an old stone wall, which provided wind and sun protection for them in winter and trapped enough snow to cover them over. The first year they were in their permanent homes we protected them with stakes and burlap, as is our practice with other broad-leaved evergreens. Many were severely burned, and several were killed completely to the ground. Clearly a single piece of cloth was not barrier enough against the severity of the winter. So each plant is now covered with its own large box — crude, heavy wooden affairs that block out all wind and light. They are not attractive, and as the plants will keep enlarging, putting them on requires first that the fattest specimens be corseted up with baling twine and sometimes with wide bands of burlap or old sheets.

Wonderful breeding work has recently been done with cultivars of Korean box *(Buxus microphylla koreana)*, chiefly to eliminate its tendency to pigment with an unattractive russet brown in the cold. Korean boxwood is much hardier than English box, so we are testing the new cultivars elsewhere in the garden — particularly in the rhododendron garden, where their small leaves and rounded shapes form a valuable counterpoise to the broader, coarser foliage of the rhododendrons. We doubt, however — even should the Korean boxwoods prove winter-hardy without protection — that we will give up our old specimens of English box. They have been with us too long; and besides, we have the boxes. It is also a happy ritual to uncover them in April, and to enjoy again their splendid dark green formal shapes against the daffodils and the first coppery growth of the peonies.

Our covering of the boxwoods marks definitively the end of our active involvement in the outdoor garden for the year. From now until early March — perhaps longer — we will not so

much walk through the garden as traverse those paths kept open in the snow, to feed the cows, to de-ice and start the car for errands that are unavoidable, to haul in wood for the fires, and to visit the lower greenhouse. There, much of summer's wealth — cuttings taken from tender perennials, tubs of agapanthus, rosemary standards, and shrubby daturas — have all been squeezed together like passengers in a subway car for the long trip through the winter. But some of its occupants are not sleeping out their journey; they are just waking, to the fresh growth and flower of their proper season. Especially wonderful among them are the many bulbs we grow for winter flowers.

One of late autumn and early winter's most immediately rewarding tasks is the preparation of bulbs for forcing. We have been growing bulbs in pots for winter and early spring flowering for as long as we have gardened. At first we grew only the easiest bulbs — paperwhite narcissus and hyacinths that had been pre-cooled by the growers and were ready, when placed in pots of earth, to flower. Neither positively needs earth, even, but will bloom in trays of gravel or in vases of water. We have never grown them that way, for there is something morbid to us in the idea that they will immolate themselves to flower for the gardener's pleasure. Paperwhite narcissus, being a tender bulb, is never worth the trouble of carrying on for a second year of flowering, even when it is grown in pots of earth. Hyacinths, however, if kept cool and well fertilized after their blooms have past, can be successfully established in the garden. And though one will never again see fat, tightly packed drumsticks of flowers, so much the better, for once they have passed their overfed stage and have adjusted to a realistic garden diet, they will achieve a grace and beauty that are really preferable to the corpulent perfection Dutch growers admire.

But even if one has no interest at all in saving the potential wealth in a forced bulb, there is still something wonderful, something appropriate somehow, in growing them on naturally for late winter and early spring flowering. No fragrance is more evocative, more blood-stirring, than that of a pot of daffodils, narcissus, or hyacinths in late February. But if it is mixed with the smell of rich earth, and perhaps that of a mossy clay pot, its power is all the greater. And one can enjoy it with the assurance that one can, if one wishes, plant the bulbs out later in light woodlands or among the shrubs of the border, for additional years of pleasure. For that reason we turned away from paperwhite narcissus, and even from hyacinths, preferring instead the tiny, shy species crocus; *Iris reticulata*s of incomparable blue with a smell to them of violets; ephemeral snowdrops; and longer-lasting species of muscari, called "grape hyacinths" for their clusters of cobalt blue bells.

We also force larger bulbs, narcissus and tulips, both of which we plant in great quantities in the garden in autumn, and doubtless always will for as long as we garden. From each mesh bag of two dozen bulbs we select out the plumpest five or so, choosing always double narcissus bulbs (for they give twice the flower), and put them aside to pot in shallow clay bulb pans.

Most spring-blooming bulbs are easy enough to force, asking only a cold dark place to root in their pots for twelve weeks or so and a cool sunny place to develop their leaves and flower buds. For the rooting process, temperatures that hover about five degrees above freezing are ideal, and a sunny windowsill, perhaps in an unheated guest bedroom or sunporch where temperatures remain between 40 and 50°F, produces the strongest leaf and flower. Lacking a cold basement or insulated bulkhead for rooting, we use a refrigerator — not the one were we keep our food, for there is something unsettling about earthworms next to the roast beef, but a clunky old one from the 1950s that we acquired for five dollars and the hauling. For continued growing, we use whatever sunny space there might be in the winter garden, where, happily, the ideal temperatures for flowering camellias coincide with the needs of our bulbs. We have had great success, sometimes producing five or six pots in peak flower at the same time, to make corners of the living room and the dining table rich with their beauty.

What comes after forcing was a great problem at one time, for we cannot bear to throw anything living away, and so we would continue growing all our forced bulbs, fertilizing them every week with half-strength 20-20-20 water-soluble fertilizer for vigorous growth so that they could eventually be planted in the garden. Shabby maturing foliage is of course what one pays for the beauty of any spring-blooming bulb, and while in the garden there are ways of disguising this price, in the conservatory there are not. Perhaps for that reason — or perhaps we simply became bored with the process — we no longer force many of the traditional bulbs for spring blooms. At bulb-planting time, it is always an effort to bury all one's wealth in the ground. While holding a particularly plump narcissus or tulip bulb in one's hand, one thinks for a minute, "Well, maybe just *one* pot for forcing." But in it goes. We do other things now.

For our choice of late winter flowering bulbs over the last ten years or so has become more rarefied, and works according to a firm rule we have established, that each season of the year has its own pleasures and its own

In addition to the hues found in willows, fine winter color is provided by the stems of several dogwoods.
Best for vivid red are Cornus alba 'Westonbirt' and C. alba 'Cardinal', and for yellow, Cornus stolonifera
'Flaviramea'. One might think it a good idea to mix them together, but in fact the yellow turns dingy in
such a planting, and so is best seen alone.

horticultural challenges. We wait, therefore, until spring for our daffodils, crocuses, and tulips, devoting our winter efforts and our greenhouse space to African bulbs that bloom normally in winter, albeit far from the lands where they originated. We began with fresias, which have been one of the great pleasures conveyed on us by the acquisition of a greenhouse. These South African bulbs, among the richest for fragrance that one can grow, are not particularly rare. Pots of them can be found at any good florist's, which is nice, but not as nice as growing them at home. They do require cool conditions and good light from their first emergence until flowering; and as their natural tendency is to flop, they should be carefully staked from the beginning, and not when they eventually need it. Slender bamboo stakes may be inserted against the inside edges of the pot, and an almost invisible network of nylon filaments laced between them to support the growth as it extends. Because fresias are cheap to purchase as dormant bulbs, we do not save them from year to year.

Anyone who has ideal conditions for growing fresias, however, can also grow hundreds of other fascinating bulbs native to South Africa, all of which should be carried on from year to year. Fortunately that is a very easy thing to do. For the natural tendency of all of them is to dry out completely in summer and quicken into growth and flowering through the winter months. So just when the greatest demands will be made on home greenhouses to start seedlings for summer bedding and the vegetable garden, they will be preparing for their dormancy. Water should be withdrawn in spring, allowing the foliage to ripen until it turns papery and brown. The pots are then set out of the light in a dry place and ignored completely until late autumn or early winter.

Then, if the bulbs have not become overcrowded, it is enough simply to cut back the withered stems and begin watering for a new season of growth. Most South African bulbs are very prolific in their increase, however, growing technically from corms, as do crocuses, and forming quantities of small cormels around each flowering-size corm each year. So every two or three years it is a good idea to empty out the dry pots onto sheets of newspaper and sort the corms by size, returning the largest, blooming-age corms to the pot to continue growing, and giving away or discarding the smaller, nonflowering cormels. When growth begins, the pots should be fed rather liberally, once a week with half-strength 20-20-20, drenching both the new soil and the foliage. This regimen should continue until flowering, but then fertilizer should be withdrawn so the plants will begin to ripen and prepare for their summer dormancy.

Among the South African winter-flowering bulbs we have grown are several species of gladiolus, sparaxis, watsonias, babianas, homerias, and ixias, all but one of which – the gladiolus – might be quite unfamiliar names to many gardeners, unless they are lucky enough to live where these plants flower naturally outdoors in winter. Among the best of them for us has been *Gladiolus tristis,* with its fine, grasslike foliage the thickness of a pencil lead. It grows to three feet tall and produces slender wands of flowers, only three or four to a spike and of the palest yellow. We have only just gotten a *Gladiolus orchidiflorus,* but we have seen it blooming on a chilly February day in the conservatory at Wave Hill in the Bronx. We shamelessly begged a handful of corms from the gardeners there and they already, this December, show great promise. We must wait another month – maybe a little longer – for the flowers, which are pale greenish yellow, hooded in the manner of some orchids. But they should be a great addition to what is surely to become our gladiolus collection.

Probably none of the South African bulbs we grow will ever surpass *Ixia viridiflora* in our affection, in part because it is so beautiful and in part because our first corms were given us eight years ago by Marshall Olbrich, a great plantsman and a cofounder of Western Hills Rare Plant Nursery in Occidental, California, where so many of the great treasures in our garden came from (as did, indeed, the inspiration for its making). From grassy tufts of self-supporting foliage about two feet tall, it produces each year little inch-wide starlike flowers of a clear celadon, just the color of priceless old Korean pottery and of a shade unmatched by any blossom we know. In the center of each is a stain of cold black, creating a strange art deco effect. It is somewhat fussier to grow than the gladiolus, requiring annual repotting in rich free-draining compost and the best light and most faithful fertilizing we can give it. But it blooms reliably in late February, though never as abundantly as we might wish (for who could have too much of it?). To us it is a precious reminder of a great plant scholar and, until his death in 1990, a very generous friend.

Though so much of the interest of the gardening year must now shift inward, we still believe that a real garden has beauty every day of the year. So, though most shrubs and trees in the garden are bare and gaunt, even their naked forms offer delight. To find it one must look past a great deal of homeliness — bleached flapping burlap, practical but not very attractive boxwood covers, bare crusted dirt where the snow has disturbingly departed and evergreen boughs not put down to take its

place. Above and through all that plainness, however, one can, by a mental effort at exclusion, admire the muscular pale gray bark of the magnolias, densely clustered at their tips with furry mouse-gray buds, the thick congestion of the smaller, lighter trees — the hawthorns, crab apples, and birches — the creamy mottling on the older branches of the stewartias, the polished cinnamon brown of the paper-bark maple, *Acer griseum.* These are muted colors, of course, a play on gray, buff, and sienna brown; but even at this season the garden offers flashes of more brilliant color, of scarlet and egg yolk yellow.

We have planned it that way. One of the greatest contributions, of both color and form, comes from the willows. Willows are endlessly obliging trees. Most will root simply by sticking a bare branch a foot or two into moist spring earth, even one as thick as a broomstick, making an instant bush and very quickly a tree. They accept, indeed relish, soil that is too boggy for most deciduous plants, and by careful pruning one can give them almost any shape one pleases. Though the garden is rich in willows of all kinds, for winter color by far the best are two cultivars of *Salix alba: Salix alba* 'Chermesina', with vivid orange stems shaded to yellow, and *Salix alba vittelina,* with contrasting stems of strong yellow burnished with rust. Both were chosen at just this season in Harvard's Arnold Arboretum in Boston, where we were generously given permission to take cuttings, strong straight branches about three feet in length and the thickness of a wooden spoon handle. Because of the season, we "struck" them into quart pots of potting mix, and then put them against the foundation of the house to wait out the winter and root if they could. Being willows they of course did, and we were ready to plant them out by late spring. We established them along the steep bank of our stream, where they grew lustily. We trained each one to a strong stake, and when they reached six feet, we removed all side branches, allowing the tops to thicken. The third year we pollarded them by cutting them back at the top to three or four stobs about five inches long. They quickly produced mops of vividly colored branches, which we could admire in the darkest times of the year from the living room windows. Now, after ten years, the trunks have thickened enough to be self-supporting, and each spring's pollarding produces an ever-denser head of stems. (It also provides, incidentally, the best garden stakes for perennials — limber, twiggy, and with impressive tensile strength. It is only important to store the trimmings for a week or two in a dry place, or else every one will root, turning the summer perennial border into a willow thicket.)

Equally valuable for winter color, and equally obliging, are several cultivars of dogwood. Though the most familiar dogwoods are cultivars of *Cornus florida,* graceful understory trees with starry white spring flowers, we grow those only barely and with the most careful siting. But the dogwood family is a large one, containing several serviceable shrubs, a few of which color vividly in winter. Most beautiful, perhaps, is *Cornus alba* 'Siberica', a super-hardy shrub that quickly reaches eight feet in height, providing quick filler for slower-growing shrubs and evergreens around it and a dense mass for privacy or any type of screen. Like the willows, the shrubby dogwoods root readily from bare branches stuck into the soil in early spring; like willows also, the most vivid color is achieved from forcing young growth by cutting out older branches in late winter, though they should be cut at ground level.

The showiest of this group is certainly *Cornus alba* in its selected form, 'Westonbirt', which has stems of a brilliant sealing-wax red, gorgeous in the snow. But we also treasure *Cornus stolonifera* 'Flaviramea', which has stems a duller yellow than those of *Salix alba vittelina* but still cheering on moody, cloudy days. The important point is never to plant it intermingled with the red-stemmed dogwoods, for both go muddy in conjunction with each other. It is far better off alone, perhaps with a black-green backing of evergreens to bring out its color.

The greatest feast of color in December by far comes not from twigs, however, but from berries. The three shrubs that hold their magnificence the longest are *Viburnum opulus* and two species of deciduous holly, *Ilex verticillata* and *Ilex decidua. Viburnum opulus* is a serviceable, old-fashioned dooryard shrub that persists in thickets around old farmhouses long after they become forgotten cellar holes. With a form and vigor equal to common privet and an ultimate height of about eight feet, it is strictly a one-season shrub, and its coarse thicketed growth, its healthy two-inch-long leaves, and its dull white flowers in late spring qualify it only for background plantings. But its one season of glory is a long one, stretching from early November to late February, and then, when it festoons itself with translucent scarlet berries, down-hanging in clusters and each about the size of a large pea, it cannot be ignored. The fruit is too sour for the birds, and it withstands subzero temperatures without ever losing its color, which glistens against the snow. We plant it wherever we can (for it is inexpensive) at the back of woodland walks and on the sunny edges of the woods, where it steps forward in late autumn and winter to become the chief beauty to be found there. Those who are interested in growing the

Our baffled neighbors ask us, sometimes, "When are you going to get round to paintin' your house?"
We never will, of course, and we are never so glad of its weathered face as when Ilex verticillata *extends*
in naked, scarlet sprays before it.

widest possible range of fruits for consumption might well pass over *Viburnum opulus* in favor of *Viburnum trilobum*, an American species similar to it in most particulars, but dissimilar in that its berries can be made into a quite palatable jelly. The cultivars 'Wentworth', 'Haws', and 'Andrews' are all excellent old forms, but the same lack of extreme sourness that makes them useful for preserving also makes them attractive to birds, and so their decorative season in the garden is much shorter than that of *Viburnum opulus*.

Equally brilliant in the winter garden, though different, are the fruits of *Ilex verticillata* and *Ilex decidua*. Among the hollies, they provide considerable compensation for the lack of berries in our one remaining American evergreen holly, *Ilex opaca*. By careful siting in the winter shade provided by the woodshed and by faithful applications of antidesiccant each year, we have succeeded in growing one specimen of *Ilex opaca* to an impressive, symmetrical ten feet. All hollies are dioecious, meaning there are separate male and female plants; both are required for berries. We have, alas, lost our male, and keep forgetting to replace him, so all we see from our old evergreen holly is its beautifully crafted leaves. From the two deciduous hollies, however, we see an abundance of fruit that is the greatest glory of the garden from late November into January.

Both *Ilex verticillata* and *Ilex decidua* are much

hardier than any evergreen holly. *Ilex verticillata* generally appears in colder regions, as far as Zone 3, and *Ilex decidua* appears farther south, in Zone 5. Intermarriages produce offspring that can survive well into Zone 4. When we first built our house, a simple clapboard center-chimney cape, we bypassed the obvious front foundation planting it seemed to demand: two symmetrical trimmed yews at the door, a massed line of low shrubs in front, and perhaps some sturdy lilacs at either end. Instead, we planted four female specimens and one male of what we thought were *Ilex verticillata,* in such a way that they would form a cool green curtain before the windows in summer and in winter would ornament the front of the house — which is sheathed in redwood and left unpainted — with sprays of scarlet berries. The house has weathered to a pleasant gray, tawny in patches, and the hollies, limited to four or five sturdy trunks per plant, have spread out before it in just the way we anticipated. It appears, however, that they are in fact *Ilex decidua,* for they stubbornly hold their foliage throughout October and even into November, looking more and more sad as the leaves blacken on their branches.

But in December, as the weather comes nearer to the full bitterness it will achieve, they drop their leaves to reveal naked stems thickly clad with scarlet berries. It is a picture we enjoy from without, but even more from within, for from there one views the garden — gray and cold and black-green from the conifers — through a scrim of the clearest red. Purple finches and yellow and purple gros-

beaks come to eat the berries as we watch from just inside the glass. To them there seems to be a greater palatability in *Ilex decidua* than in *Ilex verticillata,* and its berries remain in good condition much later into the winter; so, for the pleasure the birds give us on our living bird feeder, we are not sorry to have been misled about the species. Still, being greedy, we have planted the true *Ilex verticillata* — or so we assume — away from the house in the newer portions of the stream garden, for it will grow in permanently moist soils or even standing water. And it has forms that bear fruit not only of the typical scarlet, but also of orange and even yellow. We have planted these various color forms one against another, so that the shades intermingle with a painterly effect.

People who come to visit in December sometimes ask, "Where is your Christmas tree, your holiday greens and decorations?" We answer that they are all outside. Except for a pot or two of early bulbs, or perhaps sprays of tawny witch hazel or pale pink, fragrant *Viburnum x bodnantense* harvested on the odd day when it is above freezing, allowing for forcing indoors, what is festive for us still exists outside our windows. Besides, as gardeners, the real festival for us is the winter solstice. For from the end of December, once it comes, the days lengthen, imperceptibly at first, though we deceive ourselves easily into thinking that the minute or two of light we gain each day may really be perceived. Psychologically, it is, signaling the turning of the earth back to light and warmth and hope. Still, the worst of winter, which is January, is before us.

January

*I*F throughout autumn we cast our thoughts back toward the luxuriance of the garden just past, by January we have let go of the last season and have begun thinking of the next. The snow and ice give us no choice in that, for when they come, with the attendant bitter cold, we must be in. It is not pleasant, or even actually possible, to wander in the garden. When, from sheer necessity, one must go "out there" — to empty kitchen waste on the compost heap, to scatter a thick blanket of fireplace ash around the trunks of lilacs, to check for signs of the deer's depredations — one does not so much follow familiar paths as forge them anew, struggling for each footstep in snow deep enough to find its way over the tops of boots and into them. The highland cows, whose vast weight and stubby legs make it difficult for them to plow very far through the snow, constrict their movements to the

feed lot and a watering hole kept open through the ice on the stream, wearing a short, safe path between. They sleep a lot, standing only to receive their bales of hay — two in the morning and two at twilight — and to amble the short distance they must go for a cold drink (and, of course, to enrich their chosen bedding spot even more, creating the rich mine from which we will harvest, come spring, buckets of sustaining compost).

Snow is, actually, the best thing about January. Though each morning's weather forecast includes the total minutes of sunshine for the previous day and adds them all up at month's end, no gardener needs to be told that January is the darkest month of the calendar. It is obvious, not only out the window, as one leaden day succeeds another, but in one's spirits, which *will* decline, no matter how firm-minded and optimistic one is determined to

We try to remember, when contemplating the snows of January, how privileged our garden climate is, with
its cool summer nights, its evenly spaced rainfall, its rich woodland soils, and its thriving
colonies of Meconopsis betonicifolia. *Even the heavy snow is a blessing, as it insulates*
the earth, protecting the crowns of fragile perennials and ensuring an even flow of water from our well.
In January, particularly, we try to remember all that.

be. January is, quite simply, the year's low point for gardeners. For though one may take brisk walks, weather permitting, or hit the ski slopes, or the treadmill in the bedroom, though there may be a fragrant fire of birch logs on the hearth (one saves birch logs for January, when one needs them most) or a savory pot on the back of the stove, though one has recently been meaning to reread *Anna Karenina* and is grateful for the chance, and though the pileup of a whole year's correspondence waits to be answered — still, January is, as far as gardening goes, not a whole lot of fun. The first snowdrops and aconites are two months or more away, and though one is grateful for forced bulbs and greenhouse flowers, they are not substitutes. They ask so little, and the lift and stirring of the heart they cause can issue into no real action, as, for true gardeners, such stirrings always should. It is too early even to prune, for the bitterest cold can still lie before us, and it is not a safe thing to lay bare sensitive inner bark to temperatures that can descend to −20°F or even lower.

Snow is, therefore, the great blessing of January. It has tremendous practical value for the garden, for a thick blanket of it — say three or four feet — will complete the work of covering-over tender perennials and shrubs that began with evergreen boughs in December. Even more crucially, it insulates the ground, preventing the frost from going so deep as to lock up sustaining roots in ice and make it impossible for them to supply moisture to evergreen needles or leaves. But the snow is also a psychological event, a little festival arranged by nature to relieve the tedium of one gray day succeeding another.

There are as many sorts of snowstorms, it seems, as there are days on which they occur; and as one often has little else in January to stare at, out the window, we have become connoisseurs of them. The prettiest, always, are the ones made of great heavy slow-falling flakes that seem to fill the air and catch on every twig and branch, returning briefly to the garden something of the volumes it possessed in full summer leaf. But there are fierce ones too, coastal storms that make their way this far inland on howling winds laden with icy grains that cut against the skin when we go out, and that patter insistently on windowpanes all night long, finding their way under doors and window sashes we thought securely sealed up. Drifts build against the back of the house, sometimes hip deep, scoured into fantastic patterns of white on white. The bitter air that often follows crusts the fine grains so firmly that one can sometimes walk atop a drift without breaking through. But though January is typically our coldest month, it, too, partakes of the capriciousness that is always part of New England weather. Sometimes a snowstorm will occur when temperatures are just above freezing and the air is laden with moisture. Such storms are the ones schoolchildren love and gardeners fear, for a little more warmth turns the snow to freezing rain, making roads impassable to school buses or any other traffic, and catching and freezing on every exposed surface — twigs, branches, and evergreen needles — burdening trees and shrubs until they crack under its weight. It never serves, in such a storm, to thwack at evergreens bent to the ground or to shake the crystal coating from deciduous shrubs and small trees, for the violence of one's actions might just provide the extra pressure that finally causes them to snap. Better simply to wait until the temperature warms, or an agitating wind comes to shake the carapaces of ice to the ground in a rain of half-cylinders and ice

Lovely though a heavy snow is, one must take care to remove it from evergreen branches before it freezes into ice, for then snow drag can fracture even the sturdy branches of the yews. It never serves to thwack violently with the kitchen broom, however. Rather, each branch should be gently prodded until it releases its weight of snow — one hopes not down the collar of one's coat.

straws. Such storms can be quite beautiful, if one can take one's mind off the hawthorn threatening to split under pressure out in the front border.

If it is true, however, that snow is generally a friend to the garden and a diversion to the gardener through a long month in which little else happens, it also, ironically, brings to the garden its greatest threat. The rural, wooded area in which we live is rich with deer. The progressive reforestation of the state over the last forty years or so, together with the elimination of all natural predators save people, has caused a huge increase in the herds. Though the annual hunt in November — with bow and arrow, conventional rifles, and even front-loading muskets — is pursued with an almost religious fervor by our townsmen, the number of deer killed is by state law in strict proportion to those who hunt them. As the number of hunters has declined with a decrease in the local population, and the number of deer increased with an abundance of food and the absence of other predators — big cats and wolves — a huge problem has developed for gardeners. For in a winter deep with snow, when the deer have exhausted woodland forage and cannot get to sources of food in open pastureland, they move into gardens. Once they have found their way they settle in, coming stealthily at twilight and remaining until dawn, stripping the garden of everything that is palatable to them and much, as they grow desperate, that is not. They begin with yews, arborvitaes, and junipers, stripping away the needles patiently as far in as they can reach. They will paw up and devour certain perennials with avidity, particularly the dianthus and the *Alyssum saxatile*. Euonymus, if they can find it, is a particular delight. From these palatable plants they will descend to less

favored species, taking all the buds and tender tip growth from deciduous azaleas, evergreen rhododendrons, and even magnolias. Then they proceed to bark, stripping away beyond repair the skins of newly planted or young fruit trees.

When we first came to Vermont, the sight of deer along the highway or in the meadows up above the house was always a particular pleasure. For they are beautiful, gentle-looking creatures, always shy of presence and delicately made. Years of experience with their destructive ways (especially the winter of 1993, the worst in the history of our garden) has altered our attitude. A casual glimpse of one along the highway, or even a silhouette sign signifying a favored crossing place, causes in us a shudder of disgust. Someone has called deer "rats with hooves," and anyone who has woken to find a treasured evergreen stripped beyond recovery, the choice variegated *Alyssum saxatile* called 'Dudley Neville' ripped from a wall where it had finally been coaxed to grow, or a row of young apple trees just reaching bearing age reduced to raw broomsticks, ought to sympathize with how we feel.

But not everyone does. There are many who post "No Hunting" signs on their land, motivated by the belief that in providing a safe haven for the deer they are acting responsibly toward the environment and reducing by their own small fraction some of the dreadful brutality wreaked by humanity on our planet. It is a terribly wrongheaded notion, as anyone who has seen the sick and starving herds in Connecticut would realize. Those who have the misfortune to garden near heavily posted land must simply give up growing large numbers of plants, perhaps all plants whose leaves and twigs persist through the winter. For deer prefer to remain within one square mile of the place of their birth. They will leave that approximate area only with the greatest unwillingness, and not until they have stripped it of any living thing that will give them nourishment. Many will stay on even then, dying of starvation or disease.

So, with the judicious advice and approval of our state game wardens, we have declared a sort of holy war on deer. For years our front line of defense consisted of methods that would not destroy them, but only gross them out. On every bush we knew to be most susceptible to their depredations we hung bars of soap, as strong-smelling as we could buy, cutting them first into quarters or eighths with a sharp knife and wrapping the pieces in bags of nylon mesh. When that failed, we went to dried blood, since the smell of blood is terrifying to a deer. First we simply spread it around, but as each snow or rainfall diminished its odor, we began to put it by half cups into plastic sandwich bags, tying each with a strand of woolen yarn from which it could dangle along a branch after being pierced with a skewer. Piled in a basket as we made them they looked like some sort of macabre party favors, but outdoors they seemed to work, for a time at least. We also tried various commercial deer repellents, as well as solutions made of Tabasco sauce, cheap perfume, liquid soap, human hair, rotten meat, and even-less-mentionable substances. All were successful, to greater or lesser degrees, for deer are very cautious creatures, and anything they do not recognize as familiar they perceive as frightening. Eventually, however, a combination of familiarity and real hunger bred contempt for all our methods, and the deer appeared ready to have their supper, even liberally laced with vile substances, rather than to greet the dawn hungry. Who could blame them?

Our next defense was to acquire a dog, a rough-coat collie, for we had been assured that the breed was highly territorial, would not roam, and would energetically drive off any intruders. And so, at first, it was; for George, as he was named, was an exemplary dog, and the slightest shuffle or snort in the night would set him to barking and to a limited pursuit. No one told us, however, that rough-coat collies retire early from their jobs, preferring at a certain point to sleep out the night than to continue slaving away for the general good. We lived in a sort of deerless paradise for five years, until George got weary of it all, and though he continues to enrich our lives in many important ways, he is not, deerwise, the dog he was. It is hard to think of getting another, which prudence would argue and George enjoy; for rough-coat collies are large animals, and our kitchen is small, and wall-to-wall dog, with all that brushing and shedded fur, is more than we can face.

So we have gone to the last lines of defense, which are a sturdy five-strand electrified fence eight feet tall and a hit man. We have hired a good-natured lad, a skilled hunter, to patrol the garden for a couple of hours each night, watching with rifle ready for any deer that find their way somehow through the fence. (For deer may be legally shot at any time of the year in Vermont if it can be proven that they are destroying valuable property. Alas, the proof is all too palpable on every bush.) Neither of these options is particularly pleasant, for the fence causes the garden to look like a concentration camp, and the sound of shots in the night is not conducive to anybody's rest. Those who do not garden must think our behavior very odd, even sinister, perhaps immoral. They may think what they please. For us, who love animals, saving the garden from irreparable damage is still our main concern.

Not all of January, however, consists of trench warfare. It is an irony that the oldest part of the garden, at this season, is full of light and warmth and is rich with flowers and fragrance. It is the winter garden, a small but precious space fourteen by twenty-four feet, built into the southeast gable of the house. It employs the same heavy timber and modified post-and-beam construction as the living room and kitchen, the only other rooms on the ground floor. So when one peers down into the winter garden from a pair of barn sash windows over the kitchen sink, or descends the three steps into it from the French door just opposite the dining table, it seems an integral part of the house. It is not at all like a conventional greenhouse, perfunctorily stuck on, and still less like a sunporch or sunroom. It is in fact not a porch or a room at all, though it has windowed glass walls and a glass roof. What it hasn't, that porches and rooms always do, is a floor; for between its four-foot-deep frost-walls of poured cement is the living earth, as fecund and full of life as we could make it with manure, peat moss, wood chips, sharp sand, and rich native clay. And growing in that earth, with the drollest complacency, are camellias, sasanquas, tender ivies, delicate tropical rhododendrons, sheets of tiny species cyclamen, and what is probably — without much contest — the largest specimen of *Leptospermum scoparium* 'Ruby Glow' in Vermont.

Originally the winter garden was a conventional greenhouse, bisected along its length by a straight path of the same old brick that paves the kitchen floor. The outer wall against the glass was occupied by a waist-high bench on which we staged a large collection of potted plants. Along the inner, house wall was a bed

planted with large shrubs, which we hoped to train or espalier, that would be of interest primarily in the winter, when we needed them most. First to go in, and still thriving, was the *Leptospermum scoparium* 'Ruby Glow'. We had admired it in California, and we had read in the *Sunset Western Garden Book* that it was a compact, upright, six- to eight-foot shrub with dark foliage and profuse three-quarter-inch-wide double oxblood red flowers in winter and spring. (The book said the "entire shrub looks red.") The height seemed right, since the lean-to roof of the greenhouse reached ten feet in the spot where we hoped the leptospermum would flourish. And we thought that an entire bush looking red with double oxblood flowers would be just the thing when viewed from below against a cold blue late winter sky. It has never let us down, though it exceeded its promised height of six to eight feet within four years, and tactful pruning is now required in early spring to keep it from pressing against the glass and trying to enter a world in which it does not belong and would not be at all happy.

To keep the leptospermum company, we also planted *Magnolia grandiflora* 'St. Mary', said to be compact, and *Ceanothus* x 'Julia Phelps', which was to be pinned around the kitchen windows. It was all too much. For in addition to the unaccountable burgeoning of the leptospermum, the magnolia grew with such vigor that — after presenting us with three eight-inch blossoms on the same day in its second year — the pruning it required took off all its later buds, and we never saw it bloom again. (We know now that we should have planted the diminutive cultivar 'Little Gem', though it was unavailable to us then.) The ceanothus was admirably cooperative in allowing itself to be trained against the wall, as it is in the best English gardens, and for three years it was

January begins the camellia show, and the first is a curious Japanese form in the higo class called 'Yamamato Nishiki'. It is a single one, with a thick boss of yellow stamens and unpredictable carmine variegation across its white petals.

sheathed in early March, ground to rooftop, with flowers of a heavenly violet blue. It had a wonderful scent, too, both from its flowers and its resinous leaves, as of lavender growing near a pine wood. But after its three years of glory, it developed a case of scale that resisted the most noxious of sprays far better than the person washing dishes at the open window. So it was decapitated (the magnolia had gone the year before) and replaced with a winter jasmine *(Jasminum nudiflorum)*, a plant we had first seen starred with yellow flowers at Kew Gardens in January, and later met again with pleasure in the glassed courtyard of Boston's Isabella Stewart Gardner Museum in earliest spring.

The jasmine grew magnificently, as if to show that it could rival the ceanothus in our affections, and soon covered the wall around the kitchen windows. But, alas, it suffered from an acute case of modesty, refusing to throw off its glossy three-part leaves to display its two-inch chrome yellow flowers. A *Jasminum nudiflorum* that is never nude offers at best a restricted pleasure, and so it was sent the way of the magnolia and the ceanothus, making us feel embarrassingly like wicked sultans in a harem. But the jasmine's replacement, a camellia of the higo type called 'Yamamato Nishiki', has proven an exemplary plant, about which nothing bad can be said at all. Its growth is compact, its leaves are handsome, and its flowers, born for two months from December to February, are beautiful on the bush and a lavish gift to those for whom we really care. The flowers on this form are single, but this simplicity is contradicted by a baroque arrangement of thick gold stamens against a white ruff irregularly streaked with clear carmine. It pointed us the way we might have gone from the first.

But although the bed against the house wall provided some interesting experiments and two splendid successes, it was the bench on the opposite side that absorbed most of our attention. On it we grew just about every plant we could acquire that would grow in a pot, bloom in the dead of winter, and remind us of climates we loved, far from our home in Vermont. We had begonias, pelargoniums, winsome blue felicias, and a large collection of species orchids. We forced azaleas and tender rhododendrons, and at one time there were even two huge potted citrus, which bloomed in late winter and attracted hosts of bees through the first open windows in early March. There were also pots of early spring bulbs — crocuses, grape hyacinths, paperwhite narcissus, daffodils, tulips, and fritillarias — that we managed to have in steady succession from Christmas to early April. It was a grand illusion of a four-month spring.

It was also a damned lot of work. We spent hours each week picking off dead flowers and leaves, sweeping up debris, restaging the best things for maximum display, scrubbing the bricks free of slime and algae, and finding a place where ailing plants, or those past their best but still too valuable to chuck, could be stored unobtrusively so as not to spoil the general effect. Aphids were a nightmare. Fungus was rife.

Nevertheless, we might have gone on with our traditional staged greenhouse bench except for three black moments. On two successive winters, power failures cause the greenhouse temperature to drop below freezing, carrying off our best and tenderest things, some of which we had been growing for twenty years. The first occurred while we were on vacation in California. We heard of it by phone, and optimists by nature (as all gardeners must be), we merely felt it provided us with the occasion to buy up and bring back a host of plants we had wanted to grow but for which we had not previously had the space. (We even acquired an elegant plant of *Tulbaghia violacea variegata*, the famous "society garlic," but it stank so badly of rancid onion that we had to abandon it in the Chicago airport.) The second disaster occurred in late March, during a short trip to Boston, and was far worse. The temperature dropped from a daytime high of 70°F to an overnight low of 20, just as most of our plants had broken dormancy and commenced their soft spring growth. When we returned, most of the greenhouse was a black mess, including many of the new California plants that we had not yet brought to flower.

But it was the last of the three disasters that proved definitive in turning our greenhouse into the winter garden. We had called in a carpenter, a local handyman, to install an automatic ventilator, having become tired of opening and closing windows in chancy March weather. We were at lunch when he interrupted to say that there was something that needed our attention. We went with him into the greenhouse, where he pointed out rot in a dozen places, poking his screwdriver here and there into beams that appeared solid but that were eaten from within. The bench itself was the worst; the whole structure was held up by cobwebs and needed instant attention. The only solution was to rebuild.

It has always been our conviction that the disasters and disappointments any gardener must face are opportunities to rethink and recontrive. They cannot be cheerfully faced otherwise, lest what ought to be an activity full of joy becomes simply a passage from one agony to the next. It is also a nice feature of that part of one's life that is devoted to gardening (in contrast to whatever part might be left over) that so cheerful a veil of optimism may be thrown over the inevitable setbacks Nature contrives. Following this rule, we reasoned that if the greenhouse had to be rebuilt, it should be done in a way that would give us new pleasure and a new interest in the space. This time around we vowed also to be practical, or at least as practical as any greenhouse owner in Vermont might be said to be. We retained the structure's original design, which had pleased us for more than ten years. But we followed our handyman's advice to use pressure-treated lumber. Each piece came with a reassuring tag guaranteeing it for years — long enough, it appeared, for us. And since we had lost so much to power failures, we decided to eliminate all the tender plants that could not endure one. Further, as our attempts at pot culture had come to seem more like work than pleasure, we decided to refashion the space into a true winter garden, in which all but a very few treasured plants would grow directly in the ground.

The brick path was removed and replaced with large old Vermont fieldstones, against and among which we could plant with greater flexibility. We ripped out the bench against the window, and in its place created a deep fertile bed in which to plant more camellias (following the lead of our success with 'Yamamato Nishiki') and three sasanquas, thereby extending our season by two months, as the sasanquas begin blooming in October, followed by the camellias in December and January. Under and around the camellias we created an understory of tender rhododendrons, chiefly of the maddenii sorts, which we had come to love on our trips to the West Coast, and which bloom in March and early April just as the camellias are finishing. In such space as was left at the

edges of the beds and beneath the larger
shrubs we planted small tender treasures and a
few larger perennials we cannot grow outdoors.

Among the first of these plants to go in was
the wonderful scarlet- and green-flowered
Alstroemeria psittacina, scorned by gardeners
where it is hardy as a noxious weed but precious to us under glass. We planted also a
Helleborus argutifolius, whose lime green pinwheels and marbled foliage are handsome from
November to April. But perhaps our greatest
success, and certainly among our greatest pleasures, have been masses of tiny winter-bloom-
ing species cyclamen that have "naturalized"
(if such a word can be used of such a space)
under the shrubs, along the path, and even
between the stones. All originated from a
handful of seed-grown bulbs bought from
Nancy Goodwin's Montrose Nursery, now,
sadly, out of business. They seem to have
found our winter garden the perfect place in
which to flourish and increase. We are glad we
got the last she had to sell.

But like rare animals in a zoo, the plants in
our winter garden haven't a clue about what
has been done to ensure their comfort. For in
addition to all the snipping, spraying, training,
pruning, and deadheading that keeps any other
sort of garden healthy and pretty, this garden
must also be heated in winter to a minimum
of 40°F at night — not an easy thing when the
temperature falls to −20°F outside and a violent wind howls across the glass. It is on its
own heating zone, since 40°F, though comfortable to the plants we grow there, tends to
penetrate even a third layer of sweater added
by the person unlucky enough to be washing
dishes at the kitchen sink in January. Heat,
such heat as is required to keep the frost out,
with a barely safe margin, is supplied by the
house furnace; fueled by oil, it heats water that

then circulates through copper pies. Can there
be another leptospermum in the world whose
toes are curled comfortably around subterranean and permanently warm copper pipes?
Recently a friend visiting from California in
mid January looked up at it and said, "How
strange. How very strange to see that here.
Mine at home is in full bloom too, and looks
just the same."

Strange it certainly is, but it keeps us going.
Still, we realize that if our winter garden were
not so precious to us, it might seem a bit of a
joke, if not a folly. It is perhaps one more
place in which very moralistic people, having
made careful studies of heating systems and
the globe's shrinking resources, might find us
guilty of criminal waste for our own selfish
pleasure. Indeed, we are sometimes asked by
practical, energy-minded people (who know
well, as do we, that cement floors store heat
and earth ones leach it away) how much our
winter garden costs to heat and whether we
gain much warmth on sunny days and lose
much on cold, cloudy ones. The questions are
always couched in a sniffing, catching out kind
of smugness that prejudges whatever answers
we might make as incriminating. And so they
are. For we would say that such calculations as
we could make of heat loss, using infrared
photographs and carefully collated fuel and
temperature records, would still render conclu-
sions quite irrelevant to the pleasure our winter garden gives us in the darkest days of the
year. For every winter morning finds one or
the other of us (there is not really room for
two at a time) strolling about, coffee cup in
hand, to see how things are doing. Perhaps a
single flower has appeared on an *Iris ungucularis,*
of the most vibrant blue and strongly violet-
scented. Maybe the first wine red cup of the
camellia called 'Tinsie' has opened, or the

Some of the small-species cyclamen, such as Cyclamen hederifolium, *will survive outdoors for us, blooming in autumn. We envy gardeners who can grow the others, especially* Cyclamen coum, *under their outdoor rhododendrons and other shrubs. We must be content with our small patch in the winter garden.*

conch-shell pink of its neighbor, 'Berenice Boddy', is blossoming beneath glossy, dark green leaves, a promise of the abundance to come. Certainly there will be a flower to pick off the camellia 'Silver Waves', for it is never sparing with its five-inch-wide, gold-stamened blossoms (one of them is enough to decorate the coffee table for a week). Maybe, with luck, there will even be a few weeds to pull, though their removal is a pleasure that must be saved and shared between us, as there are never really enough to go around. At the least there will be the smell of the living earth and the promise of what will come, while all outside is still frozen deep and spring is months away.

We built our winter garden because of the extraordinary harshness of the climate we live in, because our great love of gardening demanded (just like other great loves we can think of) at least a little tactile expression in the downtime. So the winter garden is actually a little hug, a pat on the hand, an affectionate wink – nice in itself but also a promise. For we would frankly have to place ourselves among those scorned by John Donne in "A Valediction, Forbidding Mourning" – those "dull sublunary lovers" whose "love . . . cannot admit / Absence, because it doth remove / Those things which elemented it."

Whether, then, the catalogs that begin to arrive in January should be viewed as love letters or as frank pornography we leave an open question. It is true only that we love getting them, even in duplicate, and that we pour over every one. What is worse, perhaps, is that there is not one – not even the most lurid tabloid picturing rosy gluttonous infants sickening themselves with both hands on strawberries (get one packet for a penny if you order two at regular price) – not one that doesn't contain some plant or seeds we'd like to have.

Love, at least of the rather carnal sort that we confess for gardening, is certainly sometimes blind. But it is always greedy.

Such misery as we feel about that (a misery expressed more in the end-of-month bank balance than anywhere else) is certainly not unique to us. For every garden writer who has ever had to consider January falls eventually to discussing the latest catalogs, their offerings and their deeper meanings. Few have done it as wittily as the late Katherine White, who made her career as a writer reviewing seed catalogs for *The New Yorker,* and whose first sentence in her collected works, *Onward and Upward in the Garden,* speaks for us all: "For gardeners, this is the season of lists and callow hopefulness; hundreds of thousands of bewitched readers are poring over their catalogues, making lists for their seed and plant orders, and dreaming their dreams."

Though Katherine White searched out and carefully considered the catalogs of seemingly every small nursery in America, she would be amazed at how the mail-order business has burgeoned in the years since her death in 1971. There is a powerful renaissance throughout American gardening at present, causing us all to think that there never could have been a better time to garden in this country. A happy consequence of this resurgence has been the growth of dozens of small mail-order nurseries specializing in unusual plants; the simultaneous growth of quick-delivery services guarantees that plants and seeds will get to the gardener quickly and in good condition. While word of the existence of these nurseries has passed quickly from gardener to gardener, they have all been gathered together in Barbara Barton's wonderful book, *Gardening by Mail,* now in its third edition. Just about any interest a gardener might have is referenced and cross-

At any season of the year a green flower is a pleasure, but in winter, when one is so hungry for green, flowers of such hue can be doubly wonderful. This single specimen of Helleborus argutifolius *in our winter garden is far from its Mediterranean island home (it comes from Corsica and was once called* H. corsicus*) — how little sense it can have of the trouble we took to secure its January flowers.*

referenced, from tiny alpines to antique shrub roses to cannas, camellias, and heirloom vegetables. For those who have had to depend on their local garden center for plants, Barton's book opens a vast dimension of possibilities and a thrilling winter of browsing.

Among the many small nurseries supplying plants by mail, several have offered irresistible riches to us each year. Among the most exciting has been Nancy Goodwin's Montrose Nursery, which began by specializing in seed-grown hardy cyclamen, a welcomed response to the fact that most nurseries' cyclamen corms are collected in the wild, thereby critically reducing natural stands. During its ten years Montrose also offered a host of other wonderful plants, beautifully grown and beautifully shipped. Alas, however, 1993 was its last season in business, since its owner decided to devote herself full-time to her beautiful garden, and to writing. It was wonderful while it lasted; but from the writing, other gifts will come.

And there are other wonderful small mail-order nurseries, offering plants probably unknown to most gardeners, and more of them than most gardeners have space to grow. John Wittlesey's Canyon Creek Nursery (3527 Dry Creek Road, Oroville, CA 95965) offers a catalog with an extensive list of old-fashioned dianthus and many other perennials, including a dozen American asters of species other than the familiar Michaelmas daisies. From him you can also buy five agastaches with brightly colored tubular flowers in terminal spikes that bloom all summer, and twenty shrubby salvias — for the ground if your garden is warm, or for pots if it is not — of which the best perhaps is *Salvia guaranitica* 'Argentine Skies'. (We do not know what the skies of Argentina look like, never having been there, but we hope they are just such a limpid, clear blue as is this tall,

spiked flower, raised by Charles Cresson from seed and named by him.)

The specialty of Richard Weaver and Rene Duval's We-Du Nurseries (Route 5, Box 724, Marion, NC 28752) is neglected American plants, wonderful roadside "weeds" that our national prejudice against our own has barred from our gardens until recently. But they also offer rare woodland natives and ferns that often can adjust as contentedly to a dank city backyard as to their native forest floor. A special interest of We-Du is in what botanists call "congeners," plants that share a common genetic heritage but developed divergently as continental land masses separated. An example, which We-Du can supply, is *Eomecon chionantha*, which they describe as an Asiatic counterpart to our bloodroot: "Stoloniferous perennial with long-stalked, heart-shaped leaves; racemes of white, poppylike flowers in May. Pops up here and there in the garden." Oh, how we wish! So far, we have failed with it, either because it is not hardy enough for us, or because we have yet to find it just the right spot in which to pop. We'll try again. And for the truly adventurous gardener, We-Du also offers a list of mosses and liverworts, known mostly to gardeners as flattened lobes of green that appear on seed pots when they are kept too wet. We doubt if many gardeners will choose to grow liverworts deliberately, though it is pleasant to think one could if one wanted to.

From Siskiyou Rare Plant Nursery (2825 Cummings Road, Medford, OR 97501) one can secure treasures without number, chiefly alpine and woodland plants and their dwarf conifer companions. Particularly rich is their listing of saxifrages, tiny, fragile-looking plants whose Latin name nevertheless means "rock breaker," from their habit of seeding into crevices in seemingly solid outcroppings and thriving there. Within the many divisions of this vast group of plants, our favorites are those whose tiny spatulate leaves are thickly crusted and beaded with the lime they have extracted from the soil or the rocks where they love to grow. Whether they have formed this habit for protection from the fierce cold of their native mountaintops, to make themselves unpalatable to creatures that might otherwise munch on them, or simply for the fun of it, their beautifully symmetrical rosettes look permanently frosted, or dipped in granulated sugar like crystallized fruits. So tiny are many of them that they have lived for years in stone troughs in our garden, spreading slowly into mats of rosettes as hard to the touch as carved stone, but topped in early spring with a froth of white, wind-tossed flowers. Siskiyou offers a large selection of these plants individually, and special collections for the uninitiated of eighteen plants in six different kinds. They also include a note that, should you be looking for a specific saxifrage not listed in their catalog, please inquire, as they presently grow many others in quantities too small to offer.

During its first three years, Dan Hinkley's Heronswood Nursery (7530 288th Street NE, Kingston, WA 98346) has managed to stun the most knowledgeable gardeners in America with the richness and rarity of its offerings. It has been, in the words of J. C. Raulston, Director of the University of North Carolina Arboretum at Raleigh, "a brilliant comet streaking across the sky." Brilliant it surely is, judging from its catalog, for on every one of its eighty pages are plants the most experienced gardener has never heard of. But we must hope it outlasts a comet, for it is the only source we know of in America of ornamental rhubarbs, seven species or which were listed in the 1992 catalog. It is the most

complete listing we have ever seen of gentians and border geraniums. A Heronswood specialty — one, apparently among many — is hydrangeas, of which its catalog lists thirty-nine species and cultivars.

The catalog from Forest Farm (990 Tetherow Road, Williams, OR 97544-9599) is one the late Katherine White would have approved of, for she did not merely peruse a catalog, she *read* it, savoring its particular style and searching for pungent observations and bits of plant lore. Forest Farm's catalog is enlivened with quotations on nature, the environment, and gardening, suggesting the distillation of a whole winter's reading; but its densely printed pages offer perhaps the widest selection of trees, shrubs, perennials, and rock garden plants available in this country by mail. One is glad for the quotations, but the plants are the main thing, and it is always wise to take on Forest Farm after one has filled out one's orders for other nurseries; for then, at least, you can rule out what you've already sent for. There'll be enough left over.

For camellias, sasanquas, and azaleas, the venerable Nuccio's Nursery (P.O. Box 6160, 3555 Chaney Trail, Altadena, CA 91001) really cannot be topped. Now in its second generation of management, its catalog contains enough to strain the resources of a large southern plantation. Most exciting, perhaps, are unusual forms of *Camellia japonica,* such as the higo, profuse in blooms of a beautiful single plum-blossom shape rich with stamens, and the small-flowered rusticana, or snow camellia, from the higher elevations of Japan, compact-growing and so floriferous as to be completely covered with blooms. But all of Nuccio's camellias are interesting, and only the most sophisticated specialist would fail to find within its lists a form he was searching for.

The name of the camellia called 'Berenice Boddy' always sounds more appealing when it is pronounced with a French accent. She has other problems, too, in a lax, weeping habit that makes for difficulties in a small, narrow space. Still, we would not give up the precious elegance of her blooms, a tender, silver pink, or her fidelity in producing them from January until March.

Best of all, Nuccio's shipping methods are among the best in the business; though they don't guarantee it, they can ship a plant of blooming size to you with every bud, and often fully opened blossoms, in perfect shape.

Finally, every season we wait with trepidation for the catalog from Gossler Farms Nursery (1200 Weaver Road, Springfield, OR 97478-9691). Trepidation is the word because Gossler specializes primarily in magnolias, but includes dozens of other rare shrubs and trees. From Siskiyou all the plants one might crave will arrive in a carton hardly bigger than a shoe box; but from Gossler it will be a crate. Though magnolias are not ultimately the largest things one might think to plant, they are big enough, and every one of the seventy-seven species, cultivars, and hybrids Gossler lists seems to have some special beauty to recommend it: Many are not hardy enough for us, of course, but enough are — too many, in fact, for a garden that, though large, still makes a quandary of the placement of a tree that will achieve an ultimate height and spread of thirty feet. So we study the Gossler Farms catalog with a strict quota in mind; *one* magnolia is the limit (and maybe a few shrubs). Last year's was the amazing new one called 'Elizabeth', developed at the Brooklyn Botanic Garden, a cross between *Magnolia denudata* and *Magnolia acuminata.* It is super-hardy, and its flowers, as large as the three-inch-high cups of *M. denudata,* are a bright, clear yellow. We know, for the little plant that came to us, hardly three feet high, had four buds, all of which opened in its first year in our garden. Such experiences make self-imposed limits very hard to adhere to.

These favorite catalogs, and a wealth of others that all get better and better, richer and richer — or so it seems — do much to lighten the burden of January, heavy as it can be. Further, they cause one to feel, paraphrasing Wordsworth, that it is good to be alive, and to be a gardener is very heaven. It is a marvelous thing, too, that when one gardens in the mind, one can edit out all the really irritating questions, such as where one would put all the plants one fancies, how they might all compose together, and who will water and feed and fertilize them until they have "caught" and can make it on their own. Truly, as Katherine White said, "this is the season of lists and callow hopefulness." And if spring were really near, things would not be so bad. Perhaps the real trouble with January is that it is not followed by April.

February

TWO Februarys are possible in southern Vermont. The second, praise Heaven, blessedly is rarer than the first. What might be called the ideal February, the best that can be hoped for, occurs when the arctic air mass that deep-freezes our state extends far to the south of us. Though the consequence of that can be some of the bitterest weather we can endure, it also brings a series of crystalline skies and unblemished days through which the sun shines with determined persistence. The thermometer may still read below freezing day after day, and three or four feet of snow may still lie on the ground (and should, for the protection it provides is as needed now as ever); but light streams into the house, illuminating corners of rooms that have not been bright since October. The last vestiges of ice from the storms of January melt from the roof of the winter garden, and the precious

illusion it was built to fulfill, of spring in the dead of winter, becomes reality (or as much reality as gardening ever is). Under the increased light and heat, the camellias continue to open their improbable blossoms, the leptospermum bends low from the sheer weight of its thousands of carmine flowers, and the buds of the tender maddenii rhododendrons begin to expand, showing the strange, rich purplish mauve that will later fade to white. A small window is cautiously opened for some buoyant air, and shirtlessness — at least under the protection of the glass — does not seem a bad idea.

Impassioned gardeners that we are, it is nevertheless on such days that we find ourselves turning to the needs of the house in which we must live. There are, of course, many garden chores that could be done in February, and that must be completed before the end of the month. Pruning, particularly, should be

For display on the dining table, the florist's cyclamen (Cyclamen persicum) *and a tender primrose* (Primula obconica) *will flower all winter if one remembers to put them in a quite cool place at night. Though pussy willows wait until March to flower outdoors, a few branches brought into the warmth will quickly display their mouse-gray catkins, dusted over with yellow pollen.*

finished before the sap begins to rise. And as we've stared out the window at the shapes of the bare trees all winter long, we know exactly where cuts should be made. But the job can be put off a little longer, at least until the end of the month, and the work we must undertake now, while our spirits are up to it, is the work necessary to keep ourselves decent indoors. For soon — with luck — there'll be no time for house chores, and certainly no willingness.

So heavy gallons of white paint are bought, rooms are cleared of furniture and objects (and dust — how could so much have built up?) and newspapers are laid over the floor in a triple thickness. (It is only in February, at painting time, that one realizes how much news one has missed throughout the year.) As the fresh skin of paint goes on, we are always surprised — shocked, actually — by how dull a winter's worth of wood smoke has made the walls. It takes a full day to paint a room, and a second to rub a thin coat of tung oil into the pine floors. But the third is our reward, for as each piece of furniture is waxed and put back into place, each picture polished, each object scrubbed of its dulling coat of grime, we feel somehow as if we had come into a fine inheritance. When all is done, the concordance of the next day's bright morning, the pristine whiteness of the newly painted walls, and the new brilliance of polished glass and waxed furniture all combine into as intense a feeling of joy as we can know before the first fine days of gardening. The smell of beeswax and turpentine, tung oil, fresh latex paint, and glass cleaner mark for us the end of winter and, spiritually at least, the advent of spring.

That is one kind of February, and four years out of five it is the one we get. But then there's the other, what might be called "Black February." It occurs when the seam between arctic air and the warm southern flow from the Gulf of Mexico lies close enough to us to make for a whole month of storms. One succeeds the other, with only periods of preparation in between. So when it is not actually snowing, or sleeting, or drizzling freezing rain, the sky is gray and brooding, looking as if one had merely to pull a chain to cause something dreadful to come down. It is as if February never actually happens, but instead January is fifty-nine days long. And so we return to January's activities, poring over catalogs for treasures we missed, giving more thought to whether it might not after all be nice to order yet another kind of fancy-leaved elderberry, taking such pleasure as we still can in well-laid fires, fresh-baked bread, and the middle of the longest novel on the bookshelf. (*Clarissa* and *The Tale of Genji* are neck and neck.) No rooms get painted, no windows washed, no floors oiled. We just tidy, and wait a little longer for the light.

Actually, it is in this kind of February that the pruning always gets completed on time, if grimly, simply because one is driven out to it. Fortunately, pruning is one of our favorite jobs, even without the warmth of the new sun. It is wonderful to see graceful shapes emerge slowly from a congested tangle of twigs and crossed branches. So the pleasure of the work causes us to forget even sodden boots and socks — at least until the end of the day, when we find our toes are not working quite like they should. And as with all garden work, even the least pleasant, there is always the double satisfaction of seeing the work completed well and of doing it when it ought to be done. The best time to prune most trees is as brief as with other garden chores. That time is, first, when the trees are dormant and their skeletons are clearly revealed without the distraction of leaves. Not that a well-pruned tree isn't obvious even in the full luxuriance of its summer's green; for pruning is concerned above all with balance and proportion, always there to see (or not). But it's almost impossible to know where to make major cuts when the tree is in leaf — one just can't see into it. And there's waste in pruning a tree in leaf, even when one can, for one is cutting away energy already spent, which the tree might have put into fresh growth that fulfills the gardener's vision of its best form.

It is just as important to prune when temperatures are consistently cold, preferably below freezing. For then one avoids many diseases borne by insects. A scourge of all fruit trees, particularly, is fire blight, a bacterial disease that enters their systems when insects light on open wounds. There is no cure for fire blight once it has entered the sap, and its progress is sure and fatal. A young tree — and sometimes even a mature specimen — will be in fine leaf one week, and blasted as if by a blowtorch the next. As there are not many insects flying about in Vermont in February, our best chance to avoid such acute distress, to the tree and to us, is to prune then.

But pruning in cold weather, before the sap really begins to rise, has another advantage as well. It avoids the excessive discharge of sap through fresh cuts — appropriately called "bleeding" by gardeners — which can be as debilitating to the tree as it is to the gardener's spirits while he watches the tree's life fluids drip from wounds he inflicted. Some trees pruned in February will bleed in any case, particularly maples and birches. Native Americans first learned to boil down the mildly sweet sap of *Acer saccharum*, the sugar maple, a knowledge they passed on to the first white settlers. It is now, of course, a major industry in Vermont and, when each tree along the road bristles with

buckets, a sure sign of spring. There are trees in our neighborhood that have been tapped to catch the daily rise and nightly descent of sap in early spring for two hundred years, and they are still hale and full of vigor. One might reason from this that maples too might be pruned without harm in February. But two or three half-inch holes bored into the bole of a tree are one thing; a major branch is quite another. And so, as maples are not subject to fire blight, when one of ours must be pruned we carefully note the branches that must be removed and wait until midsummer to make our cuts. And as no one that we know still brews birch beer, we avoid bleeding the birches by deferring their pruning until then as well.

Pruning is now a major activity for us, the first of the new gardening year. But in our first late winter at North Hill, there was precious little to prune. The garden was still being cut out of the mature woods and we were years from planting anything likely to need much more than a judicious snip here and there. But we were longing to garden in all its forms. So, that first February, we strapped snowshoes to our feet and hiked ever so far (really only half a mile or so) to a lovely meadow that lies at the back of our land. It was our first winter struggle through the woods, cumbersome with our attempts to master the skill of snowshoeing, but full of the joy of new possession and discovery. Our purpose, however (for anything is made better if it possesses what the world calls a purpose), was to do some pruning.

Long before we came to unite the destiny of this property with ours, it had been made salable by carving it out of a much larger farm, and the bulk of a hundred-year-old apple orchard lay just over our property line. But for some inexplicable reason — perhaps an ancient oak or towering white pine that provided a

In February, Cyclamen coum *still blooms along the path of the winter garden. This one, selected by Nancy Goodwin of Montrose Nursery for its gray foliage, is called 'Pewter Leaf'. It is joined by a surprisingly early show from a grape hyacinth, which in a protected environment will produce its foliage in autumn and its first flowers in February.*

landmark once but is now long vanished — five old apple trees were left on our side, neglected but (or so our real estate agent, who knew the land from boyhood, assured us) still fruitful. "You could do a lot with those trees," said Stub Burnet on the late April day we first walked the land, "a whole lot, if you were minded ever." Clever man, Stub Burnet, who must have known how to make his sale on us. For minded we certainly were.

The varieties of our five trees we neither knew then nor know now, though there are great scholars of apples who would know, and perhaps we will some day search out one to tell us. For it is nice to call an old tree by its name, to know its parentage, its year of introduction, its whole family history and what it was once thought best for, whether for fresh eating, for keeping, or for cider. Our trees, so far as we could tell, had been good only for deer fodder for thirty years or more, and might, for all we knew, never be good for much else. They were all still hearty (a word with new resonance for us), showing no signs of internal rot within their great solid trunks. But otherwise they were a neglected mess. Still-living branches had been wrenched and splintered by years of storms; others were dead and bearded with lichens. Water sprouts, the upright twigs that grow on apple trees once they have been pruned, had developed into thick branches crossing and congesting the centers, into which light should always shine. But beneath the tangle of dead and overly vigorous branches, each tree displayed a solid and potentially shapely form, showing that someone a century ago had judiciously overseen their early development. The living tips of each branch terminated in thickened spurs, promising, if not usable apples, at least apple blossoms. In any case, we were now the

stewards of these ancient trees, responsible for giving them as much more of life as they could have. And as the house was brand new and the garden hardly more than a thought and a hope, we had nothing else to do.

The work took thought and patience, the more so because we did not then own a chain saw or the courage to use one, and so had to go slowly with handsaws and unformed muscles. That was not a bad thing, as it kept us from being hasty and wreaking a havoc we could never repair. We first removed all dead branches and those that had been damaged beyond restoration. We then looked for branches that crossed the center of the trees or blocked the light, sawing them off flush with the trunk. Enough of the structure of each tree was then revealed to judge its balance and symmetry, and to remove branches from the heavier side so that weight would be evenly distributed throughout. Finally, we thinned leaf- and (we hoped) fruit-bearing growth at the ends of branches by about a third, so that new vigor would pour into them.

It is easy to anthropomorphize any plant, especially a great old tree, thinking that it smiles on one's efforts and is grateful for its new and un-looked-for chance at a longer and better life. We assume that is not the case, that nature in any form is oblivious to human ministrations, even when their results are as benign as they are meant to be. It was difficult, however, when we had finished our work, to feel that the pleasure had been all for us. But doubtless it was. Even so, the trees responded the following spring by showing clouds of blossoms, and in the late summer and early autumn they were laden with fruit. Only one of them, as it turned out, bore apples that were any good for eating fresh, though it gave us beautiful ones, pale yellow streaked with red on the outside, crisp and sweet within. The other four were clearly cider trees, though we found them perfect for pies. And to our cows, heritors now of the extra bounty that once fell to the deer, it makes not much difference.

We have kept up with our apple trees, though they have, of course, never since required the radical surgery of that first year. But it was a good way for us to begin as pruners, for it taught us much about what to plan for in a mature tree and what not to let happen. So when the following spring we came to plant new apple trees within the garden-to-be, we knew already, not so much from books as from this direct experience with our ancient survivors, the forms we should plan for.

That spring saw a great planting of trees generally. The conifer screen — of pines, spruces, junipers, and arborvitaes — was put in place along the roadside in the upper section of the garden, as were two Merrill magnolias (*Magnolia kobus* x *stellata*), a single shrubby *Magnolia stellata*, and several aristocratic small trees that our more experienced garden counselors and the books we read assured us could never survive in Zone 4. (They have all been proven wrong.) We planted *Stewartia pseudocamellia*, with its elegant teardrop form, its brilliant scarlet foliage in autumn, its cream-colored bark mottled with plates of gray, and its two-inch-wide flowers like single white camellias in midsummer. We had fallen in love with an old paperbark maple (*Acer griseum*) at the Arnold Arboretum — the oldest specimen outside China — a muscular twenty-five-foot-tall tree with a polished mahogany trunk and wings of cinnamon brown on younger branches where the bark had peeled away. We thought we should have one of those, too. And we had seen an autumn-flowering cherry (*Prunus* x *subhirtella* 'Autumnalis') at the base of Boston's

Beacon Hill, unaccountably in bloom during a midwinter warm spell. We thought it would be a splendid effect in Vermont. (It has, of course, never flowered here in February, and never will, but it is a cloud of tiny, candy-pink blossoms in April, and that has proven good enough.)

It was odd planting those trees, so small and inconsequential, amid thickets of wild blackberry and the stumps of felled beeches and maples. But we had already made that leap that has come to be our most important skill in designing other people's gardens, of seeing a garden in the mind that isn't on the ground, isn't yet but will be. And the presence of those newly planted trees gave us goals, targets to work toward, as we cleared away brambles, section by section, to fashion new borders at their feet. Time is the most important dimension in garden design, not just in how the garden will look next season, or five years hence, or twenty, but in the benefits the gardener hopes to leave to others, in that distant, teasing time that stretches beyond his own life. Our old apple trees taught us that as well, and so we were careful, in our first planting of trees, to include some of those.

We planted four that first spring, across the back of what was soon to be our first vegetable garden, and subsequently the perennial garden. It came to be bounded on the house lawn side by a hedge of yew; on the road side it was already defined by a privacy screen of arborvitae. But the view across its back was of our neighbor's beautifully tended meadow, with his cow barns picturesquely in the distance. So, though we wished to create a boundary there, we also wished to preserve at least glimpses of the beauty beyond. We planted semi-dwarfs that nevertheless achieve twenty feet in height and take on, with the

Generally, only a single stripe of carmine will appear on the flowers of the camellia 'Yamamato Nishiki', though sometimes, out of boredom, we suppose, it will show a blossom that is rich pink all over. Though a two-month blooming period is not extraordinary for a plant, in the depth of winter the persistence of this camellia counts for a great deal.

years, the stern nobility of standard-size trees (which dwarfs never do). Of the hundreds of varieties available, we selected two that would give us apples early in the season, 'Yellow Transparent' for August fruit and 'Rambo' for early September, and two for later, 'McIntosh' and the wonderful (and wonderfully named) 'Cox's Orange Pippin', which is perhaps, with its winy complexity, the best of all apples for eating fresh. Long before they bore fruit, we were careful to give them the type of wide, outward-branching scaffold of major limbs that we had admired in our old, inherited trees. But as they were meant to feather the view of the meadow and provide a foreground for it, they were also allowed to branch low, about four feet from the ground, with their tops interlacing. Now, after seventeen years, they have achieved the dignity of mature trees, and their flowers and fruit-laden branches provide as satisfying a background for perennials as they might have for the vegetable garden, had it not been moved away.

In February, late or early, it is to these apple trees that we turn our attention. They require little pruning, only the elimination of water sprouts, the occasional removal of a secondary branch that has grown across another, and the thinning of fruit-bearing twigs to encourage better apples on those that remain. The magnolias require more attention, of the sort that old gardeners called "opening out"; for as they develop, internal growth becomes congested, producing few flowers and blurring the winter beauty of the thick gray trunks and branches. *Acer griseum* and *Stewartia pseudocamellia* are among those trees that seem to be born with an innate grace; they seldom need pruning, except to eliminate crossed branches. But *Prunus* x *subhirtella* 'Autumnalis' might need a

snip, here and there, to open its center and give it greater poise.

It is always tempting with fruit trees and spring-flowering trees, when one has finished the job and sees the resulting tumble of severed branches and twigs, to take up those that are shapeliest and most covered with buds for forcing indoors. Of them all, *Prunus* x *subhirtella* 'Autumnalis' is the easiest to force — it will even open a few flowers outdoors when temperatures remain above freezing for a week. It asks only to be put in water and kept in a cool but bright spot to burst into bloom. Generally, however, spring-flowering trees will force readily only when cut close to their natural blooming times. As apples and deciduous magnolias naturally bloom in May in Vermont, we have had little success forcing them. Those blossoms that do open are wan and stunted, looking as if they wish they hadn't been made to. And our fear of fire blight prevents us from snitching a few twigs in March to hurry their season.

But the garden is now full of spring-blooming shrubs which are very easy to bring into bloom out of season. Though *Viburnum* x *bodnantense* 'Dawn', *Cornus mas, Daphne mezereum* f. *alba,* forsythias, and the two species of flowering quince (*Chaenomeles japonica* and *C. speciosa*) have a month or more to wait before they will flower outside, if we are willing to wade through the drifts to pick them, they will willingly open in February, and sometimes even earlier. *Viburnum* x *bodnantense* 'Dawn' is really better for us as a forced than as a garden flower. An occasional spell of warm weather any time in the winter will cause its flowers, tightly packed inch-wide bundles of dusky pink, to begin to open. But their optimism is quickly nipped in the bud, for they are likely to be blasted by late arctic cold snaps. Picked and brought inside, they can do what they prefer, which is to bloom in these late winter weeks without the fear of harmful frosts. The others are all quite reliable flowers for the garden, but still we pick them now, so impatient are we for the coming of spring.

None of these shrubs is particularly rare or difficult to grow, and forsythias are positively common. The old hybrids of *Forsythia suspensa* and *F. viridissima* grow everywhere in American suburban gardens, a fact that only exacerbates the general vulgarity of their display. For the whole thrust of hybridizers in creating these plants was to produce ever-brighter shades of chrome yellow, and ever more of it. These hybrids, varieties of *Forsythia x intermedia,* are represented at their best (or worst, we would say) by the cultivars 'Beatrix Farrand', 'Karl Sax', 'Lynwood', and 'Spectabilis' – all rather stiffly upright growing with large flowers of a brassy, screaming yellow. Though we are generally champions of good plants scorned by gardeners because they have become overused, we would not grow these hybrids even if we didn't object to the violence of their colors. For they are not bud-hardy in Zone 4, and the effect of that is an odd sight, for they generally bloom only around their base, where snow has protected the buds, each looking like a bush in a bright yellow skirt.

But there are other forsythias, cultivars of the Korean species *Forsythia ovata,* that are much hardier than *Forsythia suspensa, F. viridissima,* or their hybrids. It is a species that was scorned by early breeders because the flowers are small, of a softer yellow and more sparingly produced (they do not cluster the branches thickly like yellow bees in a swarm). It is just for these reasons that we treasure it, especially two of its varieties. The one called 'French's Florence' has tiny, pale yellow flowers like little elf's caps, and 'Minigold' has somewhat brighter but

equally tiny flowers, and with an upright, angular habit that makes it look from a distance like *Hamamelis* x *intermedia* 'Arnold's Promise'. Both have a refined elegance in the garden and in a vase. Cut on a day in February when the temperature is at or slightly above freezing, they will open indoors in about eighteen days; they will open sooner if picked in early March. And their hardiness ensures that gardeners in Zone 4 will enjoy abundant blooms from top to bottom. Gardeners may also have as much of it as they have room to grow, for like all forsythias, cultivars of *F. ovata* root very readily, simply by sticking a dormant branch into evenly moist soil in early spring.

A plant much like the forsythia, and of the same family (Oleaceae), is *Abeliophyllum distichum,* sometimes called the "white forsythia" (it ought not to be, for it has abundant virtues of its own). Its flowers are milk white, emerging from grape purple buds and almost black twigs. It blooms a bit later in the garden than the forsythias, and so, if one wishes a forced bouquet of the two mixed together, it should be cut a week or so earlier. (To such a bouquet it will also add sweetness, for it is fragrant and forsythias are not.) *Abeliophyllum distichum* is listed as hardy only to Zone 5; and as its buds, like all spring-blooming shrubs, are formed in autumn, it should receive the protection of a house wall or a larger evergreen shrub. But we have seen it flower reliably in Vermont for ten years, planted against a yew hedge, where its glistening flowers are particularly beautiful against the backdrop of dark green.

Another old-fashioned shrub that is excellent for forcing at the end of winter is the flowering quince, in two species, the Chinese *Chaenomeles speciosa,* and *C. japonica.* Though it was introduced to western gardens as early as 1800 and was once planted abundantly, even as hedges, the plant has fallen out of favor with modern gardeners, perhaps from overuse or perhaps because many cultivars come in hard colors like watermelon pink and orange-red. Certainly they are dreadful when planted next to yellow forsythias, as was too often done, or even in the same garden with the bright purple rhododendron 'PJM'. But they can be splendid if cut in February for indoor bloom in early March. They will be paler when forced than they are in the garden, and so an out-of-the-way place should be found for one or two. Softer colors have been bred, however, that make fine additions both to the spring garden and to a late winter vase. One of the loveliest is the tall, open-growing form of *C. speciosa* called 'Toyo Nishiki' in Japan and descriptively marketed as 'Apple Blossom' in America. Its flowers are a pale, delicate pink irregularly mottled with deeper carmine. The snow quince, *C. speciosa* 'Nivalis', is an elegant pure white, beautiful outdoors and in. Though cultivars of *Chaenomeles japonica* are generally only four feet tall, and so fail to produce the long angular branches one wants for forcing, a hybrid of it and *C. speciosa* called *C.* x *superba* 'Cameo' inherits enough height to make it useful — especially as its warm, orange-pink flowers are of a rare and wonderful color. From this group Marshall Olbrich gave us another, shortly before his death, called 'Oka', with flowers of a pale yellow. Flowering quinces actually benefit from having older, congested branches cut from the center of the plant, so one can take a few quite large ones without feeling guilty. One should not be too greedy, however, for it takes three or four years to build up the stern, oriental-looking wood that is the plant's main beauty. In any case, some flowers should be left for the spring garden and to produce the curious, knobby fruits, one

or two of which, chipped fine into an apple pie, will give it added tartness and the smell of honey. Gathered just before the heavy frosts and arranged in a bowl, they will also perfume a whole room.

Most flowering shrubs picked for forcing will require a little patience before they may be tricked into opening their flowers, though they may be speeded by crushing the bottoms of their stems with a hammer and immediately putting them in tepid water. The best and brightest flowers are produced by keeping them in a cool, sunny place, 55 to 60°F being ideal. Even so, the earlier in the year one cuts the branches, the longer it will generally take for them to bloom. Some, particularly *Prunus* x *subhirtella* 'Autumnalis' and *Viburnum* x *bodnantense* 'Dawn', will show their first flowers within a week or two. Others, such as *Hamamelis mollis* 'Brevipetala' and *Daphne mezereum* f. *alba* will open in a day or two, the thready little flowers of the first and the four-petaled, intensely fragrant white stars of the second waiting only for a bit of warmth, indoors or out, to unfurl. But unless February has been unusually mild, forsythias may take three weeks and flowering quinces even longer.

But one group of shrubs, the willows, need not be forced at all, for even in February some have begun to show fully expanded buds, mouse- or pink-gray, despite the cold outside. They charm the simple and the sophisticated alike. Children, particularly, delight in their kittenish beauty, and experienced gardeners will find themselves begging cuttings of any new ones they chance upon. Willows are, of course, one of the easiest of all shrubs to root, usually even in the vase; but as water-formed roots have trouble accommodating themselves to soil, a better way is to stick thick stems a foot or so into the squishy soil of March.

It is useful to know that many plants will achieve a zone or two of greater hardiness, and will flower precociously, if their roots are established near a stream where water percolates throughout the winter. Situated in such a spot, our plant of Hamamelis mollis 'Brevipetala' will furl and unfurl its threads of rusty petals from January to March. It should always be picked for indoors, where it will shake out its rich scent to perfume an entire room.

Among willows grown for their early spring catkins, *Salix discolor,* the much-loved native pussy willow of swamps and marshy places all along the eastern seaboard, is not the first to flower. Its spanglings of silver on glistening dark brown stems wait until late March to appear in Vermont. Earlier by a month is *Salix chaenomeloides,* called the "giant" pussy willow because its catkins are as big as thimbles. Even before opening they are encased in showy red sheathes, which split as the buds enlarge and may linger on their tops when they are fully expanded, causing them to look like small gray birds sitting in a row along the branches. *Salix chaenomeloides* will quickly grow to twenty feet or more. Like all willows grown for their catkins, new growth should be forced periodically by cutting out older stems about eight inches from ground level. The result will be several long, straight rods and much larger catkins, perfect for cutting.

Salix alba var. *caerulea* is as tiny as *Salix chaenomeloides* is large. It is called the "cricket bat" willow because its wood is the preferred material for fashioning the implement used in that sport. We'd be sorry for the cricket player who had to use a bat made from our plant, however, for its many branches ascending from the ground have never reached more than five feet in height and a diameter of less than an inch. ("Cricket wicket" willow would suit it better.) Though it is useful for no game, *Salix alba* var. *caerulea* can be the earliest willow of all to show buds, tiny catkins lined along its stem. They are not blue, alas, as the species name *caerulea* promises, but a smoky silver-mauve that is pretty enough. Improbably, they appear as early as the end of January, remaining all the rest of the winter until the pollen-laden flowers open briefly in April and then drop. Not so early, but still appearing by the middle

of February, are the catkins of *Salix gracilistyla* 'Melanostachys', rather sparsely produced but as close to black as any blooming thing we know. It is dramatic when cut and brought indoors, but even more so when one views its inky catkins against the snow.

Pussy willows reach their peak long before any other flowering shrubs have yet begun, save *Hamamelis mollis* 'Brevipetala', which may appear with *Salix alba* var. *caerulea* in January and will wind down with the last willows in March and April. Those late willows are wonderful, too. The native wilding, *Salix discolor,* shows abundantly wherever moist, open ground exists; but it is a good garden plant too, and absurdly easy to root. *Salix gracilistyla,* known for years now as the "rose-gold" pussy willow, a name attached to it by some enterprising nurseryman, adds tints of pink to the pale silver catkins of *S. discolor. Salix caprea,* the rather elegantly named "French" pussy willow (though it is native throughout Europe and northern Asia), also appears with *Salix discolor,* though its catkins are larger by half. It is the willow apparent in florists' shops at this season, usually in bundles on the sidewalk to entice flower-hungry urbanites inside. Pretty as it is, we like it better in its weeping forms, the old cultivar called the 'Kilmarnock' willow and the newer, female form called 'Weeping Sally'. (Willows bear male and female flowers on separate plants, and with willows — for once among plants — it is the female that is larger and showier.) Both forms will make a small haystack of tangled branches on the ground; they are much nicer trained up on a single stem and allowed to cascade from the top to the bottom. It is worth noting about all these comparatively late-flowering *Salix* species that they may all be forced with great ease in January and February. As they all require periodic cutting back in any case to

Though it is the large, almost Victorian camellias that we like best, there is great charm in the tiny bells of the camellia 'Baby Bear', abundantly studding its chubby three-foot-high bush in February. It also nicely conceals the pot in which Phormium tenax *is growing, tucked behind it and waiting for its placement in the summer garden.*

ensure abundant and large catkins, much is gained by pruning them then.

Flowering shrubs and plants are not the only thing we force to lighten the last dark days of winter. Odd as it seems, one vegetable — chicory — also reaches its prime during this month. Called "Belgian endive" and sometimes "witloof" in stores, it always fetches a high price; but it can be had almost as easily at home, and for no money beyond the cost of a seed pack. The seed must be sown in spring, at the time one sows lettuce and other salad greens. But the object in growing chicory for forcing is not the summer leaves, which are tough and very bitter, but the roots. The plants should be thinned and fertilized to produce the largest possible, and when the tops are quite blackened by heavy frost, they should then be dug. The tops are trimmed away, taking care not to cut into the growing tip of the root, for it is from there that the winter chicory will sprout. The roots can be stored for several months in plastic in the refrigerator and taken out and potted, a dozen or so at a time, from the beginning of December until early February. The pots should be large enough to accommodate the full length of the root and about six inches beyond; we use a huge old terra-cotta pot that is planted with annuals in the summer, but a large black plastic nursery can or even a small garbage can would serve, provided holes were punched in the bottom to allow for drainage. Almost any soil will do, if it is open and loose. Once the roots are in place (touching shoulders, if one wishes to do that many at a time) they should be covered with more soil, to a depth of six to eight inches. The pot should then be watered well and stood in a cool place, preferably one that hovers between 40 and 60°F but never freezes. In a month or so the

noses of some of the plants may break the surface of the soil. If they are tardy, one can reach one's fingers down into the top layer of soil to feel for their fat expanding shoots. When the shoots are between four and six inches long, the entire plant should be extracted with a gentle but persistent tug, and the root cut away. (It can actually be repotted to make a cluster of new sprouts, never again as elegantly loaf-shaped as the first and never as large, but still delicious. Or, if one likes the blue flowers of wild chicory along roadsides and in meadows, the spent roots can be returned to the refrigerator and planted in early spring to beautify a piece of wild or waste ground.) By potting up a fresh supply of roots each week, one can have fresh salad throughout the winter. With home-forced chicory, however, it is necessary to split and wash each one very carefully to free it from grit, or — even better — detach each pale ivory leaf patiently from the core and wash it in cold water like loose leaves of lettuce.

Winter chicory is the last fresh vegetable we can enjoy from our garden (via the greenhouse potting shed) — or perhaps it is the first, if one wishes to put a really optimistic bent on things. Even if, as we have often heard, decent crops of the hardiest vegetables might be grown — or at least kept still — in carefully protected cold frames, we are not sure how we would get to those cold frames through the snow, never mind prying up their lids. Because our house is a new one, its cellar is poured concrete, and well heated, denying us the luxury of a fully stocked root cellar. So for storage of the last crops from the vegetable garden, we depend on the same old refrigerator we use to force spring bulbs. Piled inside are jumbles of beets, carrots, turnips, leeks, and celeriac — not, we would say, always at peak freshness, but still an important component of our winter diet, at least for soups and stews. Cabbages, selected from the sorts that keep well through the winter, are heaped in a loose tumble in a dry corner of the potting shed, covered with insulation to keep them just above freezing. As late as the end of February, one head might still be extracted fresh enough from under its outer covering of papery brown leaves to serve for a stir-fry. And our potatoes, all of them of the rarest and choicest antique varieties, are still sound, and will be until potato-planting time in May. Still, of course, one does long for something fresh and green beyond forced chicory, precious as it is.

For years there used to be grown a variety of kale in America called "Hungry Gap." Its name made perfectly clear its primary value, for if planted with a little shelter, and perhaps protected in early winter by an overturned wooden box with a stone on top, leaves could be harvested deep into the winter and again in earliest spring. Perhaps its race was allied to the ornamental kales that one has seen lately contributing their depressing note of Pepto-Bismol pink to the fronts of shops well after Christmas. Or perhaps it came from a more dignified lineage. Its seeds might still be available from the wonderful conservation banks and growers committed to keeping alive strains of antique vegetables. Or perhaps there is another, similar variety available, equally hardy though surely not so well named. The trouble, though, is that we have never developed a taste for kale of any kind. In that we may be like a very young friend of ours, who declined the offer of boiled shrimp with a polite, "Thanks, but I haven't come to like shrimp . . . yet." Meanwhile, we descend from our conviction that one ought to eat according to the seasons. We scan the vegetable displays of the supermarket for produce of reasonable freshness, organically grown, and as appropriate to the end of the season as can be. And we wait, with unrequited hunger, for the first wild dandelions of March.

March

THERE is a point, usually toward the middle of March, when a stroll around the garden — just to escape the house, just to get some air — takes on a quite different quality from the ambles of deep winter. The ground is still frozen hard, the tender perennials and heathers are still swathed in evergreen boughs, and the boxwoods are still sleeping under their ungainly crates. There is detritus everywhere: sodden perennials and annuals that the autumn left no time for cutting away, rotting leaves swirled among the shrubs, snow compacted into stubborn, heel-bruising ridges of ice, and even less mentionable things — a winter's leavings from household pets, perhaps even a full vacuum cleaner bag put out the back door and forgotten beneath an obscuring fall of snow. There is little that is beautiful, and such as there is — the somber forms of evergreens, the courage of witch hazels, the enameled stems of willows and shrubby dogwoods — has been celebrated too much, fed on for too long to be of continuing interest now. But still, in the middle of this most dreadful of gardening months, one feels a difference in the garden, and in one's own personal chemistry. It is not so much in the behavior of the plants, though to very attentive eyes the willow buds are certainly swelling, and the snow around plantings of galanthus begins to be pierced with curious spikes of celadon. But the tap one feels on one's shoulder, the rise in one's heart, is from a sudden gust of warm, moist air. The direction of things has changed. Tentatively, shyly, like the first promise of very young love, the new year has begun.

Though the first promise of spring begins in the air, its strongest consequences are in the gardener's sleep. One wakes in the night realiz-

Our winter garden is not a greenhouse, but a real garden, open to the earth and with a path of the same stone used in the garden outdoors. One can of course tell that it is not outdoors, from the opaque plastic winter sheathing, made milky from the snow beyond. Still, after a dousing from the hose, it is not so hard to pretend that one is in San Francisco or the warmer parts of England.

ing that one has been dreaming of the garden, and one stays awake, continuing the dream into waking by making plans, forming lists of what — this year — one is surely going to do. *That lilac will be moved early, so its growth will not be too much disturbed. The lawn has surely been needing humus, and now — tomorrow — would be just the time to spread peat over it. The fireplace ash stored in the basement from a long winter of fires would do it good as well, and wasn't there a bag of phosphate rock somewhere in the back of the garage? Those Siberian irises in the perennial border were horribly infested with witchgrass last summer, and one could twitch it out now, for it will be green and easy to pull before the irises wake. Could there be a stone terrace built in the backyard, where the lawn chairs sit? With the press of other garden chores, it would not be possible to do it later in the spring, but if one started early, the work might be done before the daffodils bloom, and the rawness would be healed by June. The* Crambe cordifolia *showed corky knobs of growth above ground in the autumn cleanup. Some could be broken off rootless and potted into Pro-mix, for another clump would be nice opposite the old one. There are those packets of larkspur and poppy ordered last year but never sown. If they were sprinkled on the cold earth now, would they have enough viability left to sprout? It is worth a try.* And so it goes, until, bit by bit, one sees the garden that will be in one's mind, and one begins to doze off again, vowing this year to stake the delphiniums . . . just . . . as they . . . should be.

It is most certainly in the mind, and in dreams, that most of the charms of March exist. For beyond the odd gust of heart-stirring southern wind, it is in the main the most blustery, the most frustrating month that northern gardeners know. Like November, it marks the passage of one season into another; but whereas November ushers the gardener into the long sleep of winter — a rest he generally craves — March rouses him violently with the

pangs of a slow birth. Violent weather forces contend for the right to hold the garden: the warm, gentle air from the south is assaulted — initially with complete success — by the still-not-vanquished cold from northern Canada and the Arctic. Fierce winds and driving rains or snows — or worse, what lies in between, storms of ice — characterize March. In old country lore there was an adage for every season. The personality of March is so consistent, however, that its tag, of all the months, has remained in the popular imagination. At the post office, in the filling station and the supermarket, people will say, relentlessly, that it comes in like a lion and goes out like a lamb. Happy for us all if so, but our experience is that it is likely to exit in the same manner as it entered. Any person who possessed the characteristics of March would not be a person one would want to make a friend of.

For March, with its violent vagaries, is the season of greatest disasters in the garden. Or perhaps they are merely the most visible, for March, with all its force, displays a certain frankness. An unusually mellow autumn that suddenly dives into a bitter December, or a pronounced January thaw that coaxes up the sap — only to be frozen — leave corpses in the garden that one does not find until much later, when one wonders why, exactly, they died. But one can see the havoc March causes. Rhododendrons, already depleted by the frozen earth and winter winds, shrivel visibly under March's sun. The heavy rains that can fall, a hopeful sign of course, fall on still-frozen earth, cutting channels across the garden and exposing the bulbs and roots of daffodils, touchingly naked. Alternate freezes and thaws make tiny dirt-colored towns, fortresses, and castles in the flower beds, like an evil gnome's rendition of the *Très riches heures du Duc de Berry.* Nearby, a primrose may rise up on the stilts of its roots, its crown desiccated in the air. Rains may freeze as the temperature drops, turning the garden into a crystal miracle, beautiful to anyone but the gardener, who will see the exposed yellow flesh of hawthorns, crab apples, and cherries as their branches split apart under the weight of the ice. Most sinister is snow drag, when a winter's snow, like goose down when it fell, now compacts from freezing and thawing into a solid pack of white, drawing down toward the earth and carrying with it the branches of rhododendrons, azaleas, and other brittle shrubs, splitting them off from their sustaining sap. And the deer, desperate from hunger, may come even in the day to feed on the yews and arborvitaes, staring you in the eye and resisting your shouts, contending boldly, in their misery, for essential rights.

For all that, March is a beginning. At other times in one's life, there may have been — there may be still — struggles and hardships that signal not loss but gain, not defeat but victory. Just precisely in the pains of March is the assurance that winter is over. The worst it brings can generally be repaired. Plants heaved out of the earth can be pushed back in — never the way to plant anything, but the combination of the softness of the mud and their strong wish, now that spring is here, to live means that few will perish. Furrows and trenches cut into the garden can be filled with compost or with duff bucketed in from the woods, and the beds will be the better for the addition of this new rich humus. Stones on paths can be scraped clean of mud and reseated where they have sunk, or bigger, better ones brought in to replace them. Even ice-fractured trees or shrubs delimbed by snow drag can be pruned and rejuvenated, making them more resistant to next March's ravages. And the yews browsed by deer

can be brought back to better shapes — for they were overgrown anyway, and as they must resprout, they might as well do so in more pleasing configurations. (Only, next autumn, better provisions must be made against those deer. March is full of resolutions.)

Besides disaster, March is also full of hope, though outdoors it is expressed in the littlest of signs. For even in March, despite its vagaries, there are flowers again in the garden, later than we would like them but still earlier than we have a right to expect. Along the path that leads from the drive to the front door is a large collection of snowdrops, now perhaps more than a thousand, though initially we did not plant so many. They have multiplied happily in the rich leaf mold that accumulates there, and we have been careful to divide clumps whenever we could, just after flowering and while the leaves are still fresh and green. For it is a mistaken notion among gardeners that bulbs can only be planted when dormant, in the fall. Almost all — and certainly snowdrops — will easily accept division while in full growth, and that is a great convenience when one wishes to increase existing stands in the garden; for in autumn, one will have forgotten exactly where they are.

The snowdrops always bloom in March, regardless of the severity of the weather. Through frozen ground or even a thick crust of snow they will pierce their folded leaves, revealing soon a flower that seems so tiny and fragile (the only lack of candor their guileless blossoms possess). For snowdrops are in fact incredibly tough, bending their nodding bells to the ground under icy blasts but straightening up, fresh and clear, the moment the weather shows the slightest modification toward warmth. Beyond their simple beauty it is their intrepidness that we most treasure, for in that they seem so fitting an emblem of March.

Someone has commented that gardeners make such large collections of snowdrops — and garden writers blather on about them so endlessly — simply because their is little else to admire in the garden when they bloom, never mind to write about. We hope that is not so, though whether from their precocity, their tiny stature, or their modest beauty, they do require a gesture of obeisance one might not perform for another flower, later, when there are so many. One must go down on one's knees before a snowdrop in order to appreciate it fully; it is an uncomfortable posture, with one's limbs still stiff from winter and one's knees blotting up moisture from the cold, slushy snow. Still, at this season at least, it is worth the discomfort, for one can see within a snowdrop marvelous things. The commonest snowdrop — and still always the nicest — is *Galanthus nivalis*, which has an entirely felicitous arrangement of three large down-facing petals and three smaller, inner ones stained green at the tips, the whole forming a tiny cup. All flowers are wonderful and all carry, to greater or lesser degrees, a resonance that strikes the heart of the viewer. But there are a few — and snowdrops are the first of that few — that seem, quite simply, perfection. One cannot stare at them too long. Curiously, also, one does not wish to pick them. That is not only because later each blossom will enlarge into a fat, pea-size seed capsule, bending away from the mother clump as it enlarges and containing a whole generation of future snowdrops, every one of which will come to maturity. It is also because snowdrops, of all flowers, seem to belong outdoors. They have chosen their own proper element. And besides, there is so little else out there at this season.

For all these reasons, the gardener is apt to make a great collection of snowdrops. *The Plant Finder*, published in association with the British Hardy Plant Society, lists almost eighty species and varieties of snowdrop, with information on where — if you live in England — you can buy them. It is a gauge of how far one might go, in the snowdrop line; given time, we will doubtless go as far as we can. At this point, however, our collection consists only of five or six forms. There is the species, *Galanthus nivalis*, which in its simplicity really cannot be bettered, though in a self-seeded population the very attentive will notice minute variations, of larger flowers or deeper stains of green. There are also two giant forms — or giant at least for a snowdrop — 'Samuel Arnott', at almost a foot in height, and the nicely named 'Mighty Atom', only slightly taller than the species but with flowers twice its size and of even stronger substance. There are doubles, too, if one wishes to add baroqueness to so sublimely fashioned a flower. The double form of the species breaks its innermost petals into many fragments, forming a tiny, green-stained rose. 'Lady Elphinstone', also a double, is supposed to be marked with yellow instead of green, though it may take a long time — even a gardener's lifetime — for it to settle down to this remarkable characteristic.

It seems true of all the most special forms of common bulbs that they must really be at home in the garden before they are willing to show off the qualities for which they are celebrated, and for which — usually — one has paid quite a bit extra. So it is with Lady Elphinstone, who was given to us by Charles Cresson, a great gardener and an even greater connoisseur of snowdrops. She lives in a pot, because we are eager to increase our stock, and we think we are better able to keep track of her in

Among the most improbable plants we grow in Vermont, one of the oddest is the Chatham Islands forget-me-not,
which begins to achieve perfection in the lower greenhouse in March, never willing to believe that our winter
is not the summer it knew in its home east of New Zealand. Its first production is of splendid leaves,
more varnished than any we know and fully six inches across.

the cold greenhouse. There she blooms in February, and her flowers are quite pretty, though they are stubbornly marked with green. When we have enough bulbs, we will try her in the open garden, and there – in two years, or five, or ten – she may show the chartreuse for which she is celebrated. We'll wait to see. But whether the autumn-blooming snowdrop, 'Queen Olga', ever escapes her pot is in great doubt. In an odd, eccentric family, she is the most peculiar, choosing to bloom not in earliest spring, but in October. That is a very odd time for a snowdrop to bloom, since usually there isn't even any snow. But when one comes to love any group of plants, one loves them even in their eccentricities; so we take care of Queen Olga, and we enjoy, at the end of autumn, her sense of humor.

Though March turns the gardener's attention outdoors, in his waking hours and even in his sleep, much of his gardening pleasure must still be indoors, in the greenhouse and – if he is lucky or improvident enough to have one – in the winter garden or conservatory. Spring has been in force there since January, and its beauty is far from spent. The leptospermum is still a haze of red against the glass of the roof, and though most of the sasanquas and many of the camellias are finished, there will still be a perfect blossom or two, tardy in opening because it was nearer the wall or was shaded from the heat of the sun. Jasmine wreathes the door, a foam now of scented white flowers. *Helleborus argutifolius* makes its pinwheels of acid green, and *Iris unguicularis* produces a long succession of short-lived, violet-colored and violet-smelling blooms. Most beautiful now, however, are the maddenii rhododendrons, whose proper season, here under glass and outdoors where they thrive, is March.

As a clan, the genus *Rhododendron* is so rich with treasures that it would be absurd to single out one group as most specially beautiful. These tender rhododendrons, however, seem to us the most beautiful we grow (that being, of course, a tiny fraction of the genus). We loved them when we first saw them, over twenty years ago, in the gardens around San Francisco on one of the first of our now annual flights from the grayness of the early New England spring. But really we loved them before that, in descriptions within David Leach's remarkable book, *Rhododendrons of the World*, published in 1961 and now, sadly, out of print. We have had cause to note David Leach before in this book, since so many of the rhododendrons out in the garden are the product of his work. He has spent a lifetime of labor – still continuing – breeding hybrids as hardy as any, and as luscious, in shades of yellow and peach, pink, cream, and white. For those who live in really frigid climates, and who still must have rhododendrons, his has been a gift of mighty importance to gardeners. For us this would be enough to be grateful for, though we have an overplus of gratitude for his having introduced us, through his book, to the wonderful tender rhododendrons we grow in the ground of the winter garden.

In his discussion of "Rhododendrons for the Cool Greenhouse," Leach remarks:

> Some of the most impressive of all Rhododendrons are too tender to be really satisfactory garden decorations anywhere in America except in the San Francisco region of California. Their usefulness in the British Isles is equally restricted to the most favored gardens of Cornwall and of the West. Elsewhere under glass many of them produce sumptuous flowers of luxuriant proportions and delicious fragrance.

It was that comment, more than any other thing — even more than the indisputable harshness of our climate (so far from San Francisco, never mind "the most favored gardens of Cornwall and the West") — that hooked us on the folly of a winter garden in the first place. For what gardener could resist the promise of "sumptuous flowers of luxuriant proportions and delicious fragrance" at any time, not to mention at just those times — the bitterest depths of late winter and the cold teasing days of earliest spring — when one needs such wondrous things most? Were we as rich as the late Doris Duke, we would doubtless have had a whole acre under glass. In it we would have grown all of the sixty or more tender rhododendrons listed by Leach as among the very best. For, as he notes under the section devoted to larger greenhouses, "greenhouse Rhododendrons are really at their best in ground beds and this is the way they should be grown." Naturally we wanted them "at their best," and that is therefore the way we decided to grow them, though not (for reasons too obvious to enumerate) beneath an acre of heated glass.

Our winter garden is only twenty-four feet long by fourteen feet wide, is entered from the dining area off the kitchen by a French door, and is visible from the sink by a pair of barn sash windows swung open during the winter. It is a restricted space, to be sure, since among the rhododendrons we also cultivate camellias and sasanquas, two small trees and a host of early blooming tender perennials. But all gardeners — Doris Duke included we suppose — must eventually settle down to the space and the ground they have, however deep their pockets or however ungoverned their passion. So of the tender rhododendron species and hybrids recommended by Leach as possessing

four stars or three (which is to say, as with restaurants, the very best) we have grown twenty or so in our winter garden. That number, however, is still winnowing down, as some plants — fortunately our favorites — have burgeoned in their little world and crowded out others. Once, years ago, we saw a picture of a huge, single plant of *Rhododendron* x 'Fragrantissimum' in full flower against the March sun, apparently the sole occupant of the English greenhouse in which it grew. We doubt that we will come exactly to that, though the sublimity of such a solitary and treasured plant has its charms, like the single great grape vine snug in its own house at Hampton Court. For the time, however, our winter garden contains five or six splendid tender rhododendrons, all of which we can recommend (under the proper circumstances) for cold places like Vermont.

Among them will always be 'Fragrantissimum', though it has received only three stars in its rating from the American Rhododendron Society. That is presumably because, though its flowers are splendid three-inch flared bells born in a truss of four or five and smelling halfway between nutmeg and honey (richly earning its name), its growth is lanky and its leaves scarce. Indeed, when Allen Haskell gave us our plant twenty years ago, growing in a pot of fibrous peat as all this group should be when they are not in the ground, we remember commenting on its rather skeletal form and its scanty foliage. The comment was about the plant, not the gift, for which we were deeply grateful, but Allen's reply was swift and sure: "You don't realize, yet, how long it has taken me to get it looking even that good. And further," he continued, for Allen's scolds never come in halves, "you don't realize the treasure you have. But you will."

By the first week of March, the rhododendron 'Fragrantissimum' reaches its peak of flower, still silhouetted against the snow of the outdoor garden. 'Elsie Frye' joins it a week later, and it is hard to know, in the medley of their flowers, which is in fact "most fragrant."

We have. Once liberated from its pot, 'Fragrantissimum' has achieved a rangy four feet in about fifteen years, and never fails to justify itself with "sumptuous flowers of luxuriant proportions and delicious fragrance," just as David Leach promised. Because it is so much leg and so little leaf, however, we have squeezed it against the inner wall of the winter garden, between the tall, rich pink, formal camellia called 'Katie' and the venerable, blood red 'Professor C. S. Sargent'. To mask its one fault, we have also "faced it down" with 'Elsie Frye', a plant of thick growth, abundant with two-inch quilted dark green leaves, and full of flowers. It blooms a little earlier than 'Fragrantissimum', usually in the first week of March rather than the third. The flowers are shorter and broader, more out-flaring, and they possess perhaps even a stronger fragrance than 'Fragrantissimum' (for all this group smells wonderfully the same, with, to a fine nose, only a little more nutmeg in one, a little more honey in another).

A third member of this group, though across the path from the other two, is 'Countess of Haddington', an open, vigorous, tall plant with thick, polished, brownish red stems rather like those of the tall California madronas. It is the last to bloom, at the very end of March and into early April. Its flowers are larger, too, five-inch down-hanging bells, four or five in a cluster. All these rhododendrons have the habit of showing a deep mulberry stain on newly colored buds that persists, when the flower is open, as a beautiful flush against the white, like a bit of good burgundy spilled on an immaculate linen tablecloth. It is an oddly felicitous effect — luscious, we would say — proving once again that a white flower is doubly beautiful when it carries a tincture of some other color within it.

'Countess of Haddington' is, of all the tender rhododendrons we have grown, the best at contriving this magical effect, and for that reason we tolerate her somewhat rangy growth and the ragged untidiness with which she carries her blossoms. We have read, however, that others are even better, for Leach remarks under "favorite sorts" for the cool greenhouse that his own personal favorite is *Rhododendron formosum.* "It has large white flowers with yellow throats and a red band on the outside of each 'petal.' Seen as a pot plant about two feet tall it is remarkably beautiful and its pervading fragrance scents a large room." In hopes of bettering even that description, we have planted *R. formosum* 'Edinburgh', said to have even stronger maroon markings and to be an even more beautiful plant than the straight species. So far (which is to say, in fifteen years) our plant has grown strongly, but has failed to produce much in the way of flowers. It isn't particularly happy with us, probably because of the shade cast on it by our tree of *Leptospermum scoparium* 'Ruby Glow'. We would never give up that tree, now that it has thick ropy trunks and has rewarded us, for many winters, with such a wealth of cherry-colored flowers, high against the roof glass. So, in so small a space as we must work with, *R. formosum* 'Edinburgh' will perhaps have to go. That loss might be great gain, for we are always craving space for more camellias, and a new one would flourish in that shade. We will see.

One other plant in the winter garden deserves special mention for its beauty in winter and early spring, and that bears the impossible name of *Xanthorrhoea quadrangulata.* A native of southern Australia, it flourishes in America only in the most privileged garden sites, which is to say the southern parts of California. We fell in love years ago with a sin-

It must surely be the case that we possess the finest specimen (if not the only one) of Xanthorrhoea quadrangulata
*this far north. We would not waver in our affections for this plant even if we knew of an older, better one, for
we are not competitive in that way. If it should ever die, however, we'd mourn its splendid symmetry,
its ease of culture, and, most particularly, the way a casual brush of the hand causes the whole mass to quiver
as if it were a sentient being. Perhaps it is.*

gle specimen in the Strybing Arboretum, of
about the height of a person and with a person's presence. It is a very old plant, its rugged
black trunk topped by a perfectly symmetrical
explosion of perhaps a thousand out-facing
bluish green leaves, each the thickness of a fine
knitting needle, but so flexible that brushing
one's hand among them causes the whole mass
to quiver. Of course we had to have one, and
we secured a small plant from a nursery south
of Santa Barbara. Because of the beautiful
symmetry of the plant, it would have been lost
to us had it been crammed into an open space
of the winter garden among camellias and
rhododendrons. So it has grown in a huge clay
pot for fifteen years, elevated on an ivy-covered
maple log (for we will never see much trunk
on it, though someone might, some day) so
that its plume of foliage is silhouetted against
the icy glass. In the summer, to give it a sort of
vacation, we move it out to stand by the steps
leading down to the holly court, on a platform
built into the wall just for it. But, curiously, it
has never reversed its conviction that our winter, which is the Australian summer, is the
proper time to grow. So starting in January it
steadily increases its production of knitting
needles, becoming thicker each winter until the
end of March, when it rests. It is, among the
many plants we grow, a sort of pet, and our
affection for it causes us to hope it will have a
long, long life.

All during the winter and into spring, our
winter garden supports us psychologically with
its wealth of flowers and its improbable
beauty. The lower greenhouse, by contrast, is
essentially asleep. But gardeners, true gardeners
(if one can use such a phrase of distinction,
for all gardening, even the simplest, is "true")
do not always need richly colored flowers,
heady fragrances, or rare, luxuriant leaves to

feed their passion. The bare scaffold of a
sleeping standard fuchsia, showing only tiny
mouse ears of new leaf, the quickening of a
cutting, the sprouting of early seed — all in
their way can be just as sustaining as an armful
of camellias and tender rhododendrons. So,
throughout the winter, we take the long slog to
the lower greenhouse through the snow, enter-
ing its cool but protected world to check on
things, to fill the water barrels from the
stream, to clean and feed — generally to putter.

That greenhouse came into existence when
we made the decision to convert the one off
the kitchen into a real garden where plants
could grow in the ground. The rewards of
such a space were almost immediate, but its
conversion left us with no space for the many
activities — so many of them rather untidy —
that must occur under glass to support the
summer garden. So we made the decision to
construct a working greenhouse for these purposes, located — for reasons more aesthetic
than practical — at the bottom of the garden,
far from the house.

It is a structure forty feet long and fifteen
feet wide, and we remember thinking ner-
vously, when its concrete slab was poured, how
close its general shape was to a trailer. When
the building went up, however, it had enough
complexity — even quaintness — to cut against
that impression. For it is not a prefab greenhouse of aluminum ribs, expanses of reflecting
glass, and practical, elaborate gadgetry. Such
structures can, of course, be very beautiful,
when the patina of age is on them, when they
are visually anchored to the ground by a foundation of mellow old mossy bricks, and when
streaks of real whitewash have dulled the glare
of their glazing. But we thought that a spank-
ing-new aluminum greenhouse could hardly
provide the sort of character we wanted from a

building that was essentially to be the terminating feature of the garden. The effect we were after, from its first construction, was of a sturdy, old-fashioned garden shed. So the lower greenhouse is a distinctly home-built affair, made of solid timbers, tongue-and-groove siding, barn sash windows, and stock glazing panels for the roof.

By the time we came to build the lower greenhouse, we knew enough of what we needed from such a structure to realize that it should have two components. We envied gardeners who live in old houses for their dark, damp basements, good for so many gardening purposes. This would be our chance at something like a root cellar — not underground, to be sure, for the land is poorly drained and the cost of construction would have been increased beyond our means — but a minimally heated, well-insulated shed might perform most of the functions of a root cellar. There we could store dormant plants, force bulbs, spread out the potatoes and pile up the cabbages, accumulate potting soil for winter use, and stash — neatly we imagined — empty clay pots, baling twine, burlap, garden hoses and tools, and all the other equipment required by gardeners (and some that, strictly speaking, isn't. For who can suppose that that heavy, cast iron reel mower will ever be pushed over grass again?).

The second component of such a structure — and, of course, the primary reason for its having been being built at all — is a space for plants that are too tender for the garden outdoors in winter, but that, stood about in summer, make such valuable contributions to its beauty. We cannot imagine our garden without its potted figs, both 'Brown Turkey' and striped, its huge tubs of agapanthus in white and blue, its six-foot bay tree or rosemary standard, its white wisteria, at home now

for ten years in a square terra-cotta tank on the back terrace. We grow many boxwoods in the ground, but a few are in oversized pots — where they grow as great spreading bushes, columns, or little trees — both because we love box and because we treasure them as solid, portable accents wherever they are needed. We also maintain a host of other, lesser plants in pots, some as old as our gardening life here. There are agaves, seldom much noticed in their winter storage but essential as living sculpture in the summer perennial garden. *Corokia cotoneaster* we keep simply because it is so curious, looking at all seasons like a wad of corroded chicken wire. The 'Hidcote Beauty' fuchsia standard, now with a trunk twice as thick as a broomstick, indicates the entrance to the rose path with thick hanging bells of cameo and cream, and we cannot think of anything hardy that would do the job so well, all summer long. None of these plants need much in the winter, only enough light and heat to convince them that death is not upon them. But taken all together, they — and perhaps our Scots Highland cows — are the primary reason we remain in Vermont during the winter. For though the possibility of a winter house in some warm climate (when we grow very rich) is a tempting subject for daydreams in somber November or now in March, the cows could not be transported easily and the tender plants would have to die. It is too great a sacrifice. How dull the summer garden would be without them, how poor the soil.

From the road, the lower greenhouse presents a divided face. One half, nearest the rock garden, is the shed, with small shuttered windows, a cedar shingle roof, and a skin of clapboard, stained a gray so deep that it might as well be black. It took some courage to apply that stain, for there were those who assured us it would look quite morbid and depressing. But we took our cue from the old deacon's bench at the head of the perennial garden, which weathered down to that shade naturally and has always satisfied us. From the first it was the right color, giving the shed full weight as the terminus of the garden, and after some years of living with it we think there is no more beautiful stain for catching the light and for suavity of contrast against summer leafage or the brilliant hues of autumn. It is lightened, in any case, by the white paint of its little windows, and by the other half of the building, the greenhouse proper, which has a roof of insulted glass panels and a bank of six small-paned barn sash windows double-hung for added insulation. A pair of French doors separates the two components of the building, back and front, and a planted alpine wall, broken by them but otherwise continuous, gives unity to the face of the structure.

We must linger for a while on that alpine wall, for it is an example of so much that has happened in this garden, initially a disaster but in the long run a great gift. The wooden skin of our little building was of pressure-treated, tongue-and-groove siding, for we had a sad experience in the upper greenhouse with how quickly untreated wood could rot away in the continuous moisture of greenhouse conditions. But for thrift, the new greenhouse's lower section, both along the face of the shed and under its barn sash windows, had been pieced together from whatever was left over when the upper skin was put on. But unless pressure-treated wood is nailed firmly into the supporting beams, it will forever twist and warp under the influence of the weather. And so ours did, the little three-foot pieces curling outward along the base of the building to the point that light shone through. Though the

obvious solution was to re-side the lower section of the building with longer pieces, a better one suggested itself. We had admired Frank Cabot's wonderful planted walls at Stone Crop, in Cold Spring, New York, and we had longed for some place in our garden to build such things. Here, in our defeat, was the opportunity. So we nailed sheets of marine plywood across the wretched little pieces of siding, with copper flashing along their top edges for greater beauty, and built stone walls across the face of the building, about four feet tall and two feet wide, just under the small windows of the shed and the more ample fenestration of the greenhouse.

A planted wall is a great treasure for any gardener. Beyond its beauty and interest, there are so many plants that will flourish in such conditions but that will be usually lost — and possibly will perish — in the open garden. A host of tiny treasures — saxifrages, aubretias, campanulas, sempervivums, and drabas — love conditions where their roots are in cool soil and their tops in baking sun, for such conditions simulate their native mountaintops and rock crevices. Though many will persist in beds and borders or in rock gardens, they will never be so happy, or show to such advantage, as when grown at eye level in a planted wall. Others — cranky subjects like the compact form of *Daphne cneorum* or *Daphne arbuscula* — will seldom survive unless they are given just such conditions; and if they should, for a season or two, the gardener must go down on his knees to admire their early beauty, and perhaps to pray that it will return next year.

There are only two tricks to building any stone wall, whether it is to be cored with soil and planted, or not. The first is to follow the golden rule of "one over two, two over one," which is to say, to overlap the stones so that there is never a crevice running downward through two or more layers of stones. A crevice will act as a fault, and the inevitable consequence will be that, over time, the wall will buckle out at that point and fall apart. The second rule is to put in tie stones at frequent intervals, usually rather handsome rectangular rocks that one would rather lay with their longest face outward, to gain more distance, but that should instead be laid so their longest face points into the wall. It all sounds very easy, and to watch an experienced wall builder at work, it seems so. There cannot be a greater luxury, if one wishes to build walls and has the chance, than such watching, though one had better be very quiet, and not ask many questions. Failing that chance, however, there is nothing for it but to build, and to be prepared to tear up part of one's work the moment it seems in doubt.

In some ways, building a planted wall is easier than building one only of freestanding stone, for whether it is to be of only one face, as ours is, or a four-sided square or rectangle, the soil one packs into the center is far more stable than "chinking" (the ugly stones and stone fragments one places inside a wall to fill its core and lock each stone in place). For a planted wall, however, the filling inside should not be "soil" exactly. It is a great mistake to assume that the interior of such a wall should be of the richest, finest compost one has on hand. The plants best suited to such a structure are mostly starvelings, not wishing for, and generally not flourishing on, such a diet. Fills made of material heavy in organic elements will also inevitably decompose, shrinking in the process and causing the wall's internal support to become unstable. So to fill a planted wall, one should secure the ugliest material a gardener can confront, the reddish,

sandy, gravelly material used for road bedding, usually called "bank run." It is rich in mineral nutriments but poor in nitrogen, and is just the thing no gardener would ever think of adding to the garden. Nevertheless, it is the sort of growing medium that occurs on the barren slopes where many alpine plants flourish, and once it has settled down, it is extraordinarily solid and stable. So as each course of the wall is laid, bank run is packed behind and beneath the individual stones, and rammed or stomped down hard to support the next layer of rocks as they are put into place.

But a planted wall can only be planted as it is laid, for it is never easy or very successful to poke little plants in afterward. Therefore, one must have a good supply of choice things, in pots, ready to insert as likely places for them occur. Where there is a crevice, or a flat rock sloping downward into the bed, a plant should be tapped from its pot, the earth squeezed flat or teased away, and the roots brought in contact with the bank run behind. The next layer of rock should be laid over it, with only its tuft of foliage exposed. In that way, the wall is planted as it is built up, with the expectation that it will eventually present a face rich with lichens and studded with small treasures that will spread and multiply, clothing much of its surface with growth and presenting in April — or earlier — some of the finest, most jewel-like flowers of the gardening year. Generally, however, only the sturdiest alpine plants — *Phlox subulata*, aubretias, aurinias, sempervivums, and rock campanulas (*C. portenshlagiana* and *C. porscharskyana*) — ought to be planted along the face of the alpine wall. The great treasures — the small daphnes, tufted drabas, pin-cushion dianthus, the choicest tiny conifers — might well be saved to plant along its top, making there a little mountain land-

None of the tender rhododendrons we grow in the winter
garden may be said to be compact and tidy, but it is certain
that 'Countess of Haddington' is the rangiest. Now an
awkward six feet tall, her large trusses of claret-stained
white flowers, richly fragrant, compensate for whatever she
may lack in grace of figure.

Blue is never an easy color to photograph, especially in the
wan light of March, and especially when it is the clear, soft
shade called "China blue." That is the color, nevertheless,
of the flowers of Myosotidium hortensia, the
Chatham Islands forget-me-not. The flowers are larger
than those of the gentle border forget-me-not, Myosotis
sylvatica, or its moisture-loving cousin Myosotis
palustris. But the resemblance to both is still strong, an
odd quaintness in so exotic a plant.

scape, mulched with gravel and punctuated by small rocks with a particularly fine growth of lichens on them.

Exposed to the full force of the spring sun, warmed by the heat retention of the rocks and the gravel within, perhaps even encouraged along by some loss of heat from the greenhouse itself, it is the alpine wall that presents us in March with some of our earliest flowers. As we walk past it, to check up on things within, we may notice a tiny buttercup of *Potentilla verna*, its clear yellow all the more vivid against the gray stone. Perhaps *Eustoma grandiflorum* might be showing its first pale purple flowers against its mat of minute gray leaves. Or there could be a single yellow chalice of *Crocus ancyrensis* or one of *C. fleisheri*, their corms protected from mice by the stubborn bank run. At the least, there will be the smug little Christmas tree of *Picea glauca albertiana* 'Gnome', the smallest of all its family we grow, and now — after ten years, from an inch-high cutting — a perfect foot-tall cone of green.

Just around the corner from that tiny tree, through a French door that is the only way to enter the lower greenhouse during the winter, is a world already busy at the beauty it will produce. There is no time when it is not a thrill for us to enter that space. Even in highest summer, when it is planted with gourds — their tropical leaves and vines covering the inner rafters, their fringed male flowers perfuming the night, their bottle-shaped fruits improbably down-hanging — it is a world apart, set off for special purposes.

Throughout the winter and well into the last frosts (which can come in May), those purposes are to support the summer garden. Or at least, those are *primarily* its purposes. For though the bay tree will have sprouted new leaves by the end of March that must be trimmed away to preserve its symmetry (soft, tender leaves, deficient in aromatic oils and no good for stews, though we always try by throwing in a double handful), though the great white wisteria will begin to show its buds, first thumb-size and then ever-so-quickly elongating (how we wish it would slow down, so as not to bloom before it is safe outdoors!), though cuttings taken of *Artemesia pontica* 'Powis Castle' and *Lavatera assurgentiflora* 'Barnsley' will show, crammed into a six-inch pot of sand, that it is time to move them on (and where will they be put, now that one six-inch pot is multiplied by six?), though buds will appear on the agapanthus, and pans of seedlings will cry out to be transplanted outside (couldn't, *couldn't* they have waited just a week or two?), there are other things down there, in the greenhouse, that seem significant emblems of our gardening life.

One of those things requires a little geography lesson to understand. The Chatham Islands are a most remote corner of the world, forming a scattered cluster off the southeast side of New Zealand, about 44° south and 177° west. The group consists of three major islands and several rocky islets. There are no indigenous mammals, and the bird population, once extensive, has largely been exterminated through the introduction of cats, dogs, and pigs. For these reasons also the flora, though never very diverse, has been much reduced. However, as every good gardener knows (and to let out the secret), the Chatham Islands are the solitary home of an extraordinary plant, the unique species in its genus, the Chatham Islands forget-me-not, *Myosotidium hortensia*. The eleventh edition of *The Encyclopaedia Britannica* (1910), from which we have drawn this information, mentions in its account of the Islands only this one botanical species in any detail. Here is the conclusion of its entry on the Chatham Islands:

> One of the finest of the endemic flowering plants of the group is the boraginaceous 'Chatham Island lily' . . . a gigantic forget-me-not, which grows on the shingly shore in a few places only, and always just on the high-water mark, where it is daily deluged by the waves.

Just now, just in March, and just inside our lower greenhouse, two very large pots of *Myosotidium hortensia* are in full flower, their two-foot-high clusters of blooms looking quite like a "giant forget-me-not," each flower colored pale china blue with a yellow center. As good almost as those flowers, however, are the leaves that surround them, dark green shells, a little like a good hosta but varnished all over. They are not easy plants to grow. English gardeners — those in climates mild enough to flower them outdoors — swear by composted seaweed, packed around the crowns of the plants presumably to remind them of their shingly seaside homes. We have done very well with fish emulsion, applied directly to the soil at monthly intervals throughout the winter, supplemented by waterings from the buckets in which our goldfish hibernate out the coldest months.

Whether through these tricks or by some luck we have not calculated (which may run out, some day) our Chatham Islands forget-me-nots have flourished. Now, in March, there cannot be many gardens in North America that boast such fine specimens in full bloom. It is a curious thing about those flowers, however, that they smell faintly of rotten fish. We don't much care, for that is simply one of the things about them. And, in their exotic provenance, their botanical uniqueness, their exacting culture, their familiar, simple flowers (which look, for all the world, just like a blown-up version of the cottage forget-me-not), even their faintly "fishy" smell, they are emblems of our garden. We would put them on a woodcut symbolizing it, were we ever given to such a pretension. Meanwhile, the Chatham Islands forget-me-not blooms here in March, in our lower greenhouse, one of many reminders that the new gardening year is about to begin.

Index

Page numbers in *italic* refer to illustrations.

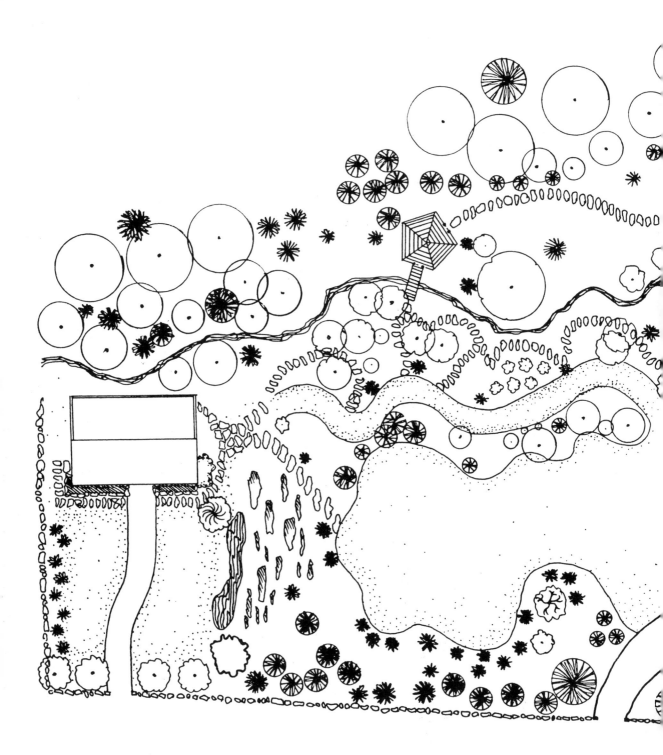